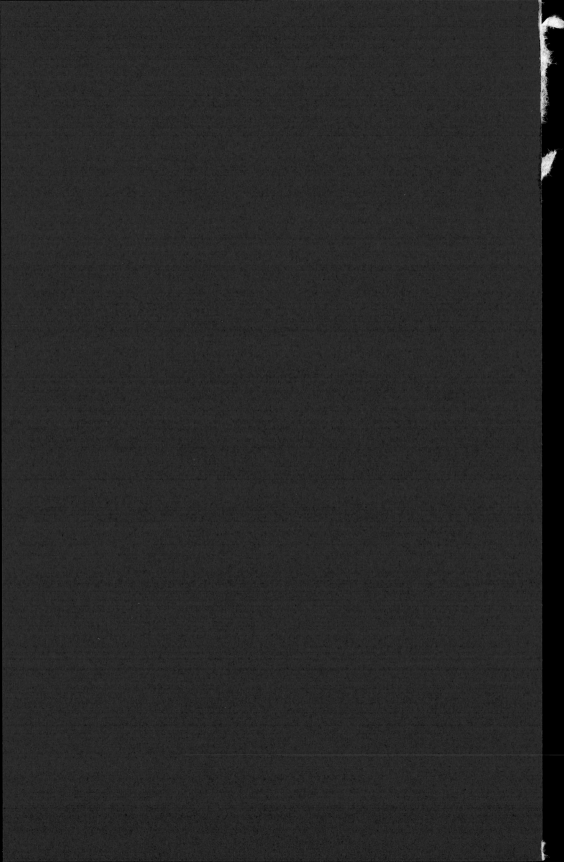

Politics, Philosophy, and Humor at the Byzantine Court

GRAPHAI

Graphai: Writings from Byzantium and Its Neighbors presents texts and translations from the Byzantine world. Ideal for scholars and students, these elegant volumes publish written material never before seen in translation and offer exciting new translations of well-known works. The series encompasses all periods and genres, and is not limited by the political boundaries of the Byzantine Empire.

An early modern engraving of Theodore II Laskaris in Hieronymus Wolf's edition of the *History* of Nikephoros Gregoras (Basel, 1562), placed just before book 1, based on a manuscript portrait of the author. Photo courtesy of Dumbarton Oaks Research Library and Collection.

GRAPHAI

Politics, Philosophy, and Humor at the Byzantine Court

EIGHT WORKS BY THEODORE II LASKARIS

Translated with Introduction and Commentary by
DIMITER ANGELOV

DUMBARTON OAKS ⁂ TRUSTEES FOR HARVARD UNIVERSITY
WASHINGTON, DC

©2025 Dumbarton Oaks, Trustees for Harvard University, Washington, DC
All rights reserved.
Printed in the United States of America.

LIBRARY OF CONGRESS CATALOGING-IN-PUBLICATION DATA

NAMES: Theodore II Lascaris, Emperor of Nicaea, 1222–1258, author. | Angelov, Dimiter, 1972– editor, translator.

TITLE: Politics, philosophy, and humor at the Byzantine court : eight works by Theodore II Laskaris / translated with introduction and commentary by Dimiter Angelov.

OTHER TITLES: Eight works by Theodore II Laskaris | Graphai.

DESCRIPTION: Washington, DC : Dumbarton Oaks, Trustees for Harvard University, 2025. | Series: Graphai | Includes bibliographical references and index. | Summary: "The thirteenth-century emperor Theodore II Laskaris, ruler of the Empire of Nicaea, is among those versatile authors of the Byzantine era who produced numerous little-known gems of literature and thought. He composed the sole theoretical work on friendship surviving from Byzantium, wrote philosophy with verve and humor, and was perhaps the most passionate advocate of the idea of a communal Hellenic identity in the Middle Ages. This volume represents the first translation into English of eight works by Laskaris. An introduction and annotations to the translations orient the reader and contextualize these fascinating pieces. The selections themselves include a satire of his tutor, his oration on friendship and politics, his oration on Hellenism, and philosophical works and musings that include a treatise filled with Socratic irony. They represent the most prominent strands of Laskaris's thought and provide the reader with a well-rounded portrait of this remarkable author"—Provided by publisher.

IDENTIFIERS: LCCN 2024042654 | ISBN 9780884025245 (hardcover)

SUBJECTS: LCSH: Theodore II Lascaris, Emperor of Nicaea, 1222–1258—Political and social views. | Theodore II Lascaris, Emperor of Nicaea, 1222–1258—Philosophy. | Theodore II Lascaris, Emperor of Nicaea, 1222–1258—Translations into English. | Byzantine Empire—Civilization—Sources—Early works to 1800. | Byzantine Empire—History—Sources—Early works to 1800.

CLASSIFICATION: LCC DF626.5 .T54 2025 | DDC 949.5/02—dc23/eng/20241204

LC record available at https://lccn.loc.gov/2024042654

www.doaks.org/publications

CONTENTS

List of Figures   ix

Preface   xi

INTRODUCTION

    The Author   1

    The Selected Works   7

    Note on the Editions and the Translations   9

    Chronology and Contexts   12
        Satire of His Tutor   13
        Memorial Discourse on Emperor Frederick II   21
        Moral Pieces Describing the Inconstancy of Life   23
        Oration on Friendship and Politics   26
        Representation of the World, or Life   30
        *On What Is Unclear and a Testimony
            That the Author Is Ignorant of Philosophy*   35
        Oration on Hellenism   38
        Letter on Royal Duty, Taxation, and the Army   42

    Style, Vocabulary, and Grammar   43

    Theodore Laskaris and Nikephoros Blemmydes   47

    Theodore Laskaris as a Literary Figure and Philosopher   51

TRANSLATIONS

1. *Satire of His Tutor*   59
2. *Memorial Discourse on Emperor Frederick II*   93
3. *Moral Pieces Describing the Inconstancy of Life*   101
4. *Oration on Friendship and Politics*   115
5. *Representation of the World, or Life*   129
       Dedications   129
       Representation of the World, or Life   134
6. *On What Is Unclear and a Testimony That the Author Is Ignorant of Philosophy*   157
7. *Oration on Hellenism*   175
8. *Letter on Royal Duty, Taxation, and the Army*   193

Bibliography   199

Index of Scriptural Passages   211

General Index   215

FIGURES

Frontispiece. An early modern engraving of Theodore II Laskaris. iv
1. Map of Asia Minor and the Balkans (1257) 6
2. Theodore II Laskaris's diagram explaining the accumulation of knowledge in Greece 181

PREFACE

This anthology grew out of my work on the historical biography of the Nicaean emperor and philosopher Theodore II Laskaris, *The Byzantine Hellene* (2019). The translations offered here are its logical sequel, for the texts, which are made available for the first time in any modern language, are among the most important sources for the biography. But also, and more importantly, they enable the reader to approach Laskaris as an author and thinker—and to obtain an idea of some of the literary and philosophical trends of his time—through his own words. I am immensely grateful to the late Joseph Munitiz for commenting profusely on my early drafts and for offering many solutions to translation difficulties. Eirene Harvalia-Crook also gave generous early help. Katerina Ierodiakonou and Petros Bouras-Vallianatos assisted me in better understanding challenging passages on logic and medicine, respectively, at a later stage of my translation work. My discussions with Martin Hinterberger and Panagiotis Agapitos have always been illuminating. I owe thanks to the two anonymous reviewers and especially to John Kee who examined meticulously all the translated texts. It is perhaps unnecessary but should nonetheless be stated that I bear the sole responsibility for the translation and the commentary, the outcome of many years of engagement with a fascinating author who has never ceased to surprise me.

INTRODUCTION

The Author

Theodore Doukas Laskaris (1221/22–1258), known as Theodore Laskaris in his lifetime and better known to us as Emperor Theodore II Laskaris, is among those versatile authors of the Byzantine era who produced little-known gems of literature and thought. His profile was anything but conventional. He was a ruler of the Byzantine state in Anatolian exile known as the "empire of Nicaea" (1204–1261), which flourished in the period of the Latin occupation of Constantinople after the Fourth Crusade. His daytime job was burdensome, yet it proved an inspiration rather than an impediment to prolific authorship. His literary accomplishments were significant and sometimes unique, more impressive than his short-lived achievements as a statesman and general. He produced the sole theoretical work on friendship surviving from Byzantium, composed original philosophy, and was among the most passionate advocates in the Middle Ages—if not the most passionate one—of the idea of communal Hellenic identity. For an author of such vision and erudition, the available translations are still regrettably few, limited to his *Encomium on Nicaea* and several letters and minor pieces.[1] This anthology presents for the first time eight of his most interesting and representative works in an English translation with commentary. This introduction gives essential

---

1 The *Oration on Nicaea* has been translated by Jacob Tulchin in Foss, *Nicaea: A Byzantine Capital and Its Praises*, 132–63. From among the more than 200 letters of Laskaris, only a few have been translated: Epp. 80, 99, 101, 124, 193, and 214 (the numbering is based on Nicola Festa's edition). See Gardner, *The Lascarids of Nicaea*, 305–7 (Epp. 101, 124, and 193); Spingou, *The Visual Culture of Later Byzantium*, 82–89, 946–51 (Epp. 80 and 99 translated by Angelov); Angelov, "Theodore II Laskaris on the Sultanate of Rum," 36–41 (Ep. 214).

biographical information about the author, discusses the chronology of individual works, and comments on important matters of composition and context.

Theodore Laskaris was born in the city of Nicaea in late 1221 or early 1222.[2] A ruler by birthright, he was the only child in the family governing the Anatolian Byzantine state, the emperor John III Doukas Vatatzes (r. 1221–1254) and the empress Eirene Laskarina. His maternal grandfather and namesake, the emperor Theodore I Laskaris (Theodore Komnenos Laskaris), had been the restorer of the Byzantine government in exile in the aftermath of the Fourth Crusade. The life of the younger Theodore Laskaris, our author, was firmly embedded in the culture and politics of the Anatolian Byzantine state. He came of age during the second decade of existence of the polity and did not live long enough to see the liberation of Constantinople in July 1261. His writings are, among other things, a key source on this special period in the millennium-long history of the Byzantine Empire.

The state of Nicaea grew in territory throughout Laskaris's life and by the 1230s encircled Latin-held Constantinople. Its victory at the Battle of Poimanenon (1224/25) led to the recovery of almost all territorial possessions in western Asia Minor held by the Latins. Expansion into the Balkans followed: modestly into Thrace in the late 1220s and later, in the 1240s and the early 1250s, farther into Thrace as well as into Macedonia and Epiros at the expense of the Latin empire of Constantinople, the Bulgarian kingdom, and the Epirote Byzantine state. Laskaris grew up steeped in the euphoria of the restoration of Byzantine power led by Nicaea, a background essential for understanding the triumphalist spirit of his *Oration on Hellenism* (composed in 1256).

As the sole heir to the throne and the living continuation of the Laskaris-Vatatzes dynasty, Theodore Laskaris was expected to carry on the successful military and diplomatic policies of his father and grandfather. In 1235, while still thirteen years of age, he was wed to Elena, the eleven-year-old daughter of the powerful Bulgarian ruler Ivan Asen II (r. 1218–1241) and his Hungarian second wife, a sister of the Hungarian king Béla IV (r. 1235–1270); the wedding took place during a short-lived Nicaean-Bulgarian alliance, which culminated in a failed joint siege of Constantinople in 1235–1236. Four daughters were born to the young couple in the 1240s and a son, John, in 1250. While Laskaris was in his twenties, he

---

2 This much-abridged account of Laskaris's life closely follows Angelov, *Byzantine Hellene*.

assumed duties in ceremonies, administration, and diplomacy, and he also assisted his father in governance, acting in effect as the coruler. He carried out local inspections, toured urban and rural settlements, administered fiscal justice, made local appointments, and at times governed Anatolia in the name of his father when the latter was on campaign in the Balkans. The right to title himself "emperor" (βασιλεύς) is firmly attested from 1241 onward and probably goes back to his childhood. The lifestyle of the Nicaean royalty was itinerant, with the heavily fortified city of Nicaea being only one imperial residence among several, in addition to functioning as the seat of the patriarchate of Constantinople in exile. Revealingly, in his *Oration on Friendship and Politics* translated here, Laskaris used the plural to refer to "the residences of emperors" (§6) from which his friends could hope to obtain precious gifts in the form of luxury garments stored there.

Laskaris took advantage of the best educational opportunities in the empire of Nicaea. In his early teens, he was assigned to a court tutor, an elderly man, who was to become the subject of a long and abusive satire (on his identity, see pp. 18–20). His duty was to supervise Laskaris's further education and his training in royal duties, such as generalship. While being supervised by his tutor, he fell under the spell of the leading teacher of the empire of Nicaea, the monk and philosopher Nikephoros Blemmydes (1197–ca. 1269). Blemmydes taught students on imperial commission at the monastery of St. Gregory the Miracle Worker near Ephesos, where he was the abbot from 1237 to ca. 1249.[3] Whether on his own initiative or at his father's prompting, Laskaris began to take lessons in philosophical subjects with Blemmydes at some point between 1238 and 1241.[4] The studies were inspiring yet brief and, as the satire suggests, met with the opposition of Laskaris's tutor. They ended abruptly by 1241 because of Laskaris's growing duties in governance as well as Blemmydes' long sojourn in the Balkans. In the 1240s, Laskaris continued his higher education with Blemmydes' ex-student, the civil official and future historian George Akropolites. He remained in communication with Blemmydes and came to consider him his mentor, spiritual father, and advisor in spite of the twists and turns in their relationship discussed below (pp. 47–51).

---

[3] On Blemmydes' life, see J. Munitiz, in Nikephoros Blemmydes, *Autobiography*, trans., *A Partial Account*, 12–28.

[4] See the discussion of the chronology of the early letters to Blemmydes in Angelov, *Byzantine Hellene*, 356–61.

Laskaris continued to visit Blemmydes in his monastery—after ca. 1249 in the new monastic foundation of Christ-Who-Is, near Ephesos—in order to obtain his writings and rejoiced in receiving his most recent compositions. Blemmydes thus sent Laskaris *The Imperial Statue*, an admonitory treatise on kingship in the mirror-of-princes genre, and Laskaris shared with Blemmydes his encomium on his father, John III Vatatzes.[5]

The educational encounter with Blemmydes was one landmark event in Laskaris's life. Another was the shattering death in 1252 of his wife Elena, which left many traces in his writings.[6] Twelve emotionally written essays titled *Moral Pieces Describing the Inconstancy of Life* bear witness to his self-reflective state of mind while he mourned the tragic loss. Another memorable event took place during the following year (1253). While his father was on a prolonged campaign in the Balkans against the ruler of Epiros, Laskaris received a large group of political refugees from the aristocratic Lancia family of northern Italy; they were relatives of his stepmother, the empress Constanza-Anna of Hohenstaufen. Later in the same year, in autumn 1253, he received an embassy arranging for their recall led by Marquis Berthold of Hohenburg, a special envoy of the Hohenstaufen king of Germany and Sicily, Conrad IV.[7] The scholars and doctors who accompanied the learned Berthold held philosophical disputations with Laskaris and his entourage in one of the Anatolian palaces. The intellectual exchanges during the reception of this Latin embassy kindled feelings of Hellenic pride in Laskaris and stimulated him to prepare for publication his *Sacred Orations*, a collection of nine works that includes the *Moral Pieces* (offered in translation here), as well as his main epistolary collection.[8]

The death of John Vatatzes in November 1254 marked the beginning of the last period in Laskaris's life. As the sole ruler for four years, he led military expeditions and launched internal reforms. The preservation of the legacy of his father was for him a powerful political argument, as we can see in his *Letter on Royal Duty, Taxation, and the Army* translated here. He was successful in keeping the

---

5 Blemmydes, *Ep.* 13, in Th. L., *Ep.*, Appendix III: *Nicephori epistulae*, 303–4; Agapitos, "Blemmydes, Laskaris and Philes," 1–6.

6 See Angelov, "*Moral Pieces*," 238–41.

7 On this historical figure, see Döberl, "Berthold von Vohburg-Hohenburg."

8 On the embassy and its influence on Laskaris, see Angelov, *Byzantine Hellene*, 145, 328–29, 351–55.

momentum of territorial expansion. The two-year campaign in the Balkans (1255–1256) against the Bulgarian ruler Michael Asen, who had declared war on Nicaea, ended with the Treaty of Regina (June 1256), which restored the earlier boundaries established by the Nicaean expansion into the Balkans in the 1240s. A marriage alliance with the state of Epiros (autumn 1256) brought the state of Nicaea into temporary possession of the city of Dyrrhachion on the Adriatic coast, an achievement flaunted in the *Letter*. Small territorial gains were also made in 1257 in the valley of the Lykos River, a tributary of the Maeander, along the frontier with the sultanate of Rum after a disastrous Mongol incursion into Asia Minor (Fig. 1).

Laskaris's internal policies were ambitious, perhaps overambitious. He enlarged the army by recruiting native soldiers in order to meet pressing needs, a policy described in the *Letter*. His childhood friend, confidant, and chief minister George Mouzalon was put in charge of the military reform and wielded enormous powers. A former page at the court educated by Laskaris, Mouzalon was the addressee of three of the works translated here: *Oration on Friendship and Politics*, *Representation of the World, or Life*, and *On What Is Unclear and a Testimony That the Author Is Ignorant of Philosophy*. The favors granted to Mouzalon and his two brothers were an affront to members of the old aristocratic families. At Christmas 1255, while residing in Lampsakos, Laskaris promoted Mouzalon from *megas domestikos* to *protosebastos*, *protovestiaros*, and *megas statopedarches*, a combination of titles and offices found in the dedicatory preface to *Explanation of the World* (p. 130 below). While the young emperor cultivated a new service elite, he purged officials from established families. His fraught relationship with the general Michael Palaiologos (the future emperor Michael VIII Palaiologos, r. 1259–1282), a well-connected and conspiratorially minded second cousin, exemplifies the tensions with the aristocratic elite. Palaiologos was tried in autumn 1253 on charges of treason, but he was acquitted and became a commander of the Latin mercenaries in the following year. In 1256, fearing reprisal, he fled to the Seljuk court, but returned to Nicaea in 1257 after receiving the emperor's sworn guarantee of his safety. Palaiologos was then put in charge of an expedition against the state of Epiros, but was soon recalled to Asia Minor and was imprisoned on suspicions of rebellion before becoming once again reconciled with Laskaris just before the latter's death.

Aristocratic opposition and an incapacitating illness threw Laskaris's policies off balance in 1258. The punishments meted out for acts of disloyalty were

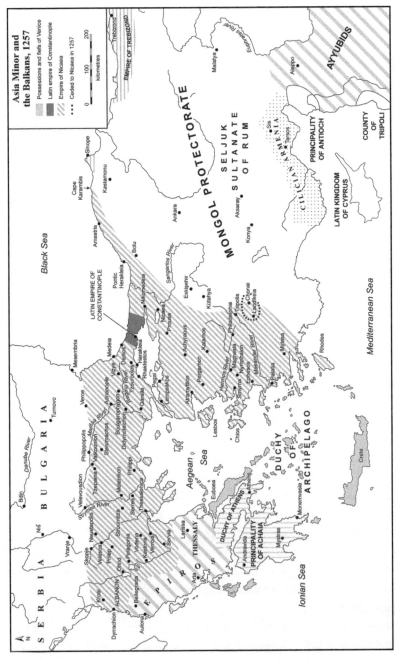

Figure 1. Map of Asia Minor and the Balkans, showing the territories of the Empire of Nicaea under Theodore II Laskaris. Map by L. Parrott.

increasingly harsh. Paradoxically, the last two years of his life proved very productive intellectually and saw the preparation of further collections with many newly composed works. To this period belong the collection *Christian Theology* and a miscellany containing letters, essays, devotional texts, and the philosophical work *Explanation of the World* with its four treatises (two of which are translated here).[9] After Laskaris passed away from his illness on 16 August 1258, the political order that he had established was rapidly transformed. Shortly before his death, he had designated George Mouzalon to serve as the regent until the coming of age of his son, John IV Laskaris. But only a few days after his demise, during a memorial service held at the Sosandra Monastery near Magnesia, the rioting Latin mercenaries assassinated Mouzalon and his two brothers. Michael Palaiologos emerged as the champion of the aristocracy, took advantage of the power vacuum, and was elected regent. In due course he was proclaimed—and in the spring of 1259 crowned—emperor alongside John IV. On 25 July 1261 Nicaean troops victoriously entered Constantinople. After the move of the court to the old imperial capital later in the same year, Palaiologos seized the throne and wrested power from the dynasty that had ruled the empire in exile for over half a century. The period of the so-called state of Nicaea thus came to an abrupt end. The writings of its ruler Theodore II Laskaris are one of the few precious voices of this special era.

The Selected Works

Laskaris was an immensely prolific author for a man who lived only until the age of thirty-six. He wrote in a wide variety of genres: epistolography, philosophy, theology, satire, hymnography, essays, and what can be called "rhetoric" in the broad and inclusive late antique and medieval Greek understanding of this concept.[10] His massive output is explainable through his literary gift, which drew the notice even of contemporaries.[11] In addition, as an emperor Laskaris benefited from the generous help and support of secretaries in the copying and the dissemination of his

---

9 On the five identifiable manuscript collections of Laskaris's works prepared in his lifetime, see below, p. 13 and n. 19.

10 For a list of his works, see Angelov, *Byzantine Hellene*, 320–23. On the varieties of understanding of rhetoric in Byzantium, see, for example, Jeffreys, ed., *Rhetoric in Byzantium*.

11 George Pachymeres, *History* 1.13, ed. Failler, 1:59.13–61.1.

works. For example, the young George Akropolites, who started his distinguished career in the civil service from the position of an imperial secretary, played a role in the preparation of the main epistolary collection of Laskaris, for which he wrote a versified preface.[12]

The eight works of Laskaris chosen for this translation are intended to introduce the modern reader to the most prominent strands of his political thought, philosophy, and self-representation. We see the political thinker who mused on rulership and social solidarity, the inquisitive philosopher who examined the principles of the natural world, the passionate proponent of Hellenism who expressed pride in his descent from the ancient Greeks, and the humorist who tried his hand at satirical and self-ironic compositions. The translated texts reveal a great deal about education and the court in the empire of Nicaea. We see his evolving relations with his mentor in philosophy, Nikephoros Blemmydes, and his political protégé, George Mouzalon. The eight works are arranged in the likely chronological sequence of their composition. The introduction and the annotations to the translations provide relevant context in order to orient the reader in interpreting these complex texts.

The translated selection is only a first step toward making the writings of Laskaris available in English. Some omissions deserve mention as a way of highlighting desiderata for future translations. The speech in praise of his father, the emperor John III Vatatzes, is a fascinating source on Nicaean diplomacy and the public image of the Nicaean emperors.[13] Laskaris's *Encomium on the Spring and the Charming Man* provides insights into Laskaris's emotional world, just as do the *Moral Pieces* translated here.[14] I have selected books 3 and 4 of his philosophical work *Explanation of the World* (namely, *Revelation of the World, or Life* and *On What Is Unclear and a Testimony That the Author Is Ignorant of Philosophy*), while not translating books 1 and 2 (*On the Elements* and *On Heaven*), which are not autobiographical in nature and focus entirely on philosophy. I have selected the seventh book of the collection *Christian Theology*, because the work in question—a speech against the Latins that I have titled *Oration on Hellenism*—conveys one of the most notable aspects of Laskaris's thought and deserves a place in this anthology.

12 George Akropolites, *History*, ed. Heisenberg and Wirth, 7–9. See Macrides, *George Akropolites*, 9–11.
13 Tartaglia, ed., Th. L., *Op. rhet.*, 24–66.
14 Tartaglia, ed., Th. L., *Op. rhet.*, 142–52.

Future translators may consider the other books of the collection—both his Trinitarian treatises, which combine geometry and theological speculation, and his treatise *On the Divine Names* (book 4 of the *Christian Theology*). The translation as well as critical edition of the philosophical treatise *Natural Communion* is yet another major desideratum.[15]

Note on the Editions and the Translations

The translations are based on the modern editions listed below. Most of the assigned English titles follow the manuscript headings found in the collections prepared during Laskaris's lifetime, which reflect the intent of the author, or at least that of his editors. That is why I have consistently translated the headings in full. The Greek text of the headings is given below. In three cases, I have preferred to assign to the translated works titles unrelated to the headings, because these new titles better fit their content: (4) *Oration on Friendship and Politics*, (7) *Oration on Hellenism*, and (8) *Letter on Royal Duty, Taxation, and the Army*.

(1) *Satire of His Tutor* (κωμῳδία εἰς τὸν βαγιοῦλον αὐτοῦ), edited by L. Tartaglia in Th. L., *Op. rhet.*, 154–97.

(2) *Memorial Discourse on Emperor Frederick II* (ἐπιτάφιος εἰς τὸν βασιλέα τῶν Ἀλαμανῶν κυρὸν Φρεδερίκον), edited by L. Tartaglia in Th. L., *Op. rhet.*, 86–94.

(3) *Moral Pieces Describing the Inconstancy of Life* (ἐπιτομαὶ ἠθικαὶ τὸ τοῦ βίου ἄστατον διαγράφουσαι), edited by D. Angelov, "The *Moral Pieces* by Theodore II Laskaris," 237–69. I have introduced only minor changes to my earlier translation. The abbreviated title *Moral Pieces* is henceforth used.

(4) *Oration on Friendship and Politics* (πρὸς τὸν Μουζάλωνα κυρὸν Γεώργιον ἐρωτήσαντα ὁποίους δεῖ εἶναι τοὺς δούλους εἰς τοὺς κυρίους καὶ τοὺς κυρίους εἰς τοὺς δούλους), edited by L. Tartaglia in Th. L., *Op. rhet.*, 120–40.

(5) *Representation of the World, or Life* (κοσμικὴ στήλη ἢ βίος), edited by N. Festa, "Κοσμικὴ Δήλωσις," *GdSAI* 12 (1899), 21–38. The treatise represents the third book of the philosophical collection *Explanation of the World* (Κοσμικὴ Δήλωσις). Two related dedicatory texts are also translated:

---

15 See below, p. 53, n. 94.

Dedicatory Letter to George Mouzalon (manuscript title: ἑτέρα πρὸς τὸν αὐτὸν πρωτοσεβαστὸν καὶ πρωτοβεστιάριον καὶ μέγαν στρατοπεδάρχην κυρὸν Γεώργιον τὸν Μουζάλωνα), edited by N. Festa in Th. L., *Ep.*, no. 187 (p. 236); *Dedicatory Preface to Explanation of the World* (incipit: Μουζάλων, τὸ ἐρωτᾶν ἀναγκαῖον), edited by N. Festa, "Κοσμικὴ Δήλωσις," *GdSAI* 11 (1897-98), 97-101.

(6) *On What Is Unclear and a Testimony That the Author Is Ignorant of Philosophy* (περὶ ἀδήλου καὶ μαρτυρίας τοῦ μὴ εἰδέναι φιλοσοφίαν τὸν γράψαντα), edited by N. Festa, "Κοσμικὴ Δήλωσις," *GdSAI*, 12 (1899), 39-52. The treatise is the fourth book of the philosophical collection *Explanation of the World*.

(7) *Oration on Hellenism* (Χριστιανικῆς Θεολογίας λόγος ἕβδομος, ὁ κατὰ Λατίνων λόγος δεύτερος, ἤγουν περὶ τῆς ἐκπορεύσεως τοῦ ἁγίου Πνεύματος), edited by Ch. Krikonis, in Th. L., *Chr. theol.*, 137-48.

(8) *Letter on Royal Duty, Taxation, and the Army* (τοῦ αὐτοῦ πρὸς αὐτόν), addressed to Nikephoros Blemmydes, edited by N. Festa in Th. L., *Ep.* 44 (pp. 56-59).

The editorial principles followed by the different Greek editions need not concern us here. Rather, a word should be said about the approach taken to vexed textual questions that have arisen in the process of translation. The notes to the translation highlight only textual issues that make a difference in the interpretation of single words or the meaning of entire sentences. In these cases, I have indicated in the notes preferable manuscript readings, have suggested textual emendations, and have pointed to the use of the interrogative rather than the indicative mood, or vice versa. I have not indicated cases in which the punctuation of the Greek might be modified otherwise. Typographical errors in the editions have likewise been ignored. I have compared Luigi Tartaglia's reliable critical editions of (1) *Satire of His Tutor* and (2) *Memorial Discourse on Emperor Frederick II* with the earlier ones by Sophia Georgiopoulou.[16] The notes indicate the few cases in which I have followed the latter's edition. In addition, I have compared Nicola Festa's edition of (5) *Representation of the World, or Life*, (6) *On What Is Unclear and a Testimony That the Author Is Ignorant of Philosophy*, and (8) *Letter on Royal Duty, Taxation,*

---

16 Georgiopoulou, "Theodore II Dukas Laskaris," 259-80 (edition of *Memorial Discourse on Emperor Frederick II*), 285-358 (edition of *Satire of His Tutor*).

Note on the Editions and the Translations

and the Army with the sole manuscript that transmits these texts, Vindobonensis Phil. Gr. 321 (*Diktyon* 71435), a miscellany produced after 1261 by a teacher of rhetoric in Constantinople who had close connections with the Nicaean milieu.[17] A similar collation has been made of (7) *Oration on Hellenism* with the two manuscripts of Laskaris's collection *Christian Theology* in which the text has come down to us: the thirteenth-century Vatican City, Biblioteca Apostolica Vaticana, Vat. gr. 1113 (*Diktyon* 67744), and the fifteenth-century Oxford, Bodleian Library, Barocci 97 (*Diktyon* 47384). Festa's editions of Laskaris's letters and of the philosophical work *Explanation of the World*, published in the 1890s, are in particular need of an update. Future editors should consider carefully the punctuation and the use of red initials in manuscripts copied in Nicaean scriptoria or produced later in the thirteenth century.

I have kept the numbered sections of the text of (1) *Satire of His Tutor*, (2) *Memorial Discourse on Emperor Frederick II*, (4) *Oration on Friendship and Politics*, and (7) *Oration on Hellenism*. These numbered sections reflect the modern editors' understanding of the text rather than the layout in the manuscripts—with the sole exception of (3) *Moral Pieces*, whose constituent essays are numbered and designated as "sections" (τμήματα) in the codices.[18] Following the practice of recent editors, I have introduced numbered sections in the three texts edited by Festa: (5) *Representation of the World, or Life*, (6) *On What Is Unclear and a Testimony That the Author Is Ignorant of Philosophy*, and (8) *Letter on Royal Duty, Taxation, and the Army*. References to the page numbers in Festa's editions are also given in order to orient readers who would like to consult the Greek text.

I have introduced three types of parentheses in the translation. The curved parenthesis "( )" indicates a digression that is part of the original Greek text, functioning in effect as a punctuation sign signifying a break in the flow of the text. The square bracket "[ ]" signals a newly inserted word or phrase in the translation that clarifies a word in the original Greek, usually a personal or demonstrative pronoun (e.g., "it"). The angular bracket "< >" also signals a newly inserted word or phrase in the translation, but one that represents an addition to the original

---

[17] On this important manuscript, see most recently Agapitos and Angelov, "Six Essays," 48–60.

[18] Angelov, "*Moral Pieces*," 251–52. The two manuscripts are the thirteenth-century Ambrosianus gr. C 308 inf. (*Diktyon* 42516) and the fourteenth-century Parisinus gr. 1193 (*Diktyon* 50798).

Greek text and complements its syntax; these brackets thus indicate a more substantial modern intervention. I have italicized quotations (both verbatim and periphrastic) from ancient authors, the scriptures, and the fathers of the church. The abbreviation "cf." in the footnotes refers to periphrastic rather than verbatim quotations and to intertextual echoes. References to classical authors follow the standard editions. The numeration of the Psalms is that of the Greek Septuagint.

Any translation of Laskaris faces the challenge of conveying in another language the literary and stylistic features of his prose (see below, pp. 43–47), in particular his wordplay and idiosyncratic vocabulary. The footnotes point to only some of the plays on words, most of which are inevitably lost in translation, and to a few problems of vocabulary and syntax. I have often broken the complex and flowing sentences in Laskaris's prose into briefer and simpler ones, preferring the readability of the translation to an imitation of the author's style. Some problems naturally arise from the differences between our world and Laskaris's. As just one example, I have preferred to translate rather than transliterate the unofficial honorific titles κυρός (the form κῦρ is also widely attested in Laskaris's time) and κυρά found in the manuscript titles. I have rendered them in English as "lord" and "lady" rather than "Lord" and "Lady" to avoid the modern and formal associations of the latter words. I have striven, as much as possible, to strike a balance between faithfulness to the Greek and clarity in English, although compromises in either direction have been unavoidable.

Chronology and Contexts

The following introductory discussion of matters of chronology, prosopography, and style aims to outline the distinct characteristics of each of the eight translated works. A summary of the content of each work precedes the introduction. A word should be said at the outset about the complex issue of dating the texts. The main—and often only—basis for assigning a date is the mention of politically significant events (e.g., imperial weddings or Laskaris's accession) and experiences connected with Laskaris's education and his relation with friends, teachers, and royal relatives. Clues are also found in chronological markers in the headings of the edited collections produced under his auspices. The circumstance that nearly all of Laskaris's writings have come down to us in manuscript copies of the collections complicates as much as it helps resolve questions of chronology, because the preparation of the collections—the process of selecting, redacting, and presenting his compositions—was in a way their second birthday (see the discussion of *Representation of the World, or Life* below, at pp. 33–35). For this reason, but also because the collections are essential for understanding Laskaris's authorial project, they should be listed here.

The eight works are interspersed among the five identifiable collections of Laskaris's literary output.[19] The *Moral Pieces* forms part of the *Sacred Orations*, a theophilosophical collection of nine works prepared in early 1254. To early 1254 belongs also the production of the main epistolary collection surviving in Biblioteca Medicea Laurenziana, Pl. 59.35 (*Diktyon* 16486), which contains the dedicatory epistle of *Representation of the World, or Life*. The *Satire of His Tutor*, the *Memorial Discourse on Emperor Frederick II*, and the *Oration on Friendship and Politics* were included in a collection of ten secular works prepared later in the course of 1254, but before his accession in November of that year.[20] The *Oration on Hellenism* was incorporated into the eight discourses and treatises of the collection *Christian Theology*, whose creation dates to the last two years of Laskaris's life (1257–1258). A miscellany collection, which contains late works and has not survived in an unbroken manuscript form, dates to the last year of the author's life (1258). This miscellany included *Representation of the World, or Life*, *On What Is Unclear and a Testimony That the Author Is Ignorant of Philosophy* (together with the other two books of *Explanation of the World*), and the *Letter on Royal Duty, Taxation, and the Army* alongside other epistles of Laskaris dating to his four-year reign.

Satire of His Tutor

SUMMARY

1. The recently deceased tutor, evil personified, was a repository of all kinds of vices. Reluctant at first to write the satire, the author does so only for the sake of his audience. In his view, the description of the tutor's shortcomings is instructive and capable of cultivating virtue.

---

[19] On these collections and their chronology, see Angelov, *Byzantine Hellene*, 324–27, 349–50; Angelov, "Moral Pieces," 246–52; Agapitos and Angelov, "Six Essays," 54–56.

[20] All ten works have been edited in the Teubner series by Tartaglia, Th. L., *Op. rhet.*

2. The tutor originated from an unknown place and was an abandoned child. His purported parents were worthy of scorn and laughter. The mother who raised him in her old age had suffered from the medical symptoms of false pregnancy. At the time of expected childbirth, the nurses put an abandoned child (the future tutor) into the empty cot.
3. The contemptible origin of the tutor matched his comical physical characteristics, especially his short stature, which made people who saw him burst into laughter.
4. The traits of his character resembled his appearance in their unseemliness.
5. His adopted mother was close to the court and arranged for his education in an imperial school in Constantinople in the late twelfth century. His studies did not, however, repair the inborn flaws of his character.
6. As time advanced, the incorrigible individual had an adulterous affair with an unnamed Constantinopolitan lady. The two lovers were caught red-handed. The tutor was punished with mutilation of his nose.
7. After the fall of Constantinople to the Latins in 1204, he fled the city and settled in the east—that is, the empire of Nicaea. When Laskaris was in the twelfth year of his life, his royal parents made the mistake of appointing the disgraced individual as his court tutor.
8. Seen in retrospect, the appointment of the tutor was part of God's plan for Laskaris to be tested through temptations and trickeries. The tutor never served as his true guardian. Furthermore, the tutor indicted him with a most absurd accusation: a passion for philosophy.
9. The deeds of the tutor in Constantinople and in the empire of Nicaea were shameful and laughable. Since joking is part of the repertory of philosophers and provides wise people with mental relaxation, the satire should be viewed as a philosophical work. Humor is one of the great inventions of nature.
10. The tutor's character was the exact opposite of that of the tutee. The tutor slandered his tutee and gossiped before Laskaris's royal parents, who turned a deaf ear to the accusations.
11. The tutor incited even the servants of the tutee against him. But the tutee paid no attention and kept his mind focused on his beloved philosophy. He progressed to lessons in logic after having studied rhetoric and poetry, in spite of the tutor's objections.

12. The grizzly-haired tutor dyed his beard black, which made him look even more laughable. He continued to attempt to draw his tutee away from philosophy but failed.
13. The tutee pursued studies in mathematics and proceeded toward advanced studies. His teacher was a great philosopher, whose immense learning aroused the jealousy of the tutor.
14. The tutor schemed against the teacher, who patiently bore the insults and was amicably disposed toward Laskaris. The tutor ignored the benefits of philosophy embodied in the first two of the six definitions of philosophy: "assimilation to God as far as is humanly possible" and "knowledge of things existent as existent."
15. The tutor ignored the features of philosophy inherent in three other definitions: "practice of death," "art of arts and science of sciences," and "knowledge of things divine and human."
16. The tutor did not pay attention to philosophy defined as "love of wisdom." The author calls upon knowledge, philosophy, and education to lament and mock the tutor. On the advice of a friend, however, the author drops the lamentation and opts to address the tutor directly in the second person about the importance of philosophy.
17. The author rhetorically urges the diseased tutor to learn about the need for philosophy. It was absurd that the tutor had withheld the knowledge of philosophy from the royal tutee, who was the heir to the throne, had public responsibilities, and therefore derived great profit from philosophy.
18. All six definitions of philosophy (mentioned in §§14–16) had a special significance for Laskaris's education.
19. The author calls upon the tutor in Hades to find an effective defender against his accusations and returns to his narrative after having addressed the tutor directly (§§17–18).
20. The foolish and deluded tutor considered himself a model of virtue and assaulted philosophy without ever being able to control it. He looked most ridiculous when he entered the palace on feast days. He wore a tall hat and shoes with high heels, attire that could not conceal his short stature.
21. The tutor devised many machinations again the author and his teacher, but God was their firm protector and guardian.

22. The evil actions of the tutor were many, but the author prefers to pass over them and focus on the tutor's death.
23. The tutor was comparable to ancient models of physical and moral degradation (Thersites, Perseus of Macedon, Novatian, and Judas), but the most appropriate comparisons were to animals and the devil himself.
24. Long digressions and poor timekeeping characterize poor rhetoricians, so the author hastens to narrate the events of the tutor's death.
25. After taking part in the celebrations of the wedding of the emperor John III Vatatzes in Nicaea, the tutor remained in the city while the emperor (Vatatzes) and his son (the author) moved with the army to Prousa. The tutor fell ill and lost weight. He left Nicaea, visited Laskaris for a week, and took up residence somewhere in the Thrakesion theme, where his health deteriorated.
26. After the doctors announced to the tutor his imminent death, he called for a last meeting with his royal tutee and devised an evil plan in order to provoke tears of lamentation. But by the time Laskaris arrived at his residence, the tutor had already passed away.
27. The satire serves as evidence that its author prizes and cultivates virtue. The audience is called to disseminate the work among the future generations.

The *Satire* is the earliest datable major literary composition by Laskaris. The work opens with a series of dramatic exclamations expressing his relief at the departure of the hated court tutor and ends with an account of the latter's illness and death, a framing that signals a date of composition in the immediate aftermath of the event. The ambiguity of the pronoun ἐκεῖνος applied to the tutor throughout the *Satire* may well have been intended: it can mean not just "that fellow" (as it has consistently been translated) but also "the late fellow."

The chronology of the tutor's death emerges from its placement within the narrative. The onset of his illness is linked with the festivities in the city of Nicaea for the marriage between Laskaris's father, John III Vatatzes, and Constanza-Anna, the daughter of the emperor Frederick II Hohenstaufen. With the help of a Venetian chronicle, the wedding has been dated to the second half of 1240 or early 1241.[21] The marriage was a memorable event in the life of the Nicaean court. The *chartophylax* at the patriarchate, Nicholas Eirenikos, composed celebratory

21 Kiesewetter, "Die Heirat."

Satire of His Tutor 17

poems, including a poem filled with solar imagery for the ceremony of *prokypsis*, the majestic, sun-like ritual appearance of the bridegroom and bride.[22] According to the *Satire*, the tutor stayed in Nicaea after the wedding and became unwell, while John Vatatzes and his son, Theodore Laskaris, moved to Prousa along with the army. The worsening illness caused the tutor to leave Nicaea and relocate somewhere in the Thrakesion theme in the southern part of the realm, where he invited Laskaris to pay him a visit on his deathbed. The royal tutee complied but did not reach the tutor's residence before he passed away. The composition of the *Satire* thus belongs to the years 1240–1241, or shortly thereafter. One of its central messages is tied to this chronology. The ridicule of the recently deceased tutor serves to voice the determination of the author to continue his philosophical studies, to which the tutor had been vehemently opposed. The *Satire* celebrates philosophy as the greatest achievement of the human mind. A part of the text (§§16–18) is devoted to a description of the six traditional definitions of philosophy, while the mockery of the tutor's vices and foibles is presented as an affirmation of virtue and wisdom. The author's anonymous "friends" (φίλοι)—who are mentioned twice, in §16 and §19—are said to gain edification from the negative example of the tutor. The audience of the *Satire* thus appears to have consisted of the circle of Laskaris's companions at the court, who appreciated the rough humor of the work and shared the author's appreciation of learning and philosophy.

The names of both the tutor and the teacher of philosophy are not mentioned, yet we can pierce their veil of anonymity, to differing degrees. The philosopher is easier to identify. Scholars have traditionally hesitated between Laskaris's two main teachers, Nikephoros Blemmydes and George Akropolites, but the sole possibility on chronological grounds is Blemmydes.[23] First, Akropolites is known to have assumed responsibility for Laskaris's unfinished instruction in philosophy

---

22 Heisenberg, *Aus der Geschichte und Literatur*, 100–105. The manuscript title of the poem refers to the "betrothal" of John III and Anna; but this should not be taken to indicate that the engagement between the Nicaean emperor and the newly arrived Western bride took place at a time other than the marriage, for the betrothal ceremony had been incorporated into marriage rituals since at least the ninth century. See Laiou, "'Consensus Facit Nuptias—Et Non,'" 190–91, with a discussion of the evidence.

23 Luigi Tartaglia, the editor of the *Satire*, preferred Blemmydes in his *editio princeps* (1992), but in the Teubner edition (2000) opted for Akropolites. See Tartaglia, *Satira del pedagogo*, 12 (*apparatus*); Th. L., *Op. rhet.*, 171.

(logic and mathematics in particular) after the interruption of his studies with Blemmydes.[24] The *Satire* describes Laskaris making his first strides in philosophy guided by a great scholar, while being under the watchful eyes of the tutor—a situation that corresponds to the beginning of his studies with Blemmydes, not their continuation with Akropolites. Second and perhaps more important, the chronology of the tutor's death (tied to John III Vatatzes' wedding in 1240–1241) corresponds to the information found in Laskaris's earliest letters to Nikephoros Blemmydes. Epistle 1 (before autumn 1241) presents Laskaris as having already studied under Blemmydes. Epistle 2 (autumn 1241) mentions the death of a patriarch in Nicaea identifiable as Patriarch Methodios II, who remained in office for a few months in 1241. It and Epistle 8 both refer to the machinations of Constantine Klaudioupolites, bishop of Ephesos and patriarch-elect of Antioch, who is attested at that time and whom Blemmydes portrays negatively in his *Autobiography* as a schemer and a personal enemy.[25]

The *Satire* gives little hard information about the life and career of the tutor. He had been educated in Constantinople before the Fourth Crusade and had been well connected with the circles of power under the Angeloi emperors (1185–1204; §5). More than thirty years later, he regaled and admonished the adolescent prince with tales of court intrigue and usurpation that he told from memory. It is unclear whether Laskaris spoke the truth or merely a salacious joke when he described the tutor's adulterous affair and punishment (mutilation of his nose) at the imperial tribunal in Constantinople before 1204 (§6). Facial disfigurement would have been impossible to hide. And yet, the tutor is consistently portrayed with grotesque features. By the 1230s, the tutor was an elderly individual and represented a precious living link with a bygone era. His familiarity with the court before the Fourth Crusade was probably among the reasons for his appointment ca. 1232 to the position of *baioulos* (or *megas baioulos*),[26] traditionally reserved for the educator of the underage—adolescent in Laskaris's case—heir to the throne. This court

---

[24] For the sequence of Laskaris's studies first under Blemmydes and then under Akropolites, see Constantinides, *Higher Education in Byzantium*, 14–19; Angelov, *Byzantine Hellene*, 81–86, 117–18.

[25] Th. L., *Ep.* 1–2 (pp. 1–6), 8 (pp. 11–13). On the chronology, see Angelov, *Byzantine Hellene*, 356–61.

[26] The term derives from the Latin *baiulus* and was used from late antiquity to late Byzantium as a court title of the officially appointed mentor to an imperial prince. See

title appears solely in the manuscript heading to the *Satire*, while the text consistently calls him παιδαγωγός (pedagogue, tutor) and avoids any mention of office holding. The only veiled allusion is the mocking description of the tutor's formal attire during receptions at the court (§20).

An identification of the tutor with a certain παιδαγωγός Zabareiotes, who was a butt of jokes in two of Laskaris's letters, was suggested long ago by Ioannes Papadopoulos.[27] Another possibility emerges from §2 of the *Satire*, which turns the tutor's birth into a parody. The tutor is mocked as an abandoned child born of unknown parents in an unknown land. The mother who adopted him is said to have suffered from a false pregnancy (*kitta*) and to have wished to avoid its shame by presenting an abandoned baby as her child. The baby "was named a conception of the labor of *kitta*" (ὠνομάσθη κίττης ἐκτελέσματος κύημα), an expression that could be a pun on the similar-sounding personal name Niketas (Νικήτας). It is therefore not impossible that the tutor was called Niketas Zabareiotes. And yet, we cannot be certain even of his surname. Elsewhere the *Satire* makes another allusion to his name, which leads toward a different interpretation. Describing how the dying tutor asked for the peace (εἰρήνη) of his soul, Laskaris comments sarcastically that he "deceived the rather simple-minded through the homonymy" (ἠπάτα δὲ τῇ ὁμωνυμίᾳ τοὺς ἁπλουστέρους) and continually conveyed the impression of peace (§26). Is Laskaris referring to the ambiguity of a prayer for peace, mocked in the same passage as the peace of demons? Or is the homonymy an allusion to the tutor's name? In the latter case, which is more likely, the tutor could have had the surname Eirenikos, and thus we could arrive at his full name as Niketas Eirenikos. Representatives of the Eirenikos family held high positions both in the late twelfth century and in Nicaea. Theodore Eirenikos had been an *epi tou kanikleiou* before 1204 and later became patriarch of Constantinople residing in Nicaea (1214–1216).[28] The above-mentioned *chartophylax* and poet Nicholas Eirenikos was a patriarchal official close to the court. The high status of the Eirenikos family certainly fits with

---

Laurent, "Ὁ μέγας βαΐουλος"; pseudo-Kodinos, *Pseudo-Kodinos*, ed. Macrides, Munitiz, and Angelov, 32.8–9, 456 (table).

27 Th. L., *Ep.*, 202.17–19 (p. 248), 216.28–40 (p. 269). Papadopoulos, "La Satire du Précepteur," called him Christophoros Zabareiotes, but this combination of names is not attested or supported by Laskaris's correspondence. The hunched individual in his entourage named Christophoros was not Zabareiotes. See Angelov, *Byzantine Hellene*, 263 n. 9.

28 Simpson, *Niketas Choniates*, 31–32.

the presentation of the tutor in the *Satire* as a politically well-connected man both before and after 1204. The two possible identifications serve only to show the difficulty of interpreting Laskaris's allusive language. The mystery cannot be resolved with certainty, beyond speculating that the name of the tutor may have been either Niketas Zabareiotes or Niketas Eirenikos.

The *Satire* mixes genres and generic modes in ways that scholars have shown to be typical of Byzantine literary production from the eleventh century onward. The overall structure is that of an inverted encomium—that is, an invective (ψόγος) as described in the *progymnasmata* of Aphthonios (fourth century).[29] The author of an invective, according to Aphthonios, has to follow the standard components of an encomium, vilifying rather than praising the family, birth, upbringing, and character of the subject. The *Satire* is structured accordingly, and the author explicitly calls the work a ψόγος (§9). At the same time, the manuscript title and the text in many places designate the work as κωμῳδία, a word that points in the direction of mocking humor. The word has been translated as "satire," although "lampoon" is also appropriate.[30] The tenth-century *Souda* and other lexica explain κωμῳδίαι as "insults," "ridicules," and "mockeries" (ὕβρεις, διασυρμοί, ἐμπαίγματα).[31] The word was used to designate the satire of Katablattas written by John Argyropoulos in the fifteenth century.[32] Laskaris frequently also calls the work a λόγος (§§7, 9, 11, 13, 14, 17, 22), translated here as an "account," for the satire not only engages in diatribe against the late tutor (as expected from ψόγος, an invective, and κωμῳδία, a mockery) but also is a narrative. The *Satire* is, in fact, a double narrative, weaving together a parody of the tutor's life and an account of the author's education. The work can be described as a combination of burlesque biography and assertive autobiography. A large part is written in the first-person singular and resembles other self-referential works of Laskaris, such as the *Moral Pieces* and *On What Is Unclear*.

---

29 Aphthonius, *Progymnasmata*, no. 9, ed. Rabe, 27–31, with the example of an invective against Philip of Macedon

30 For the manuscript title of the work, see above, p. 9. The word κωμῳδία is found in §§5, 9, 13, 16, 17, and 19. The author also uses the rare word διακωμῴδησις (§1) attested solely in Blemmydes.

31 *Souda*, kappa 2268 (ed. Adler, 3:175). The same entry is also found in Photios's lexicon.

32 John Argyropoulos, *Katablattas*, ed. Canivet and Oikonomides, 30.50, 59.446, 79.726. See Marciniak, "The Art of Abuse," 355–56.

Memorial Discourse on Emperor Frederick II
SUMMARY

1. The subject of the brief speech is the fate of rulers and generals to be targets of blame and mockery. The deplorable situation is within the nature of things: human nature tends to remember human faults and does not applaud virtuous actions. Reproach and ridicule are the perennial companions of leadership.
2. An irrational spirit of harsh criticism permeates public opinion. The ruler's accomplishments as a general are forgotten and considered blameworthy; the approach to his achievements in peacetime is similar. Aware of the normality of this situation, the ruler can still govern effectively, for he would realize that his fellow generals likewise receive no appreciation. There is a special reason for the harsh critique of rulers: the maintenance of justice arouses envy and hatred. Rulers face a stark choice: either practice impartial justice for the common good or fulfill through their leniency what is wished for. The former is preferable to the latter. The justice of a true ruler inevitably provokes envy and hatred.
3. The negative attitude toward good rulers is inspired by demons and the devil. The slanderers of a ruler who serves the common good deserve both human and divine punishment. The hallmarks of good rulership are peace, prosperity, and the growing greatness of the polity. Philosophy is the best adornment of rulership.
4. The ruler's and the subjects' wishes are at variance. Either the ruler can fulfill the wishes of everyone and be honored by everyone (a bad proposition, because harm to the realm would then occur), or he can administer justice steadfastly and incur hatred (the preferable proposition). This is a good kind of hatred, because the realm is preserved. Therefore, the ruler should accept criticism as his lot and should not protest but should seek strength both from God and within himself in order to continue to act for the common good.
5. Praises of the ruler while he is alive do not matter, for he gains nothing from them in this world and cannot benefit from them after he dies. The ungrateful multitude easily forgets his good deeds. The best and natural praise of the ruler is his work for the preservation of the realm. When the multitude continues to slander the ruler after his death, his soul is not affected. The truth eventually becomes known to those capable of reasoning. The ruler's trophies stand in his defense, leading to praises and appreciation even from enemies.

6. Petty-minded and shortsighted individuals are busy with slandering the ruler who struggles for the common good. Justice will be served, however. The brief speech has revealed the true character of the ruler and his subjects.

The *Memorial Discourse* offers fascinating musings on kingship, royal justice, and public opinion. Laskaris evidently composed the text in early 1251 in response to the death of Frederick II Hohenstaufen (b. 1194; crowned emperor in 1220; d. 13 December 1250), called "the emperor of Germans Frederick" in the manuscript title, who had been Nicaea's strategic ally for over a decade. The title designates the work as an ἐπιτάφιος—that is, a funerary speech—yet this is a misnomer. The text lacks any feature of this genre as prescribed in Menander Rhetor's handbook on epideictic rhetoric, such as praise of the family, birth, and deeds of the deceased, as well as lament.[33] Nothing immediately suggests that Laskaris's discourse was written to mourn the death or commemorate the life and career of a specific individual: there is no invocation of the audience, no reference to the grief of the Nicaean empress Constanza-Anna (Frederick II's daughter and John III's wife), and no mention of any episode from the biography of the Western emperor. Only indirectly does the composition serve as a memorial discourse. Frederick died during a raging civil war and a public hate campaign against him led by the papacy. His fate gave an occasion to his younger contemporary and fellow emperor in the Greek East to reflect soberly on the experiences of rulers: they were destined to incur hatred in their lifetime and ran the risk of oblivion after their death.

Interpreting the broader aspects of the composition and audience of the *Memorial Discourse* raises different possibilities. The work could be viewed as an elaboration on a point in Blemmydes' *Imperial Statue*. Commenting on the historical example of Nerva, Blemmydes wrote that his kindness and mercy had enabled the Roman emperor to patiently endure mockery (τωθασμοί) and scoffing (σκώμματα).[34] Yet the *Memorial Discourse* also addresses other questions, such as royal justice, and focuses on the normative consequences of the negative feelings of the subjects. In contrast to the *Imperial Statue*, the *Memorial Discourse* presents no exemplary models of rulership, instead opening with a reference to the present

---

33 *Menander Rhetor*, Treatise 2.11, ed. Russell and Wilson, 170–79. See also the guidelines for funeral speeches by pseudo-Dionysios translated in ibid., 373–76.

34 Blem., *Imperial Statue* 61 (p. 62).

times. The discourse therefore should be read as a work of royal self-fashioning and political theory, which builds on what the Nicaean court audience *already* knew about Frederick II. Information about the two excommunications and the dethronement of the Western emperor by the papacy at the First Council of Lyons (1245) trickled into Asia Minor through different channels. Laskaris attended the reception and discussions with papal envoys in Nymphaion in the early months of 1250. Frederick's letters of the summer of 1250, which were composed in Greek, apprised Vatatzes of the outcome of specific battles with papal forces.[35] In the *Memorial Discourse*, Laskaris subtly manipulated the impressions of his court audience about the embattled Western emperor and guided them toward his own ideas of royal rule.

Indeed, motifs of the *Memorial Discourse* were applied self-referentially elsewhere in Laskaris's works. In a late autobiographical essay, Laskaris discusses the bodily self-sacrifice of rulers who pay no attention to their own health during military campaigns.[36] In letters, he presents wise and educated men like himself as the targets of mockery for the common crowd.[37] The same image is implicit in *On What Is Unclear*. The *Memorial Discourse* is a special work, however, because it lays out a philosophical argument about royal justice as the root cause of this confrontational relationship. The scrupulous exercise of justice gives rise to hatred. The ruler has to understand the origin of this feeling and endure it patiently for the benefit of the political community.

Moral Pieces Describing the Inconstancy of Life
SUMMARY

1. The best cure for sorrow is the knowledge of God's existence and care. There is divine judgment and retribution before the Last Judgment. Human nature is divinely created, and even though it distances itself from its origin, it is able to regain strength from God. Corrupted over time, the human soul turns occasionally to pleasure and revolves in a vicious circle nearing destruction. The lives of mortals are filled with inconstancy.

---

35 Franchi, *La svolta politico-ecclesiastica*, 61–133; Gill, *Byzantium and the Papacy*, 89–90. See Frederick II Hohenstaufen, *Greek Letters*, ed. Merendino.
36 This is essay 6 published and translated by Agapitos and Angelov, "Six Essays," 46–47.
37 Th. L., *Ep.* 49 (pp. 67–71), 121 (pp. 167–70).

2. Humans are beset by constant misfortunes. Human nature is accustomed to value material things (food, luxury, comfort, servants, honor, and pomp), whose disappearance brings about sorrow. Human nature is capable of reason, yet it is more unfortunate than inanimate objects.
3. The author has experienced both extreme happiness and extreme grief owing to life's inconstancy. What he had once valued does not matter any longer. He laments the human desire for impermanent things that brings no profit in the end. He himself had been deluded, but now he has learned a lesson through his suffering.
4. The author had lived without any thought of death, which makes his pain worse. Life's inconstancy has destroyed what he once wrongly thought belonged to him. Worldly affairs drag the soul toward the habit of pleasure. Habit makes human nature unreceptive to virtue and leads to perdition. Suffering is a sobering experience, which enables one to rise above the corruption caused by materiality and time.
5. The crowd, however, prefers a life of material corruption. Virtue is ignored, even though it is precious and everyone ought to embrace it. Life without virtue brings about hollow pleasure and eventually sorrow. The story of sorrow is one terrible to tell. The author laments his own suffering, which he never expected to experience, and mourns human affairs for their inconstancy and tendency to lead to pain.
6. Most people tend to set store by glory, money, and luxury, but the author is amazed at the erroneous opinion of the crowd. He looks with wonderment at matter, passing away, and life's delusion. Everyone should be amazed at the inconstancy of human affairs, in order to attain the constancy of virtue. The acts of fortune are as inconstant as the passage of time.
7. Keeping the mind focused on the inconstancy of time and human affairs enables one to avoid pain and disillusionment. Everyone should consider time, fortune, and materiality nonexistent: things that are thought to exist, but in reality are nothing. Time, wealth, family relationships, and the body belong to the corruptible material world.
8. Material generation, change, and corruption happen by the force of time. Things subject to generation and passing away are nonexistent. Seasonal atmospheric phenomena reveal changes in the material universe and resemble the destructive force of fortune. The existent is constant and nonexistence

is its slave. Humans should not be the slaves of the nonexistent and should practice virtue.
9. Intelligent people should be amazed at changes in the material world and in human thoughts, not because they are unusual but because of their tendency to turn to the worse. It is easy for someone to be lured by materiality. Noble souls, however, should feel attached to intellectual things rather than materiality. True nobility is measured not by blood but by virtue, character, and care for the soul. A soul purified from corruption becomes divine.
10. One should stay away from corruptible things, which are thought to be good but are not, and should seek the company of good men, which implants virtue. Feeble individuals like the author find death frightening, but upright and stable people are drawn to virtue and find passing away desirable.
11. Nature is the beginning of motion and rest. It sets into motion generation, growth, and decay in the material universe. Human nature resembles flowers, which blossom and wither. Life is fleeting and humans are subject to material decay.
12. The author confesses that he has lived so far a life of pleasure and enjoyment without any misfortune. He had felt joy in his soul and his soulmate, his spouse. His suffering and sorrow are now immense. He and his spouse had been happier than all people, but death put this happiness to an end. He wishes to descend into the land of Hades, because he has been deprived of his life, soul, and heart as well as the salvation of his life.

The *Moral Pieces* is a personal work of reflection on the meaning of life, death, virtue, love, and other topics. As the manuscript heading specifies, it dates to the period when the author was mourning the death of his wife, the empress Elena—an event datable through Laskaris's correspondence to 1252.[38] The twelve essays constituting the *Moral Pieces* are loosely tied together, with each additional essay elaborating on a point made earlier or broaching a different theme. The style is flowing and the I-voice is omnipresent. The structure and content of the work suggest that Laskaris composed each of the twelve essays separately and later combined them into a whole. The manuscript title, ἐπιτομαὶ ἠθικαί (literally, "ethical epitomes"), itself points to a series of themes of moral philosophy that are treated

38 See Angelov, "*Moral Pieces*," 238–41.

in a succinct, summary fashion. The themes vary widely and include the changeability of fortune, the corruptibility of matter, self-remorse, the salvatory power of virtue, lament, and romantic love, which is the theme of the last and particularly dramatic essay.

Oration on Friendship and Politics
SUMMARY

1. Alexander, the king of Macedon, is honored for prizing friendship more than for his great conquests. He had five loyal and like-minded friends who helped him in his famous military campaign.
2. Alexander and his friends are models of rulership and loyalty. Three different rivers draw their water from the source of friendship. The first river is the river of pleasure. Another river flows from the same source for those interested in profit and materiality. The third river is the purest, being spiritual and intellectual.
3. Three kinds of friendship correspond to the three rivers: friendship for the sake of pleasure, profit, and the natural good.
4. The three types of friendship intersect in the figure of the emperor, who must be honored more than all friends and relatives. The natural good means peace, security, public welfare, and good ordering of the polity, for all of which the emperor serves as the guarantor. There is nothing more exalted than the emperor who is an image of God.
5. A long description is given of friendship for the sake of profit, which involves reciprocal exchanges between the emperor and his friendly subject. Most of the exchanges are phrased with the expressions "let the friend give" and "let him receive."
6. An account of friendship for the sake of pleasure follows, focusing on the resources available at the court and on royal pastimes, such as hunting and horse riding. The friend who enjoys pleasure receives praises from his master and gains the honor and respect of others, both his friends and his relatives as well as his enemies.
7. The friend of the emperor will be pleased once rumors spread of his privileged status. Pleasure, profit, and the natural good are all found in friendship with the emperor. Everyone should befriend his lord rather than relatives and friends.

8. Alexander's friends gave back many gifts to their lord, including their affection, loyalty, service, and selfless devotion. Alexander honored them with resources and status. They reigned together with him.
9. The master and his friends resemble a statue of virtues. All sovereigns and subjects are urged to look at and learn from the statue, which represents a model relationship of trusting devotion and love. The love of true subjects surpasses that of blood relatives. The audience is asked to maintain its devotion to their lord.
10. The author reminds George Mouzalon of his request that prompted the composition of this work.

There is little that can be said with certainty about the chronology of this work, except that it belongs to the period 1250–1254. Laskaris seems to have drawn inspiration from Blemmydes' *Imperial Statue* (late 1240s),[39] with which it shares a similar discourse of political admonition, the example of Alexander and his friends, and the image of the statue of virtue (§9). While 1250 is a plausible terminus post quem, the terminus ante quem revealed by the manuscript heading is Laskaris's accession as a sole emperor in November 1254. The manuscript heading is revealing in another way, because it states the addressee as George Mouzalon and adds that the author was responding to Mouzalon's question (a question repeated at the end of the text in a slightly different version) regarding the relations between lords and their subjects. The query is reminiscent of the questions-and-answers literature in Byzantium and sets up a mentoring relationship between Laskaris and Mouzalon. We are left with the impression that Laskaris, who was still the coemperor, took up the task (and advertised it through the oration) of training Mouzalon for his future position of power.

The historical significance of the *Oration on Friendship and Politics* has already been explored on several occasions.[40] Its punchline toward the end (§9)

---

39 In the *Imperial Statue*, Blemmydes alludes to his conflict with John III Vatatzes' mistress Marchesina, which is usually dated to the late 1240s. See Ševčenko, "A New Manuscript." In any case, the *Imperial Statue* was written before the *Memorial Speech on Emperor Frederick II* (datable to 1251), which borrows vocabulary from Blemmydes' mirror of princes.

40 Svoronos, "Le serment de fidélité," 138–39; Angelov, *Imperial Ideology*, 215–26; Angelov, *Byzantine Hellene*, 124–27.

lies in the "unusual" proposition that the loyalty of true friends surpasses that of many and illustrious relatives. The idea echoes Laskaris's uneasy relationship with the kinship-based Nicaean aristocracy and foreshadows his plans to promote a service elite. The subversion of aristocratic values is one striking feature of this work. Another is the silence about any official structures of authority, such as civil, military, and ecclesiastical offices. The work thus should be viewed not as a treatise on governance but rather as a blueprint for forging elite solidarity and creating a tight-knit patronage system. The appeal (§9) to a universal audience of "all potentates and subjects" (ἡγεμόνες καὶ δοῦλοι ἅπαντες) creates the impression of a political manifesto. By speaking about many lords (κύριοι) or masters (δεσπόται) and about their friends (φίλοι) or servants/subjects (δοῦλοι), the author presents a hierarchy of patronage networks and feudal-like dependencies topped by the emperor.

The literary inspirations of the work have received less treatment than its social significance and deserve attention.[41] The example of Alexander of Macedon and his friends, which serves as a rhetorical opening and as a framing device (it is repeated at the end), raises questions about the literary imagination of the author and his audience. Laskaris opens the work by alluding to an anecdote about Alexander, who is alleged to have pointed in the direction of his friends when asked to display his immense treasures. Found in late antique rhetoric, the proverbial saying was the subject of a rhetorical exercise (*chreia*) by Libanius[42] and made its way to Byzantine sacro-profane florilegia, such as the *Loci Communes* of pseudo-Maximos the Confessor;[43] it was featured in Blemmydes' *Imperial Statue*, which was probably Laskaris's immediate source.[44] Another commonplace about friendship

---

41 A recent exception is Andreou and Agapitos, "Of Masters and Servants."

42 Libanius, *Progymnasmata* 3.1; ed. and trans. Gibson, *Libanius's Progymnasmata*, 44–55. See Theon, *Progymnasmata*, in Walz, *Rhetores Graeci*, 1:208.16–18; Themistius, *Or.* 16.203bc; Libanius, *Or.* 9.8. Xenophon, *Cyropaedia* 8.2.19, attributes the saying to Cyrus the Elder, and it appears as a general maxim in the *Sententiae* of Menander, ed. S. Jäkel, 79.810 (φίλους ἔχων νόμιζε θησαυροὺς ἔχειν) and in Ecclus. 6:14 (φίλος πιστὸς σκέπη κραταιά, ὁ δὲ εὑρὼν αὐτὸν εὗρεν θησαυρόν).

43 Pseudo-Maximos the Confessor, *Loci Communes* 6, ed. Ihm, 154 (PG 91:764), attributes the saying to Alexander. But the *Florilegium Baroccianum*, known also as *Florilegium Patmiacum*, cites it as anonymous. See *Florilegium Baroccianum* (*Florilegium Patmiacum*) 11.129, ed. Sargologos, 322–23.

44 Blem., *Imperial Statue* 75–76 (p. 66), associating Alexander with Cyrus the Elder.

found at the beginning of the *Oration* is that friends resemble organs of sensation and comprehension, through which the ruler can see and hear everything.[45]

Laskaris highlights five devoted friends of Alexander who corresponded to the five senses (§1). The fascination with the number five follows the author's interest in numerology.[46] He may have modeled the five friends of Alexander on five individuals from among his own close associates.[47] A popular work of literature circulating in his time also probably influenced the focus on Alexander's select friends. The Byzantine court audience learned stories about Alexander from the Hellenistic Alexander romance, of which various medieval redactions were produced. As Corinne Jouanno has observed, the middle Byzantine recension ε differs from earlier versions in assigning prominence to several of Alexander's friends and in putting emphasis on expressions of love.[48] The evocation of kisses and embraces between Alexander and his friends are frequent in this version of the romance, just as Laskaris's oration expresses the attachment between the lord and his servants with words such as "harmony" (§1), "union" (§2), "bond" (§2), and "love" (§§4, 5, 9). The statues of Alexander and his friends and generals that were erected in the city of Alexandria, according to the ε recension, provide a curious parallel to the model statue of virtues represented by the master and his servants (§9).[49]

The theory of friendship in the oration rests on ancient philosophical foundations. The three categories of friendship described in §§3–6 derive from book 8 of Aristotle's *Nicomachean Ethics*. A bibliophile who had access to manuscripts of Aristotle, Laskaris was probably familiar with the text. He could also learn about the three types of friendship from florilegia.[50] The author approached

45 Dio Chrysostom, *Or.* 1 (*On Kingship*), 32, ed. Von Arnim, 1:6.17–20, and hence excerpted in pseudo-Maximos the Confessor, *Loci Communes* 6, ed. Ihm, 132 (PG 91:760). See also Thomas Magistros, *On Kingship* 16, ed. Volpe Cacciatore, 58.732–59.735.

46 Angelov, *Byzantine Hellene*, 194.

47 As suggested by Macrides, *George Akropolites*, 24–25.

48 Jouanno, "Alexander's Friends in the *Alexander Romance*," points to four prominent friends in this version. Curiously, the post-Byzantine vernacular *Phyllada* (§275; ed. Veloudis, 110; trans. Stoneman, 151) published in Venice in the late seventeenth century refers to five loyal friends and companions of Alexander.

49 See below, p. 126, n. 32.

50 On Laskaris's access to a deluxe manuscript of Aristotle's natural philosophy, see Prato, "Un autografo." The three Aristotelian categories, as mentioned in Plutarch, *On Having Many Friends* 94B, entered pseudo-Maximos the Confessor, *Loci Communes* 6,

Aristotle's theory from the perspective of his time. He kept close to Byzantine approaches to friendship, which emphasized practicality and reciprocity,[51] while drawing ample material from Nicaean politics and court culture. Thus, the highest form of friendship, for the sake of the natural good, is friendship with the emperor, whose duties of expanding the frontiers and welcoming refugees correspond closely to those of the Nicaean rulers (§4). The descriptions of the middle and the lowest forms of friendship, undertaken for the sake of utility and pleasure, lay out a tool kit for cultivating a loyal following. Friends had access to the luxuries and entertainment culture of the Nicaean court (§6). The term *oikeiotes*, translated here as "membership in the household," which is used (§§5, 7) to describe their relationship with the emperor, evokes the semiofficial epithet *oikeios* found among the holders of court titles in late Byzantium.[52]

Representation of the World, or Life
SUMMARY

1. The treatise is a philosophical inquiry into the lack of stability (ἀστασία) in the world and a revelation of what has remained undisclosed so far. The addressee of the treatise, George Mouzalon, is asked to receive and multiply this special gift.
2. The enjoyment of material goods is the choice of the multitude, but it goes against philosophy. The author, who has been nourished in philosophy since his childhood, is keen to share with Mouzalon his knowledge of life. The treatise shuns rhetoric. Its focus is on subjects transcending reason: the inconstancy of circumstances and individual choices. The world resembles one single city, with all kinds of pursuits and ranges of emotions. The author's own experiences serve as a proof of the things described—experiences that have shed light on many arguments.
3. The corruption of judges in the law court is the first confirmation of the lack of stability in the world. As a consequence, the Aristotelian principles of the "positive" and the "privative" (*Categories* 12a27–13a36) appear to have

---

ed. Ihm, 123–24. See also *Florilegium Baroccianum* (*Florilegium Patmiacum*) 11.60, ed. Sargologos, 303.

51 See, for example, Mullett, "Byzantium: A Friendly Society?"
52 See below, p. 120, n. 15.

Representation of the World, or Life

suffered. The principle of right timing has also been harmed. The importance of right timing is illustrated by the skills of the general and sea captain. The best things in life are those done in accordance with nature. The person who lives according to nature and possesses knowledge leads the best and most praiseworthy life.

4. Things are unstable in practice and by origin, each influencing the other in a dialectical relationship. Thus, a law that has failed leads to its correction and, conversely, an otherwise sound law can fail. The reason for the instability of the law lies in the uncertainty of human action and the craftiness of human beings. The author introduces the topic of disorder (ἀταξία) as another theme of the treatise. An example of the absence of order is the unfulfilled dictum of Plato about the philosopher-king. The author admits that he has failed to bring order among his officials. Another example of sociopolitical disorder is the greediness of tax collectors. Yet nothing remains hidden from God, and justice will be served.

5. The prophet Isaiah had once deplored Jerusalem and foreseen its fall. The author for his part laments over the "great city," evidently Constantinople. The disarray (ἀταξία) of Jerusalem had never become prevalent in lands outside of the city. The rise and fall of great leaders is explored. Statesmen in antiquity (Hannibal, Brutus, and Alcibiades) had once enjoyed moments of glory before their steep downfall. The main cause for the downfall of rulers is the duplicity of slanderers and the dissimulation of flatterers. Great rulers may be able to conquer large territories but cannot hope to exert control over the secrets of the human mind.

6. Material nature is easily weakened. The best things in life are order and disorder, each dialectically generating the other. Hidden things are found in life because people lack sincerity and dissimulate like foxes. They take on the deceptive appearance of reverence and gentleness, while in reality they harbor destructive thoughts. The human being is more secretive in his speech than are voiceless creatures.

7. The author gives a long list of observations and testimonies on deceit, insincerity, incompletion, natural disasters, absence of social order, injustice, misunderstanding, paradoxes, and curiosities. The observations and testimonies are introduced with the phrase "I saw," although some of the examples "seen" are derived from the author's philosophical and literary education. He alone

feels the pain and bemoans the reasoning of the multitude. This reasoning can be overcome only by the ruler who prevails over instability by his high rank, although the author has "seen" rulers unable to do so. The universe consists of many different components. A digression follows on another dialectical relationship, that between honor and dishonor.

8. The author embarks on describing the four seasons. The orderly change of the seasons and of seasonal human activity is set against the background of the constancy of human mistakes and transgressions. The spring is the season when living nature reawakens and when people return to their senses. The idyllic picture is marred by the demands of the tax collectors, who drive the peasants into debt. A digression on honor and nobility follows. Nobility is defined as a moral characteristic rather than as determined by blood. The focus then shifts to proper timing and the fickleness of fortune.

9. The summer season is marked by specific activities in farming, warfare, taxation, commerce, diplomacy, and medicine. It is a time when individuals can correct earlier mistakes, but many people tend to repeat them. This tendency is illustrated by the second rebellion of the tetrarchic emperors Maximian and Licinius as well as by the continual plotting of Emperor Caligula's praetorian prefect Macro. Humankind keeps lapsing into error after the Fall.

10. The autumn is the season of decay and a time for harvesting the products of agricultural labor. People who have transgressed before the coming of the autumn remain unrepentant: the seasons and the fruits symbolize the stages of progression of human faults. People who have made transgressions in the spring (their youth) and have not been corrected in the summer (their prime) are now humiliated in the autumn (old age).

11. Winter is the time of reckoning for past mistakes, a season for punishments and rewards. The author has a vision of the punishments in Hades and speaks allegorically of the extreme weather conditions in wintertime. He laments over what the multitude tends to laugh about.

12. The author leaps over ordinary human life and has a vision of Lady Philosophy. She instructs him about phenomena in heaven and in the air as well as about medicine; she reveals unfair practices at the marketplace and in the workshops of the silk weavers; she explains the craft of the silversmiths. The author learns that he still lacks full knowledge of mathematics and that people who

have indulged in pleasure and have abused their power will be found guilty for their misdeeds in the fire of the Last Judgment.
13. The author presents a vision of coherence in the universe, a coherence established by a single ungraspable and invisible nature, which lies above physical nature and above the elements. In this ungraspable and invisible nature, the monad and the triad are consubstantial. There is no "otherness" in this uniform nature. God who holds the universe together through this nature is present everywhere, just as the soul is in the body. Political power and life itself exist through God, who distributes the divine grace to everyone.
14. Human understanding is twofold: for the sake of pleasure only and for the sake of pleasure as well as acquisition. The difference is compared to a person entering the imperial treasury: he can either derive pleasure from what he sees or derive pleasure as well as acquire precious objects from the treasury. God who grants benefaction to every single person in different proportions has bestowed exceptional knowledge on the author. Laskaris dedicates the work to Mouzalon and expects him to draw knowledge from it in the future.

The treatise *Representation of the World, or Life* is the third book of the philosophical work *Explanation of the World*, which is addressed to George Mouzalon. *Explanation of the World* consists of four treatises on different subjects written at different times, which were subsequently combined, numbered, and furnished with a dedicatory preface. These treatises, or books, are the following: (1) *On the Elements*, (2) *On Heaven*, (3) *Representation of the World, or Life*, and (4) *On What Is Unclear and a Testimony That the Author Is Ignorant of Philosophy*. The dedicatory preface to *Explanation of the World* mentions the queries of the ever-curious Mouzalon as motivating the author. The instructional goal resembles that of the *Oration on Friendship and Politics*.

The chronology of *Representation of the World, or Life* is particularly tangled and can be resolved only in light of the redaction of Laskaris's works at the time of their publication in collections.[53] The dedicatory letter of *Representation of the World, or Life* as a separate work has survived among the epistles of Laskaris to

---

53 The discussion here of the chronology of *Representation of the World, or Life* and *On What Is Unclear and a Testimony That the Author Is Ignorant of Philosophy* follows Angelov, *Byzantine Hellene*, 338–42.

Mouzalon composed before his imperial accession in November 1254. A translation of this dedicatory letter has been included alongside that of the dedicatory preface to the entire four-part work. If the placement of the letter in the manuscript (Biblioteca Medicea Laurenziana, Conventi soppressi 627, *Diktyon* 15899) can serve as a guide, it was written not long before November 1254.[54] The manuscript heading of *Explanation of the World* states that the entire four-part work dates to the period before the author's imperial accession in November 1254. And yet, contrary to this chronology, the treatise comments on burning political issues from the point of view of a reigning emperor. The author speaks in the first person about his policies as examples of order and disorder in the universe (§4), refers to dealings with imperial officials (§§4, 13), and comments on the deceitful behavior of unnamed powerful individuals (§7). The allusions to Laskaris's experiences during his sole rule led Maria Andreeva in 1930 to consider the treatise evidence of the author's polemical stance toward Nikephoros Blemmydes in the last years of his life.[55] Indeed, the manuscript heading of the collection *Explanation of the World* directly contradicts a date before Laskaris's imperial accessions by referring to the addressee, George Mouzalon, with the entire range of court titles granted to him on Christmas 1255, as well as by using the term "full completeness of the imperial rule" (ἐντελέχεια τῆς βασιλείας), found only in editions produced after November 1254.[56]

The following solution to the chronological conundrum is the most plausible one. Laskaris composed the first redaction of the *Representation of the World, or Life* before his accession in November 1254. He made revisions of the text later, most probably in 1257 or 1258, after he returned to Asia Minor (winter of 1257) from his sojourn in the Balkans. The updated version entered the philosophical collection *Explanation of the World*, which was produced under his auspices and disseminated during his reign. This interpretation gains plausibility from the particularly choppy style and the long and disjointed list of eyewitness testimonies of deceptive behavior (§7). The possibility that dictation was used in the process

---

54 Th. L., *Ep.* 187 (p. 236). A note between Ep. 192 and Ep. 193 (fol. 5v of Biblioteca Medicea Laurenziana, Conventi soppressi 627) separates the previously copied letters composed before the imperial accession of Theodore II Laskaris from those copied next, composed after his accession. The dedicatory letter belongs to the former period.

55 Andreeva, "Polemika."

56 On this term, see Angelov, *Byzantine Hellene*, 328.

On What Is Unclear

of composition or revision should not be excluded.[57] The treatise exhibits a strong empirical streak. "Experience does not suffice only as experience," Laskaris writes, "but as elucidation of many arguments" (§2).

Representation of the World, or Life defies generic categories: a philosophical treatise meant to educate Mouzalon; a record book of impressions, achievements, and failures; and a personal confession of the quest for knowledge and union with God. The composition is filled with allusions to contemporary events and individuals that can rarely be deciphered. As a philosophical treatise, it combines natural philosophy with reflections on ethics and politics. The author argues that human life and the material world of nature are intricately related. The inconstancy of the physical universe exemplified by the change of the four seasons has an uncanny connection with human thought and action: it parallels the unsteadiness of the human mind. The thesis is summed up in the proposition that "one should think of the seasons and the fruits as corresponding to the concealment of thoughts" (§10). The treatise is not a religious work, even with its occasional references to an all-powerful God, the Creation, and the Last Judgment. Its opening states that the cohesive stability of nature comes from God, while instability belongs to the world of the particulars. It is the particulars in all their variety that are of special interest to the author rather than God, who remains a distant and uninvolved figure. The bulk of the treatise introduces Mouzalon to the wondrous and divinely ordained diversity in nature and in humankind through many examples drawn from readings on philosophy and history, as well as from personal experiences and firsthand observations.

On What Is Unclear and a Testimony That the Author Is Ignorant of Philosophy
SUMMARY

1. The terms "existence," "nonexistence," "understanding," "misunderstanding," "knowledge," and "ignorance" are defined. Knowledge means knowing what exists; it is a consequence of the existent and elevates one toward being. It also means knowing the properties of virtue. People who cultivate and practice virtue live in the best way. Misunderstanding and ignorance lead to the worst kind of life.

---

57 Laskaris explicitly mentions this method of composition. See Agapitos and Angelov, "Six Essays," 46.28–30, 63.

2. The author confesses to a lack of any knowledge. This ignorance means he has no hope of gaining fame and advancing in virtue. He is resolved to lift the veil covering his deficiencies and display his weakness caused by ignorance.
3. A philosopher must have knowledge of logic and be able to construct syllogisms.
4. The author confesses ignorance of logic and voices fear lest he encounter someone who would refute and ridicule him for his foolishness. He also announces his ignorance of mathematics.
5. Mathematics helps one create a connection with the intellect. The author describes and defines the disciplines of geometry and arithmetic.
6. Music, arithmetic, and geometry together constitute mathematics. The mathematical disciplines enable one to approach heaven, building a bridge to the intelligible world and enlightening the mind, which approaches God as much as is possible.
7. The author confesses ignorance of Aristotle. He urges those who are ignorant like him to go to school and acquire learning from a teacher.
8. The person untrained in rhetorical methods should not be designated as a rhetorician. If such a person tries to practice oratory, he would deploy no rhetorical device and accomplish none of the goals of rhetoric. The author himself has failed in rhetoric.
9. The author confesses ignorance of rhetoric, poetry, and grammar.
10. The capable poet uses allegory, examines old compositions, excerpts notes from books, and values word choices. Students of grammar need to distinguish between grammatical rules set by nature and rules set by convention. The meaning of words explicable through etymology is set by convention; the semantic reasoning based on the etymology of one word is not transferrable to another word.
11. The author confesses ignorance of grammar, rhetoric, mathematics, and Aristotelian science. He is blind in his mind and resembles a body deprived of sense perception.
12. He declares ignorance of the nineteen virtues appropriate for the ruler, which are described in detail.
13. He is unfit to rule because of the lack of clarity in his mind regarding these virtues. He describes the qualities of the general and the abilities of the soldier, confessing not to possess any of them. He is harmed in his soul, dragged down

by pleasure, and declares complete ignorance of everything. Being ignorant of medicine, he is incurable in his soul.
14. Crowned by God with independence and honored with the faculty of reason, he is paradoxically deprived of reason. Reason is like the talent in the scriptural parable (Matt. 25:14–30). The person who invests in studies and in knowledge will enter the kingdom of God.

On What Is Unclear and a Testimony That the Author Is Ignorant of Philosophy is the fourth book of *Explanation of the World*. Establishing its chronology faces challenges similar to those of *Representation of the World, or Life* but even harder to resolve, because no dedicatory letter to Mouzalon has survived. The best that can be offered is an informed guess. That the author calls himself "crowned by the hand of God with independence" at the end of the treatise (§14), together with the acerbity and extent of the Socratic irony, suggests that he revised, expanded, or composed the work afresh during the last two years of his reign (1257–1258). The dedicatory preface to *Explanation of the World* states that his model in the fourth and last book was Socrates, who "in his great knowledge beyond the rest said he knew nothing and so earned top ranking among all people" (p. 132). Laskaris indeed confesses total ignorance of different aspects of knowledge, such as logic, literature, generalship, and rulership, while offering detailed descriptions or interpretations of these subjects. The paradox of an erudite man professing ignorance was, of course, intentional and portrayed the author as an accomplished philosopher. The tone is highly ironic, signaling the response of a hurt and volatile man who confronted unsympathetic voices and turned the tables on his critics. The specific target of his irony eludes us today and may have been the entirety of his opponents during the last two years of his life, including aristocratic generals, officials, and his teacher and advisor Blemmydes.

One of the central messages of the treatise hinges on the different nuances of the frequently used adjective ἄδηλος (nonevident, uncertain, obscure) and the cognate noun ἀδηλία. Laskaris explores their varied nuances and ambiguity. The title of the work, "On What Is Unclear and a Testimony That the Author Is Ignorant of Philosophy" (περὶ ἀδήλου καὶ μαρτυρίας τοῦ μὴ εἰδέναι φιλοσοφίαν τὸν γράψαντα), plays on the different meanings. It conveys, ironically, the author's uncertainty about his learning and alludes, sarcastically, to his knowledge remaining nonevident to a hostile public. The translation of περὶ ἀδήλου as "on what is unclear" is meant to convey these two different nuances. Furthermore, the concept of ἀδηλία has epistemological significance and helps advance a philosophical agenda beyond the narrowly authorial one. For one thing, it leads in the direction of negative or apophatic theology. The preface to *Explanation of the World* surprisingly describes *On What Is Unclear* as a theological work, explaining that in it the author elevates the subject matter, which otherwise pertains to himself, to the level of theology. It should be added that Laskaris was particularly interested in apophatic theology and the relation between philosophy and theology.[58] The nature of the relationship is addressed in the treatise. In the section on mathematics (§§5–6), he draws attention to the obscurity (ἀδηλία) of divine concepts and proposes a method of overcoming this obscurity and approaching the divine. "The man capable of scientific knowledge," Laskaris writes, "builds through mathematics a bridge over the obscurity of the divine concepts" (γεφυρώσας τὴν τῶν θείων νοημάτων ἀδηλίαν ὁ ἐπιστημονικὸς ἀνὴρ διὰ τῶν μαθημάτων). Someone pursuing scientific knowledge (ἐπιστήμη), he points out, can use mathematics to "[build] a bridge to his intellect" and "rise from things on earth to those in heaven." The author's view of the metaphysical role of mathematics is hardly original, as it harks back to late antique Neopythagoreanism and Neoplatonism.[59] Laskaris makes Socratic ignorance an essential part of the overall structure of knowledge and assigns mathematics the role of mediator between outer and inner learning.

Oration on Hellenism
SUMMARY

1. The divine Creator introduced order in the animate and the inanimate world. Having given shape to the landmass and the seas, he established the different climate zones.
2. The natures and qualities of human beings depend on their location in the climate zones (especially in relation to temperate climate) and on their proximity to the stars. Humans have settled down all over the inhabited world, in the North and the South, in the East and the West, along the seas and on

---

58 Angelov, *Byzantine Hellene*, 193–98.
59 See below, p. 160, n. 14.

islands. God established the extent and adoption of skills, as well as different human natures, in accordance with the climate zones.

3. The Greeks surpass other peoples in their position in the inhabited world and in the temperate nature of their climate, and consequently in their nobility and scientific knowledge. The Greeks reside in the midst of the seas in the Mediterranean basin, including the Black Sea. The author outlines a series of seas, gulfs, and rivers.

4. The whole of Greece abounds in fresh and sea water, which is a cause for the agricultural fecundity of the land, along with its temperate climate. Other areas in the world that likewise are well supplied with water are less fertile because they lie away from the temperate zone. Temperate climate means good temperament: the Greeks are healthy in their bodies and intelligent by nature.

5. The Greek people who reside in the middle of the inhabited world collect the skills that have been invented elsewhere. The author illustrates his reasoning through a circular diagram. Greece lies midway between Spain and Egypt, Britain and India. Any kind of craft knowledge exported from those faraway and peripheral areas crosses the land of the Greeks.

6. The Greeks thus cultivate reason to the highest degree.

7. The author gives a list of ancient Greek writers, philosophers, and scientists. The Greeks have either discovered or perfected all philosophy, knowledge, and science.

8. Having set his argument on a firm foundation, the author rhetorically asks his Italian interlocutor why he keeps contradicting him.

9. The fall of Constantinople had temporarily deprived the Greeks of a political foundation for cultivating reason and learning, but the victories and just vengeance of Nicaea have led the Greeks to recover their true nature.

10. By nature, the Greeks are superior to the Italians. The author declares himself an Athenian in contrast to his Italian interlocutor. He urges the man to learn that philosophy originates from the Greeks of yore and that the Greeks of his time are their biological and cultural descendants, living on the same territory and breathing the same air.

11. The land of the Italians is in a state of political and military turmoil. Their embassy of "peace" is, in fact, one of confrontation. Their syllogisms on the Procession of the Holy Spirit are erroneous and arrogant.

12. The Italian interlocutor is compared to a haughty old man with grizzly hair who simulates physical activity to create the impression that he has not aged. Reason has been restored among the Greeks. The assembly is taking place only because the Latins make errors in their philosophy and theology.
13. The Italian interlocutor has invoked St. Peter, the rock of the church, but ignores St. John, Christ's favorite disciple and a mystical initiate of divine grace.
14. The author urges the Italian interlocutor to abandon faulty inquiries into theology.
15. He calls on his opponents to learn the truth from the Greeks.
16. Firmness in doctrine belongs to the Greeks, who have found the proper balance between philosophy and theology. The Italian is a transgressor of doctrine in his interpretations of the holy scriptures.
17. The Italian opponents are introducing changes in the theology of the Holy Spirit.
18. Philosophy means scientific knowledge, whereas theology boils down to doctrine. The opponents make a jumble between the two and innovate in doctrine.
19. There are constraints on human comprehension. The author cherishes the scriptural words of Peter, John, and Paul without claiming to be able to improve on them. His opponents, however, fail to obey the definitions of the fathers.
20. An investigation into theology through syllogism is a dangerous approach. It perverts the sacred words of the scriptures. The Italians have introduced a confusion between scientific knowledge and theology, whereas the Greeks are flourishing in their theological knowledge.
21. The Italians claim that their position is both philosophical and derived from the Greek one, aiming to show that philosophical wisdom is tantamount to theology, but they do not realize the fundamental weakness of their position.
22. Gregory of Nazianzus exemplifies a thinker capable of combining philosophy and theology. The author's opponents claim to be expert theologians, but they display arrogance in their investigations.
23. The author urges the assembled Greek clergy (deacons, priests, bishops, and the patriarch himself) to avoid fruitless and untimely disputations with the Italians, whose arrogance should be rejected.
24. The author pleads with the crowd to hold fast to their ancestral faith, for they are superior by nature to their opponents and surpass them in theology.

25. The author prays to the Holy Spirit and the Trinity to support his efforts and bring his opponents to their senses.

The *Oration on Hellenism* is the seventh book of Laskaris's *Christian Theology*, a collection containing treatises and speeches on theological themes. The work bears the heading *Second Oration against the Latins, or, On the Procession of the Holy Spirit*. The heading gives us a hint about the content. The speech engages in polemic against the Latins, although in fact theology is not its main subject and the audience is broader. Its position in the collection makes it a sequel to the *First Oration against the Latins*, the sixth book of the *Christian Theology*. The occasion for the two speeches was a council attended by papal envoys and Byzantine bishops. The *First Oration* addresses the papal legate and mentions the papal embassy.[60] The *Second Oration* apostrophizes (§§8, 20) an anonymous Italian and speaks of the Italians who have arrived from Rome. The same work mentions (§23) the presence of priests, bishops, and the patriarch himself—namely, Patriarch Arsenios Autoreianos (1254–1259, 1261–1264). The only known reception of a papal embassy during Theodore II Laskaris's reign, which was the occasion for a council attended by Byzantine churchmen, took place in Thessaloniki during September and October 1256. The papal embassy was led by the Dominican friar Constantine, bishop of Orvieto, whose entourage included fellow Dominicans.[61] The mention of an anonymous patriarch in the *Second Oration* fits with what we know about the council in Thessaloniki from the *Synopsis chronike* (an anonymous historical work traditionally attributed to the high churchman Theodore Skoutariotes): Patriarch Arsenios accompanied the emperor to Thessaloniki in the autumn of 1256. Arsenios's letter to Pope Alexander IV dispatched from Thessaloniki after the end of the disputations refers to "no more than thirty" bishops who were in attendance, a number corresponding to the clergy, including bishops, mentioned in the *Second Oration*.[62]

60 Th. L., *Chr. theol.*, §8, 127.92–94, §13, 128.141.
61 The date has already been proposed by the editor of the text, Christos Krikonis (Th. L., *Chr. theol.*, 61–64). On the reception of the embassy of 1256, see Gill, *Byzantium and the Papacy*, 97–100; Angelov, *Byzantine Hellene*, 162–63, 167–69.
62 Arsenios came from Asia Minor to Thessaloniki in the autumn of 1256 both to take part in the council and to perform the ceremony for the marriage of Maria, Laskaris's daughter, and Nikephoros, the son of Michael II Komnenos Doukas, the ruler of Epiros.

While the *First Oration* focuses on theology and the Trinity, the *Second Oration* can be described as a motivational speech, which exhorts Laskaris's coreligionists to avoid theological debates with the Latins. Laskaris wished to convince the assembled Greek-speaking clergymen from Asia Minor and the Balkans (as well as laymen who were probably in the audience) that they had an inalienable historical right to hold the correct position in disputes with the Latins. The Latins were latecomers to philosophy and theology, and they did not know how to draw the proper boundary between the two. By contrast, the birth of the Greeks in a blessed part of the world as heirs to an ancient and greatly admired philosophical culture awarded them a superior status and superior understanding. It is this patriotic feeling of Greek pride that Laskaris wished to awaken and inspire. The resulting vision of Hellenism is rich and without a parallel in any work of public oratory in Byzantium.

Letter on Royal Duty, Taxation, and the Army
SUMMARY

1. The duties of the emperor, the wise man, and the wise emperor are outlined.
2. The approach of Blemmydes is that of a wise man who recognizes that the inherited duty of the wise emperor is truth, discernment, and justice.
3. Blemmydes is a very close friend to the author and, thus, an ally of the authorities, although he had not always been on good terms with them. He now criticizes the judgment of Laskaris and appeals to him to change his position.
4. Blemmydes' first criticism is Laskaris's policy toward officials. The author defends himself by pointing to the example of his father, John III Vatatzes, and to the growing territory of the empire of Nicaea.
5. Blemmydes' second criticism is Laskaris's increased expenditure on the army. The author responds by pointing to the absurdity of the proposition that hoarded wealth be used to finance the army, because doing so will drain the budget and lead to debt.

See Theodore Skoutariotes, *Synopsis chronike* 527.4–7, ed. Sathas, (the detail is missing from Akropolites' account). Arsenios's letter to Pope Alexander IV written after the end of the reception of the papal embassy by his ghostwriter, the metropolitan bishop of Thessalonica Manuel Disypatos, explicitly mentions the presence of the Greek bishops. See Arsenios Autoreianos, *Letter*, ed. Pieralli, "Una lettera," 184.123–25.

Style, Vocabulary, and Grammar

6. The author further defends his position by stressing the need to maintain an effective army (especially with native recruits) and by describing his busy daily routine devoted to the army, royal justice, and diplomacy.
7. The author stresses his devotion to his royal duties and calls on future generations to assess his arguments.

The polemical letter to Nikephoros Blemmydes dates to 1257. The chronology rests on the mention of Dyrrhachion as marking the frontier: the ruler of Epiros, Michael II Komnenos Doukas, ceded the Adriatic city to Nicaea in the autumn of 1256.[63] Between December 1256 and February 1257, the *megas logothetes* George Akropolites entered Dyrrachion to arrange for the transfer of authority.[64] By 1258, Dyrrachion had fallen under the authority of Manfred of Sicily, who was building an anti-Nicaean alliance among Balkan powers, including the state of Epiros.[65] Written in a combative mode, the epistle bears witness to the strained relations between Laskaris and Blemmydes at the time (see further below, pp. 47–51). We learn about the emperor's daily routine, his army reform, and his strong sense of mission and Hellenic identity, as well as about an ongoing debate with Blemmydes on taxation and army finances.

Style, Vocabulary, and Grammar

The features of Laskaris's literary style are distinct and easily recognizable. Some can be rendered into English, but others inevitably get lost in translation. For this reason, but also because the stylistic features add to the portrait of Laskaris as an author, they deserve attention. The style is characterized by high emotional charge and free flow of the prose, which follows the author's turns of thought. Most sentences are long and rhythmic, with a poetic feel to them. Sometimes they are punctuated by terse, emphatic clauses and rhetorical questions. There are many polysyndeta connected with the conjunction καί and with γάρ. Wordplay and rare or newly coined words are omnipresent. (For Laskaris's neologisms, see the

[63] George Akropolites, *History* 63, ed. Heisenberg and Wirth, 133.12–14; trans. Macrides, *George Akropolites*, 308, 311.
[64] George Akropolites, *History* 67, ed. Heisenberg and Wirth, 139–40; trans. Macrides, *George Akropolites*, 321–22.
[65] Berg, "Manfred of Sicily and the Greek East," 272–74.

vocabulary list below, p. 46). The overall coherence in syntax and vocabulary indicates a highly cultivated hand. The general impression is of a curious combination of improvisation and authorial control.

To be sure, not all these stylistic features are unique to Laskaris. The play with genre and generic convention (noted above in the discussion of the *Satire of His Tutor* and the *Memorial Discourse on Emperor Frederick II*) is hardly anything novel. Quite a few of the features are representative of the general trends in Byzantine literature during the twelfth and thirteenth centuries. Laskaris's proclivity for coining new words follows practices of earlier Byzantine authors, such as Constantine Manasses (twelfth century) in his versified world chronicle.[66] The mixture of high-style Attic words with low-register ones, including vernacular, can be found in the twelfth century, most prominently in the schedographic compositions of Theodore Prodromos, and among later authors.[67] A general feature of literary production in the thirteenth century has been identified as the combination of excess, profuse emotionality, and generic mixtures—all features of Laskaris's writing.[68] In particular, his loose and unstructured syntax, which at times appears even chaotic, points in the direction of the writings of Theodore Metochites in the late thirteenth and the early fourteenth century.

Skillful manipulation of the vocabulary is perhaps the most outstanding feature of Laskaris's style. In *On What Is Unclear* (§§9–10), the author himself stresses the importance of word choices for good style. He selected words for added comic effect. Thus, the *Satire* (§13) compares his tutor to Hermes and his magical staff (*caduceus*) by employing the rare verb βακλίζω (to cudgel, to wield one's staff), which sounds similar to Bacchus (Βάκχος), the god of revelry, and has sexual innuendos in the context of the tutor's frequent love escapades mentioned in the same passage. Philosophical terminology projected the author's immense learning,

---

[66] See Lampsidis's observation to his edition of Constantine Manasses, *Breviarum chronicum*, 1:lxii–lxiii; 2:90–109 (*Index graecitatis*); Hinterberger, "The Language of Byzantine Poetry," 44–49; Nilsson, *Writer and Occasion in Twelfth-Century Byzantium*, 16, 68.

[67] Trapp, "Learned and Vernacular Literature in Byzantium," 124, adduces specific examples. On Laskaris's use, for example, of the vernacular verb γυρίζω, see below, p. 172, n. 60. On Theodore Prodromos and schedography, see Agapitos, "Grammar, Genre and Patronage in the Twelfth Century," 14–22.

[68] Agapitos, "Literature and Education in Nicaea"; Agapitos, "The Insignificance of 1204 and 1453."

which was important for his self-representation and served to elevate the discourse. Several sections in the *Moral Pieces* (§§8–11) are filled with terms borrowed from Aristotelian natural philosophy.

The ubiquitous puns create a lively, almost dizzying effect. The author sometimes engages in etymological wordplay: for example, a passage of the *Satire* (§19) combines the words φίλος, φιλολόγιος, and φιλοτιμοῦμαι. "As a friend of learning," he presents the composition as a gift to "my friends and fellow learned men" (ἐγὼ φιλολόγιος φιλοτιμοῦμαι τοῖς ἐμοῖς φίλοις καὶ λογίοις). Other puns are based on assonance and alliteration. The opening of *Representation of the Word, or Life* playfully juxtaposes the words στάσις and ἐξέτασις. After a long examination (πολλάκις ἐξετάζων) of nature, the author writes, he has assigned to others the study of the "stability of things unstable insofar as it is stability" (τὴν στάσιν τῶν ἀστάτων ὡς στάσιν) and has decided to devote himself to an examination (ἐξέτασιν) that unveils hidden matters. The most favorite pun of Laskaris was on the multiple meanings of words. The *Letter on Royal Duty, Taxation, and the Army* uses the word ἀφορμή with the different meanings of "asset," "inclination," and "accusation." The *Oration on Friendship and Politics* repeatedly employs the word σχέσις with a range of different meanings. I have usually translated it as "relationship" and "attachment" (and more rarely as "attitude" and "possession"). Another word about the bond between the emperor and his friend as well as between any lord and his servant is ὑπόληψις, which can mean "reputation" and "respect," but by the twelfth century had acquired the additional semantics of "trust" and "confidence." The latter meaning is prominent in the Greek vernacular romance *Livistros and Rodamne*, whose earliest version has been dated to the thirteenth century. In the translation of the *Oration on Friendship and Politics*, I have rendered ὑπόληψις in English as "trustful devotion" or simply "devotion."[69]

The proclivity for coining new words in the creative process of literary composition is a distinctive feature of Laskaris's style. The following hapax legomena and neologisms are found in the eight works (and also in other writings of Laskaris).

---

69 See the analysis of the semantics of ὑπόληψις by Hinterberger, "The Rose and the Dung Beetle: Theodore Laskaris on Friendship." In his recent translation of *Livistros and Rodamne*, Panagiotis Agapitos translates the word as "confidence" (ll. 510, 2034), "trust" (l. 1204), and "affection" (ll. 4265, 4312, 4379). See *Livistros and Rodamne*, trans. Agapitos, 69, 88, 111, 170, 171, 173.

Satire of His Tutor: ἀπερισκιάστως (without blurring), βρικαλός (swine: evidently derived from ἰβρίκαλοι, attested in the lexicographer Hesychios), γυναικωνιτικός (belonging to the women's quarters), δειλανδρισμός (cowardice), δωροδοκητικός (open to bribery), ἰνδαλματουργέω and ἰνδαλματόω (depict, represent), κερδωτικός (sly), κύταλις (snake), λειόπελμος (with flat feet), μαλακοφόρος (wearing refined clothes), ξενοσκεύαστος (strangely concocted), οὐλόφθαλμος (scar-eyed), ποντοβαίνω (be a seafarer), σαρδαναπάλιος (Sardanapalus-like), στοιχειωδία (study of the elements), τοκιστικός (usurious), χρυσανθέω (blossom with gold), ὑφαλότης (slyness)

Moral Pieces: ἁρμοτέμνω (break the shoulder joints: from ἁρμός, "shoulder joint," and the verb τέμνω, "to cut").

Oration on Friendship and Politics: συνειδότως (deliberately), τεχνεργάτης (skillful worker).

Representation of the World, or Life: ἀειρρεπής (ever-influential[?]), βριθισμός (a mass), καθαπλοῦ (simply[?]), παρυπόκρυψις (secretiveness), περιοχεύς (container), προδιαπαίζω (ridicule in advance), ἐξυδρεία (rainy wind: related to ἐξυδρίας ἄνεμος, as in pseudo-Aristotle, *De mundo* 394b19).

On What Is Unclear and a Testimony That the Author Is Ignorant of Philosophy: ἀνεμοφύρτως (blown away by the wind), διενεδρεύω (lay persistently in ambush), ἡρωότροπος (heroic in manner), ὑψηλοπρεπής (exalted), χρυσέως (like gold), ψευδότροπος (false).

Oration on Hellenism: ἀντευκρασία (harsh climate: literally, the climate opposite to the temperate climate of εὐκρασία), εὐκραταντεύκρατος (belonging to the temperate zone and its opposite), Κολασσαῖος (belonging to Colossae), ἐκπειραστής (tempter), διαθεματισμός (astrological exposition), παμφιλόσοφος (fully philosophical), οἰνοφλυγικός (drunk with wine), συνεξάρτησις (bond).

Letter on Royal Duty, Taxation and the Army: ἐκμέμφομαι (criticize).

Two patterns are worth noting. First, there are almost as many neologisms in the *Satire* as in the remaining seven works taken together. The explanation lies in the comic effect created by words such as γυναικωνιτικός, λειόπελμος, οὐλόφθαλμος, and σαρδαναπάλιος, as well as in the spirit of youthful experimentation of Laskaris's earliest major composition. Second, the new coinages often feature adjectives or epithets describing God, such as ὑψηλοπρεπής, τεχνεργάτης, and περιοχεύς. The phenomenon is not surprising, for the treatise *On the Divine Names*, the fourth book of his *Christian Theology*, contains many neologisms among the hundreds of designations of God.[70]

The grammar of Laskaris's prose features idiosyncrasies encountered among other Byzantine authors, especially in the later period. The author often uses the future participle without signaling future action or intent. In effect, the future participle assumes the role of an aorist participle, a phenomenon observed in the fourteenth-century anonymous *metaphrasis* of the *History* of Niketas Choniates into the common Byzantine koine.[71] The most striking and unambiguous case of this usage appears in *On What Is Unclear* (§1), where the expression καταλλήλως γοῦν τούτοις τοῖς ἄνωθεν λεχθησομένοις ("corresponding, thus, to these aforementioned terms") refers to the immediately preceding passage. By the same token, in *Representation of the World, or Life*, the substantive participle ὁ ἀμήσων (§3) means "one who reaps"—namely, the reaper of the crops—not the one who intends to or will reap. The future passive subjunctive, a form absent from classical Greek but present in later authors, appears frequently in Laskaris, including in the translated works.[72] The functional confusion between aorist subjunctives and future indicatives, a feature of postclassical and Byzantine Greek, is also commonly found in Laskaris's prose.[73] Rhetorical questions in the *Representation of the World, or Life* contain many examples, such as τείνῃ, νοήσῃ, δείξω, and λέξω. I have generally preferred to translate them in a modal rather than temporal sense.

Theodore Laskaris and Nikephoros Blemmydes

The translated works immerse us in the long and complex relationship between Laskaris and his teacher of philosophy, Blemmydes, which is an important topic for the intellectual history of Byzantium during the thirteenth century. The works

---

70 The treatise *On the Divine Names* can be found in Th. L., *Chr. theol.*, 99–108.
71 Hinterberger, "From Highly Classicizing to Common Prose," 186.
72 For example, *Satire of His Tutor*, §19 (Th. L., *Op. rhet.*, 181.669): the form is γενήσηται. On this grammatical development in medieval Greek, see Nicholas, "The Passive Future Subjunctive."
73 On this phenomenon, see Horrocks, *Greek*, 240, 256, 317; Horrocks, "Georgios Akropolites"; Hinterberger, "The Language of Byzantine Poetry," 52–53.

disclose the impact of Blemmydes' instruction and ideas on Laskaris, while also allowing us to trace the changing roles of Blemmydes throughout Laskaris's life: dream teacher, mentor, advisor, and critic. It is revealing that in his *Letter on Royal Duty, Taxation, and the Army* Laskaris calls Blemmydes "a very close friend to us" and also refers to times "when there was no friendship on your part toward the authorities" (§3). The hinted tension with and the changing roles of Blemmydes are best understood if consideration is given to the intellectual growth of his student. Laskaris indeed based some of his ideas on Blemmydes' teaching, but he was not a pale shadow of him.

The *Satire of His Tutor* bears witness to the awakening of Laskaris's love for philosophy, the beginnings of his studies with Blemmydes, and his determination to continue his education. The ignorance and envy of the court tutor are contrasted with the erudition and generosity of the teacher. The *Satire* signals, among other things, Laskaris's desire to learn "royal science" (§18)—that is, the principles of good government, which was the subject of Blemmydes' *Imperial Statue*. The *Memorial Discourse on Emperor Frederick II* (1251) already shows familiarity with Blemmydes' *Imperial Statue*, echoing its phraseology and vocabulary.[74] However, the perspective of the *Memorial Discourse* is that of a self-reflective ruler, and the musings differ from key points made in the *Imperial Statue*. Laskaris presents the just ruler as unpopular and hated (§4), which contrasts with Blemmydes' interpretation of hatred against the ruler as the consequence of his moral faults.[75]

A similar pattern of echoes of and divergences from Blemmydes is found in later works. The impact of Blemmydes' *Imperial Statue* is seen in the story reported in the *Moral Pieces* (§3) about the Egyptian king Sesostris yoking subject kings to his chariot and being reminded by them of the turning wheel of fortune.[76] Laskaris's familiarity with Aristotelian natural philosophy in the *Moral Pieces* (§§8–11) seems to echo Blemmydes' teaching,[77] while his interest in the concept of τὸ ὄν (that which is, the existent) in the same work has a parallel in the name

---

74 See below, p. 96, n. 12; p. 97, n. 18; p. 98, n. 20.

75 Blem., *Imperial Statue* 43–44 (p. 56).

76 Blem., *Imperial Statue* 53–55 (pp. 58–60). See below, p. 103, n. 8.

77 As reflected in Blemmydes' textbook on natural philosophy, the *Epitome physica*, PG 142:1004–320.

of Blemmydes' monastic foundation near Ephesos, Christ-Who-Is (ὁ ὤν).[78] At the same time, the description of the lowest type of friendship based on pleasure in the *Oration on Friendship and Politics* and the call on the emperor's friends to pay "homage to pleasure" (§6) run contrary to the moralizing spirit of Blemmydes' *Imperial Statue*, which cautions the emperor to "rule over pleasures."[79]

The two philosophical treatises, *Representation of the World, or Life* and *On What Is Unclear and a Testimony That the Author Is Ignorant of Philosophy*, show the growing distancing of the Nicaean emperor from his teacher against the background of continual mutual respect. Laskaris emerges as a confident and independent philosopher. In the account of his vision in *Representation of the World, or Life* (§12), he presents himself as drawing unmediated philosophical knowledge directly from Lady Philosophy. Some, but not all, of the model figures of kingship in *Representation of the World, or Life* are borrowed from the *Imperial Statue*.[80] Some, but not all, of the nineteen virtues of the ruler in *On What Is Unclear* go back to the *Imperial Statue*. Laskaris's list of virtues begins with the trio of zeal, truth, and mildness, whose importance he had already stressed in his panegyric of his father, John III Vatatzes.[81]

The divergence between the teacher and his student clearly manifests itself in their approaches to theology. After having excelled in theological disputations with visiting Latin ecclesiastics before Laskaris's accession as the sole emperor, Blemmydes addressed to Laskaris, in his capacity as the reigning emperor, a long letter on the Procession of the Holy Spirit from the Father through the Son and a treatise on theology.[82] The young emperor did not, however, favor Blemmydes'

---

78 See Nikephoros Blemmydes, *Monastic Rule*, ed. Heisenberg; and the translation by Joseph Munitiz in Thomas and Hero, *Byzantine Monastic Foundation Documents*, 3:no. 36, 1196–206. "The One Who Is" (ὁ ὤν) is among the epithets of God in Laskaris's *On the Divine Names* (Th. L., *Chr. theol.*, 101.62).

79 Blem., *Imperial Statue* 16 (p. 48), 33 (p. 54).

80 On the figures of Sardanapalus, Xerxes, Cyrus, Philip of Macedon, Hannibal, and Semiramis, see below, p. 138, n. 32; p. 138, n. 33; p. 141, n. 53.

81 See below, p. 169, n. 49.

82 *Letter to Theodore Doukas Laskaris on Some Dogmatic Disputations*: Nikephoros Blemmydes, *Oeuvres théologiques*, ed. Stavrou, 1:304–53; the suggested *termini* of composition are 1254–1256 (ibid., 285). *On Theology*: Nikephoros Blemmydes, *Oeuvres théologiques*, ed. Stavrou, 2:172–211; on the addressee and the suggested *termini* of composition (1256–1257), see ibid., 155–66. On Blemmydes' and Laskaris's diverging approaches, see the

reconciliatory approach toward Latin theology. His *Oration on Hellenism* (autumn 1256) disapproves of any intellectual engagement with Latin scholastic theologians and objects to Blemmydes' irenic attitude in his recent work on the Procession of the Spirit through the Son. Addressing the Latin interlocutors and opponents, Laskaris exclaims: "You examine the divine essence and you make syllogisms with a 'from' or a 'through.' You are in error, yes, in error, and do not hide the truth, doing this out of arrogance and pride" (§11). The combative words pertain both to the views and to the approach of Blemmydes, an expert in syllogisms, who had used his mastery of Aristotelian logic to refute Latin theologians during John III Vatatzes' reign.[83]

The *Letter on Royal Duty, Taxation, and the Army* is evidence of a direct clash between teacher and student. We know from Blemmydes' autobiography that on the accession of the emperor in November 1254 he was the latter's favored choice for the vacant position of patriarch of Constantinople in exile; instead, he received the patriarchal office of supervisor of the monasteries and came to serve as Laskaris's advisor.[84] Blemmydes touts his acts of resistance against unjust decisions made by the emperor in the last two years of his reign (1257–1258): he prevented the imposition of an ecclesiastical interdict on the entire population of the state of Epiros, intervened on behalf of an accused member of the imperial guards, and defended a long-serving palace official charged with conspiracy.[85] Laskaris's *Letter* shows a different side of the clash. Blemmydes had attacked the taxation policies of the emperor and favored the distribution of crown wealth in lieu of public taxes. In addition, Blemmydes appears to have voiced doubts about the leadership abilities of the emperor and to have objected to the increased size of the army, a stance that provoked Laskaris to defend the recruitment of native soldiers ("Greeks," Ἕλληνες). The dramatic appeal for the judgment of the later generations at the end of the *Letter* indicates the intensity of the confrontation. At the same time, the very act of writing the polemical letter to Blemmydes shows

---

observations of Michel Stavrou in Nikephoros Blemmydes, *Oeuvres théologiques*, 1:284–86, 2:155–63.

83 Ierodiakonou, "A Logical Joust."

84 Nikephoros Blemmydes, *Autobiography*, 1:74–80, 2:77; ed. Munitiz, 37–40, 80. See Angelov, *Byzantine Hellene*, 149–51.

85 Nikephoros Blemmydes, *Autobiography*, 1:81–84, 87–89; 2:78; ed. Munitiz, 40–41, 43–44), 80. See Angelov, *Byzantine Hellene*, 178.

that Laskaris still valued his opinions and cared enough to respond with counter-arguments. The same deferential attitude can be gleaned from letters that Laskaris addressed to Blemmydes in the last year of his life, in which he asked his mentor and spiritual father for medical expertise and prayers to help him to recover from his illness.[86]

Throughout Laskaris's life, Blemmydes enjoyed a special position of authority and independence in Nicaean royal circles thanks to his acknowledged status as the period's leading teacher and philosopher. When Laskaris remarked in *Representation of the World, or Life* that the "common custom" was "to exchange mutual flatteries, unless someone is a philosopher" (§7), he was doubtless thinking of the candid opinions fearlessly voiced by his esteemed teacher.

Theodore Laskaris as a Literary Figure and Philosopher

What do the translated works reveal about Theodore II Laskaris as a literary figure and a philosopher? To help readers make their own discoveries, it is beneficial to highlight several strands running through most, if not all, of the works. Four salient and pervasive strands should be stressed (and more can certainly be added): Laskaris's autobiographical impulse, his interest in ontology, his fascination with natural philosophy, and his fixation on intellectual legacy.

Laskaris deeply cared about autobiographical self-representation. The skillfully manipulated "I-voice" dominates most of the translated works. Wherever it is absent, strong authorial opinions—often couched in a combative or ironic fashion—add nuances to his self-portrayal. All eight works engage in self-representation. The *Satire* gives an autobiographical account of Laskaris's awakening as a philosopher and his educational aspirations hampered by his tutor. The *Memorial Discourse on Emperor Frederick II* is a veiled self-portrait of Laskaris as a ruler concerned with justice and public opinion. The *Moral Pieces* consists of personal musings on the meaning of life, death, love, and other topics. The *Oration on Friendship and Politics* approaches the subject of social solidarity in ways that evoke Laskaris's entourage of servants and his tensions with the powerful aristocracy of birth. The *Representation of the World, or Life* conveys to George Mouzalon a mixture of personal observations and philosophical musings on a wide range

---

86 Th. L., *Ep.* 45 (pp. 60–62), 48 (pp. 64–66).

of subjects. *On What Is Unclear and a Testimony That the Author Is Ignorant of Philosophy* is a self-revealing and dramatic work composed in a polemical spirit. The *Oration on Hellenism* can be read as the culmination of Laskaris's search, less than two years before his death, for a force of unity and communal identity in the politically fragmented world after the Fourth Crusade. The *Letter on Royal Duty, Taxation, and the Army* explains Laskaris's actions as the reigning emperor before the critical eyes of his former teacher and current advisor.

The autobiographical component running through all eight works is not confined solely to self-fashioning but features snippets of hard information about the author's life. We get a sense of Laskaris's royal upbringing and privileged existence, with the lens zooming in on details such as the food, luxury, and clothing available in the Anatolian royal residences of the Nicaean emperors.[87] We learn about the subjects he studied and the authors he read during his education, as well as about the military training he received.[88] We glean information about his routine as the reigning emperor, which included daily inspection of the army, the reception of petitioners, and audiences with foreign ambassadors.[89] We can empathize with his intense emotions: the distress caused by the passing of his spouse Elena, the special store he set by his friends and companions, and the attachment to his confidant George Mouzalon. The reader can also form an idea of Laskaris's conflict with powerful members of the Nicaean elite, the corruption of his judges, and his inability to impose order among all of his officials.[90]

The translated works open a window onto aspects of Laskaris's philosophical thought. We see his development as philosopher, from a student of philosophy in the *Satire* to a teacher and an accomplished philosopher himself in *Representation of the World, or Life*.[91] There is a remarkable consistency of philosophical ideas and vocabulary. An area of special interest for the author lay in what today can be called "ontological" questions of existence, being, and the nature of reality.

---

87 *Satire of His Tutor*, §7; *Moral Pieces*, §12; *Oration on Friendship and Politics*, §6.

88 *Satire of His Tutor*, §§13, 14; *On What Is Unclear and a Testimony That the Author Is Ignorant of Philosophy*, §13.

89 *Letter on Royal Duty, Taxation, and the Army*, §6.

90 *Oration on Friendship and Politics*, §9; *Representation of the World, or Life*, §§3, 4, 7, 8.

91 On the originality of Laskaris's philosophical thought, see Angelov, *Byzantine Hellene*, 181–201.

Theodore Laskaris as a Literary Figure and Philosopher

The concepts of "being," "the existent" (τὸ ὄν), as contrasted with "nonbeing," "the nonexistent" (τὸ μὴ ὄν), are ubiquitous. Ontology has an epistemological side for Laskaris. Philosophy focuses on the existent, for it is the "knowledge of things existent as existent" (one of the six classic definitions of philosophy). It is connected with theology because the expert in philosophy can gain knowledge of God.[92] Conversely, what is truly existent leads to understanding and knowledge, whereas the nonexistent leads to misunderstanding and ignorance.[93] Ontology also has an ethical side. According to the *Moral Pieces*, people constantly encounter in their lives a mixture of the existent and the nonexistent but are rarely capable of making a distinction—a distinction that experience has taught the author, who in turn urges the audience to discover it too (§§7, 10). The multitude wrongly considers the existent to be the result of good fortune (§6). Time and pleasure, materiality and the human body—in contrast to the human soul—are all nonexistent and nonbeing (§8).

Laskaris was fascinated with nature (φύσις) as a unitary force and attributed to nature supreme explanatory power in his philosophy. His fascination goes beyond comments on human nature or the nature of material matter, and beyond the Aristotelian physical sciences. For Laskaris, nature permeates ethics, politics, and literature. It is a universal principle of creation and cohesion. The principle of nature is contrasted with an alternative and inferior principle of convention (θέσις). In his treatise *Natural Communion*, Laskaris discusses in great detail "nature" and "convention" as the two main unitary principles in the animate and the inanimate world.[94] Echoes of this seminal philosophical treatise and of the dual principles resonate throughout the translated works. *Representation of the World, or Life* alludes to the *Natural Communion* through its opening statement that the author has "frequently examined what lies in nature and is inferior to nature."[95] Nature and convention are understood as having established a hierarchy of the

---

[92] *Satire of His Tutor*, §14.

[93] *On What Is Unclear and a Testimony That the Author Is Ignorant of Philosophy*, §1.

[94] *Natural Communion*, a treatise in six books, has yet to be edited critically and translated in a modern language. The text in Migne's *Patrologia Graeca* (PG 140:1259–396), with its accompanying Latin translation, is a reprint from an early edition by Claude Aubery published in Basil in 1571 and based on a single manuscript. For an analysis of the philosophical ideas, see Richter, *Theodoros Dukas Laskaris*.

[95] *Representation of the World, or Life*, §1.

good and as having generated order in the universe. "The best things are those done according to nature."[96] Material possessions are far removed by nature from the author, although they are mixed in him by convention.[97] "The communion of nature" is invoked to show why the Greeks are superior to the Italians.[98] Laskaris applies the principles of nature and convention to poetic allegory and to grammar. Thus, derivations of the meaning of words through etymology are based on convention, not nature.[99]

The relationship between nature and God was of marginal interest to Laskaris, even when he broached the subject in order to present nature as a divine creation and agent.[100] The *Oration on Friendship and Politics* places nature alongside God in the comment that the ruler controls his subjects "by following nature and through the lordly power of the Creator" (§6). Elsewhere nature is introduced as an autonomous generative force. The *Moral Pieces* elaborates on Aristotle's definition of nature as "the beginning of motion and rest" (§11). In other works, nature is said to do "everything in accordance with reason" and to have been responsible for the invention of humor as a philosophical method.[101] *Representation of the World, or Life* presents a vision revealed to Laskaris by Lady Philosophy of a single "ungraspable and invisible nature, by which existent things have come to be out of nothing and thanks to which they persevere and are sustained" (§13).

The establishment of a legacy was of paramount importance for Laskaris. His frequent reflections on the power of public opinion and communal memory reveal an odd mixture of amazement and apprehension. The *Memorial Discourse on Frederick II* holds a pessimistic view of the opinion of the crowd, which has the tendency to forget the virtuous characters and noble deeds of rulers. And yet, the same work concludes on a cautiously optimistic note: the trophies of the ruler that

---

96 *Representation of the World, or Life*, §3.
97 *Moral Pieces*, §4.
98 *Oration on Hellenism*, §10.
99 *On What Is Unclear and a Testimony That the Author Is Ignorant of Philosophy*, §10. In the case of poetic allegory, Laskaris does not offer an explanation of how the principles of nature vs. convention operate.
100 *On Heaven*, the second book of *Explanation of the World*, calls God "the creator of nature." See Festa, "Κοσμικὴ Δήλωσις" (1899), 14.22, 20.4–5; Angelov, *Byzantine Hellene*, 187–88.
101 *Memorial Discourse on Emperor Frederick II*, §1; *Satire of His Tutor*, §9.

remain after his death contribute to his fame (§5); God's justice triumphs in the end regardless of public opinion (§6). Laskaris anticipated, and indeed planned, the future reception of his works and ideas. The *Satire* states one of its goals as clearing the author's name from slander (evidently slander originating from the tutor) and establishing "an icon of remembrance" (§9). It ends (§27) with the expectation that the composition will circulate among future generations. His *Letter on Royal Duty, Taxation, and the Army* dramatically calls for the judgment of later generations (§7). For Laskaris, his legacy meant foremost the preservation and dissemination of his oeuvre. His confidant and student George Mouzalon was among the chosen guardians of his writings. In *Representation of the World, or Life*, Laskaris expresses his wish that throughout his life Mouzalon would serve as "the prominent guardian for all my written works" (§2). The very act of preparing several manuscript collections of his works (all datable to the period 1254–1258) can be seen as an effort on his part at preserving and shaping memory. His intention was to perpetuate his ideas and his autobiographic self-representation, intervening in this way in the process of memory creation. The curated literary and intellectual legacy of Laskaris has survived until the present day and still raises intriguing questions about the production of his texts and their varied contexts.

Politics, Philosophy, and Humor at the Byzantine Court

TRANSLATION

1

Satire of His Tutor

A *Satire of His Tutor*,[1] who was a most evil and worst man, by the same Theodore Doukas Laskaris, the son of the most exalted emperor, lord John Doukas.[2]

1. Evil has departed from amid the good things, baseness from amid the honorable, enmity from amid the peaceful, envy from the unenvious, the devil from the humans, falsehood from truth, injustice from justice, turmoil from tranquility, and a thing filled with every nastiness from all that has been well and beautifully created by God. As luck would have it, my tutor has shown this.

All lawlessness and ungodliness, covetousness and avarice, strife and envy, jealousy and pride, mad ambition and arrogance, anger and silliness, crassness and insatiate greed, conceit and superficiality, folly and foulness, and every other kind of badness, do lament! Subtracted from you has been, if not your entire force, at least most of it, which has also removed the value from the pairs, whether one might call it a matter of combination or a matter of pull and subtraction.[3] For

---

1 The tutor is called βαγιοῦλος (spelled in this way) only in the manuscript title (see above, p. 18, n. 26). In the body of the text, he is Laskaris's παιδαγωγός.

2 The author designates himself as "Theodore Doukas Laskaris, the son of the most exalted emperor, lord (κυρός) John Doukas"—that is, the Nicaean emperor John III Doukas Vatatzes (1221–1254)—in all manuscript titles in the collection of ten secular works. See the titles of the *Memorial Discourse on Emperor Frederick II* and the *Oration on Friendship and Politics* (pp. 93, 115, below) from the same collection. The formulaic phrase is featured also in titles in the collection *Sacred Orations* represented by the *Moral Pieces* (p. 101, below). On the manuscript headings, see Angelov, *Byzantine Hellene*, 148, 325, 328, 329.

3 Reading λείψεως (subtraction) with the manuscripts rather than λήψεως in the edition. The wordplay with ἐλείφθη (subtracted ... has been) is worth noting.

by nature the worse follows on the worst and *bad comes in the wake of the bad*.⁴ Therefore, by removing one member of the pair as the property and by pulling out the other as its relation, he destroyed everything altogether, leaving you in a good state, as one might say.⁵ Substances are altered by the deficiency of qualities just as they also undergo the same process by mixing with other substances. What will you all do, now that you have been reduced to half your badness, now that you have lost the chief promoter of shame, both your collaborator and also your agent? For the man indeed was evil from beginning to end, from his fatherland, parents, and upbringing, and from his actions performed in the same vein. He was entirely evil from the start, entirely evil halfway along, and entirely evil at the end: he was evil, therefore, on the whole. By having gathered together all evil, he represented through it the veritable Epicurean atom.⁶

Who can speak instead of me like Homer with *ten tongues*⁷ and assume the strength of Idiophantes,⁸ so as to complain loudly in the manner of the former about his base deeds and split up in the manner of the latter the indivisible, collect every offscouring of evil, and affix it onto him? For I lack the strength to recount all these because they are endless. So I wish to give up, because of the range of his foul behavior and out of fear that I may say a word of bad taste; in addition, there is a *law that one should not ridicule by name*.⁹ For this reason, speaking out makes for a cowardly action. Yet abandoning the subject entirely is very much intolerable to me. Since satire is appropriate for such mean-spiritedness, I shake off my doubts, spurred on by the quantity of his bad deeds, and hurry to recount his actions in

---

4 Cf. *CPG*, 1:148.2; 2:178.9, 631.18.

5 An ironic statement.

6 That is, the smallest indivisible unit of matter.

7 *Iliad* 2.489.

8 Although Laskaris spells the name as "Idiophantes," he clearly means Diophantos, a third-century Greek author of a textbook on arithmetic. Nikephoros Blemmydes (*Autobiography* 1.8.1–3, ed. Munitiz, 6) mentions Diophantos alongside Nikomachos of Gerasa when describing his own study of arithmetic. On George Pachymeres' and Maximos Planoudes' teaching interests in Diophantos in the later thirteenth century, see Constantinides, *Higher Education in Byzantium*, 62, 71, 72–74, 80, 96, 157. Laskaris may have written "Idiophantes" as a sort of joke. On the same problem, see below, §13.

9 Hermogenes, *On Issues* 11 (in *Opera*, ed. Rabe, 88.11–14). See also below, *Representation of the World, or Life*, §2; Th. L., *Ep.* 52.1–2 (p. 75).

order to put to shame all his badness, *girding myself* with strong zeal as my *belt*.[10] Therefore every listener will grant me forgiveness if I ask for it and everybody unacquainted with evil will have experience of impieties unlike him through the record[11] of this shameful person. And something unusual will happen: one will be able to draw endless virtue from the fountain of evil. For many evils are there in his life, and whoever flees from them escapes, as if escaping a fire, from the depths of shame, from utter disaster, and (to sum up) from all danger. All these he has around him.

2. The fatherland of that fellow was nameless, or rather it was neither existent nor known, and this was a work of God's providence intending to show that evil is without foundation and so are those individuals who accidentally arise from that. No historian can give an account of the fatherland, nor can any geographer shed light on it, no land survey can ever measure it, because it is beyond division and is more immaterial than the atoms themselves. What can I say? His fatherland was a no-man's-land. The parents were completely ridiculous, to the point that they provoked great laughter both with their names and with their affairs in life. His mother was not a mother but a false pregnancy (*kitta*),[12] a certain malaise that befalls women, swells their bellies, and makes them think falsely that they are about to give birth. Customarily, when affecting some woman it has convinced her to devote herself to this false impression. When the time for childbirth arrived and all the midwives gathered, the thing conceived resulted in shaming the woman in labor. Wind[13] came out instead of a child, as usually happens with false pregnancy, which hinted at the abnormality of the birth. Then the alleged mother, out of shame, ordered the nurses to take some child from wherever they could find it, throw it into the cot, and joyfully sound the cymbals. When an old woman in truth gave birth to a child (for the woman who produced him was ancient), the midwives collaborating in the deceit took up this hobgoblin, which was found at

---

10 Cf. Ps. 108:19. See also Pss. 17:33, 64:7.

11 "Record" (ὑπόμνησις): the Greek word can refer to an administrative document, a memorandum. See Dölger and Karagiannopoulos, *Byzantinische Urkundenlehre*, 82–86.

12 The Greek word κίττα means a "magpie," but also refers to a medical condition: the craving of pregnant women for food. The author understands κίττα as a false pregnancy in light of his satirical agenda.

13 The Greek word πνεῦμα means both "wind" and "soul." The joke is followed up a few lines below in the comment that the newborn "also had to have" a real soul.

the doorstep at the precise moment of the crime of Cronus;[14] and having ensouled with their breath the creature that had emerged from her, as it was right (for the thing also had to have such kind of soul), they patched up the unstable being and made masculine the half-man, or rather the aborted fetus, with rejoicing and much dancing. This was shrouded in silence yet was in fact known to everyone. Such was the mother of that fellow and of such origin. But if someone wishes to learn about his begetter, let him consider him to be a pile of vegetables and pulses. For they produce winds that swell the belly in a way similar to false pregnancy (*kitta*). Once born and swaddled in complete evil, this baby was named conception of the labor of false pregnancy (*kitta*).[15]

3. Who knows parents of such noblest and most exceptional origin, resembling the wake of a seafaring ship and the echo of cymbals, the steadiness of dust and the solidity of a wave? For my part, I am completely astonished by this, namely, how a nonentity could acquire a name other than nonentity itself. For things that are never and in no wise are truly never and in no wise, just as is this glorious human being whom we now depict. For he was a nonentity coming from nonentities; from a malady, a malady; from something foul, a piece of dirt; from stench, a stench; from insult, an insult; from misfortune, a misfortune; from shame, a shame; from a breeze, a wind; from a *kitta*, a son. What kind of child did the sun see, what did heavens behold, what did the earth receive, what did people see? The son of an ape, the ruler of monkeys, the lowest of beasts! The great fellow had a harmonious bodily shape, too, complex as well as dexterous. For he was *bandy-legged* and *pointed* <in his head>,[16] with bow legs and flat feet, dissimilar from the top of his head to the tip of the toes of his feet,[17] broad-bellied (this was due to his outrageous acts) and narrow-chested (this was caused by the brave constitution of his soul), dark-skinned in color and curly-haired, snub-nosed and squint-eyed as well as scar-eyed, hunched and long-necked, one cubit tall in all and entirely evil. Accident shaped him in this way and completed him into an organic whole, so that

---

14 That is, the abandonment of the infant.

15 See above, p. 19.

16 The author borrows epithets (φολκός, φοξός) from *Iliad* 2.217–19, lines that describe Thersites, an ugly and physically deformed warrior among the Achaeans sailing to Troy.

17 For similar phraseology, see Deut. 28:35.

Satire of His Tutor 63

those who saw him could burst into laughter and those who listened to him could clap their hands.

4. His inner unsightliness did not fall short of his outer one. For he was filled with malevolence and great slyness, teemed with evil, and was shifty in his purpose, and was inconsistent, timid, and petty-minded, mercenary and nosey, double-faced and speaking with many nuances, saying one thing but hiding another in his heart,[18] a depository for all sorts of trickery, power-loving and Sardanapalus-like,[19] money-loving in the extreme, refraining from good things and frank about evil ones, a womanizer and womanish, very much—and recognizably so—belonging to the women's quarters, an offender by his actions and irreverent in his words, very foolish and poor in memory, a store of envy and a high point of antagonism, a glutton and a guzzler, insatiable, impertinent, an overthrower of the sacred laws by frequent remarriage.

5. Even if his code of conduct was filled with every illegality—so far it lay beyond the law and so great was the lawlessness—still that fellow possessed in his body and soul all the things that the satire most clearly will assign at the right moment, as is right. After his birth, he was brought up with these assets and with a nurture fit for Satan and the devil. His adopted and supposed mother entrusted him to the emperors,[20] so that his shameful garment might be stripped away and he perhaps might win fame through endurance—for education is a kind of second nature. But again darkness remained darkness, for the Ethiopian could not be turned white;[21] he engaged in his education like vinegar with honey and in his training in refined matters like dung added to perfume, and the evil man altered the natural good,[22] as I wish I had never experienced.

---

18 A notable Homeric echo here (ἄλλα δὲ κεύθων φρεσί) from *Iliad* 9.313.

19 The Assyrian king Sardanapalus was notorious for his hedonistic lifestyle. See below, *Representation of the Word, or Life*, §3, p. 138, n. 32.

20 These emperors must belong to the Angelos dynasty (1185–1204). See the comment in §9 below, p. 67 with n. 43, about the emperor Isaac II Angelos being the tutor's "master." The Constantinopolitan school attended by the tutor is, unfortunately, not mentioned.

21 A reference to a Byzantine proverb regarding things that cannot be changed. See *CPG*, 2:258.1.

22 On "the natural good" (τὸ φύσει καλόν) as the highest good, see below, *Oration on Friendship and Politics*, §§3–4.

6. As time went on and he advanced without making the slightest visible improvement, this Mr. Mackerel fell in love with Lady Tuna,[23] who took a certain pride in her shamelessness, and one fish augmented the joy of the other by returning its love. But the nets of investigation[24] arrived, caught Mr. Mackerel, and carried him onto the driest shore of the palace. He was voiceless—for he was caught inside the loop[25]—and flapped his gills and wagged his tail, for this Satan had a tail. The legal judgment polished its sword, the sentence came, the punishment was imminent, and the wretch trembled. Although he escaped beheading thanks to the entreaties of certain people, he had his nose slit and through the penalty became a symbolic example of his mode of life.[26] Nonetheless he remained the same, for he was born incorrigible.

7. As God wished that the Queen of Cities be handed over to her enemies[27]— surely, I think, for absolutely no other reason than for containing inside so great an evil, as the account suggests—this person, too, stealthily slipped away along with the rest.[28] Having committed a thousand misdeeds and while remaining in the East and avoiding death (for he was advanced in years), he bided his time to become my tutor until I left my mother's womb in order to do his evil work in me, for he knew that I would cultivate philosophy. For I think he sometimes practiced witchcraft, because he displayed some of his worst qualities even unwittingly, especially when he kept company with Dionysus,[29] which he did frequently.

---

23 The mackerel who falls in love with the tuna is a Greek demotic proverb, with ancient antecedents, referring to scoundrels associating with each other: compare the English proverb "Birds of feather flock together." See Strömberg, *Greek Proverbs*, 20–21.

24 See above, p. 18.

25 Reading ἀγχόνῃ (in the loop) rather than ἀγχόνη in the nominative, as in the edition.

26 Mutilation of the nose was a legally prescribed punishment for adultery. See *Ecloga* 17.27, ed. Burgmann, 234; Leo VI, *Novels* 32, ed. Noailles and Dain, 127–29; Constantine Harmenopoulos, *Hexabiblos* 6.21.4, ed. Heimbach, 736. Blemmydes describes a monk living in his monastery whose nose was amputated for an unknown reason. See Nikephoros Blemmydes, *Autobiography* 1.40, ed. Munitiz, 22.

27 That is, Constantinople, which was captured by the armies of the Fourth Crusades on 12 April 1204.

28 The pithy phrase "along with the rest" (σὺν τοῖς ἄλλοις) encapsulates the mass exodus of the Byzantine elite from Constantinople after 1204.

29 That is, he kept company with wine.

After time passed and I came into the world, I was brought up as usual for royal children. I was soon of the right age, and when I was in my twelfth year, he was appointed my tutor. O dear me, what a great absurdity, one not willed by God, while Destiny, to put it in the words of the Hellenes, had fallen asleep! I have no idea how this slipped past the shrewd mind of my lords and parents,[30] by whom every piece of knowledge was tested, as the saying goes, *with a Lydian stone*[31] and with *the Rhine, the river of the Celts, the test for bastard children*.[32] I think that perhaps old age as well as his slyness and underhandedness tricked them—for nobody could ever escape from a schemer. So they believed in all their sincerity that all people were good, but everybody was acting according to his own lights.

8. But why am I talking so much and do not hurry on to investigate his foul practices, even if this may seem to me difficult and burdensome? And why does my head become dizzy from the memory and hardly persuade me that I am capable of looking back at this? This happened, this really happened, and wickedness was assigned to me as my tutor in my simplicity! I do differentiate in my mind as to whether God brought this about, the Maker and Improver of all things, or whether it happened by chance. I am persuaded it was God with the goal of instructing my rather simple nature in some sort of complexity. For this is indeed also good in a way. At the same time, the saying of the prophet was fulfilled. *The wolf guided the lamb*,[33] tutoring me or rather bringing me to the precipice. So I was advancing troubled among the whelps[34] and after leaving the dry land of freedom was wandering over the dark waters,[35] exchanging the ocean storm for serenity and a loud roar for quietude. For that wretch who abandoned any occupation of his own set

---

30 That is, the emperor John III Vatatzes and the empress Eirene.

31 That is, an ancient touchstone for testing gold, which became a proverb referring to the precise assessment of things and situations. See *CPG*, 2:186.15–16.

32 According to a Byzantine proverb, submerging newborns into the Rhine River tested their legitimate parentage. See *CPG*, 2:569.10–11: Ὁ Ῥῆνος ἐλέγχει τὸν νόθον. The author uses the word ἀμβλώματα (aborted children) rather than νόθοι, although the proverb makes sense only with "bastard children." On the proverbial usage, see also Kosmas of Jerusalem's commentary on the poetry of Gregory of Nazianzus in *Commentary*, ed. Lozza, 335–36.

33 Cf. Isa. 11:6, 65:25.

34 Cf. Ps. 56:5.

35 Cf. Ps. 17:12.

his sights[36] on trapping me. Even though the impious man had the dedicated duty to serve as my firm guardian, he closed his eyes, put on many-colored clothes, and donned the darkness of fraud. He never said he raised his eyes to see the truth and was conscious of the end result of his tricks, as to whether at least profit might be gained. For the crook knew how to blind his conscience. Thus, this Proteus who gathered together all the evils *from the wagon <of abuse>*[37] had them loaded onto me as an unbearable burden and indicted me with the charge of philosophy.

9. *Hear, O heaven! Give ear, O earth!*[38] As he conceived in this way of every slander, he heaped it onto me, who was patient at that time. He added insults to insults, suspicions on top of suspicions, and prejudices on top of prejudices, a man who had never seen a book of rhetoric! I would willingly ridicule him with a dozen rhetorical circumstances[39] should such exist, so that if he becomes somehow extended[40] by the satire he would not be comparable in body and in insults. Looking for the opportunity that I should seize, whether actions or speech or some other occasion given by that fellow, so that I do not compose his invective in incomplete or unsophisticated manner by leaving out the actions, but multiply them [his actions] with additions and fashion a complete portrait of his shamelessness, I find myself unable to do so. For when I set my mind to the earlier events, I am moved to recount things from the beginning. Once I explore the beginning, I see an unreal birth; parents who reek and are not his parents, originating from the flatulent *Pneumonics* of Heron;[41] a fatherland that is unreal and nameless;

---

36 Reading ἐνεώρα rather than ἐν ὥρα. The emendation has been suggested by Georgiopoulou, "Theodore II Dukas Laskaris," 299.189.

37 The phrase ἐξ ἀμάξης is proverbial, going back to Demosthenes, *De corona* 122.6, and refers to public rebukes and ridicules, as in an ancient festival. See *Souda*, epsilon 1530 (ed. Adler, 2:300); *CPG*, 1:453; 2:212, 656. See also Blem., *Imperial Statue* 207 (p. 112) (translated as "from the wagon").

38 Isa. 1:2.

39 According to Hermogenes, *On Invention* 3.5 (in *Opera*, ed. Rabe, 140.16–141.3), there were six "circumstances" (περιστάσεις) for the composition of a compound dialectical argument (ἐπιχείρημα) in rhetoric: place, time, manner, person, cause, and action, with a seventh one, material, later added by the philosophers.

40 Literally, "undergoes extension" (εἰς ἐπίτασιν πέσῃ), which may be another jibe at the short stature of the tutor mentioned in a humorous way in §3.

41 Reading Ἥρωνος rather than Εἴρωνος as in the manuscripts and Tartaglia's edition. The textual emendation was suggested by Georgiopoulou, "Theodore II Dukas Laskaris,"

an upbringing that was altered from good to the worst because of his worst purpose; deeds, judgments, and retributions in his youth, about which Stentorian voices scream in rather piercing tones; his departure from Constantinople with so many tricks, so much oath breaking, and such foulness and crudity toward those who then ruled.[42] In the end, he witnessed his own master murdered through poisoning[43] and arrested earlier because of the plot of certain individuals, perhaps also because of the advice of this man, as he often described the events, even if unwillingly, when as an old man he spoke about the past, for he always was a great babbler. Who is there who could examine his stay in the East after the conquest <of Constantinople>[44] as well as his acts of foulness and crudity? Surely nobody! For he was evil right from the start and right up to the end.

At this point, adopting my own good sense as a counselor, I wish to leave aside all those early doings of his lest I seem to be inventing them, especially as *sight is more reliable than hearsay.*[45] I avoid in this way the accusations coming from the latter [hearsay] and welcome the trustworthiness of the former [sight]. I therefore keep silent about what I learned from others, although it is worthy of a lengthy account. But I will speak in God's name about what I witnessed, even if I alter this slightly for the sake of propriety. I will speak about his every impiety truthfully and as it took place, and will present to those unfamiliar with evil an account of evils, to those who are most honest an account of underhanded deeds, and to everyone the maliciousness of that fellow. In this way, I know I will gain an icon of remembrance in the eyes of the future generations and a clearing of my name, things in which everyone profits who by nature seeks to attain goodness.

301.213. Heron of Alexandria (first century CE) was an Alexandrian mathematician and engineer who authored the *Pneumatics* (Πνευματικά). There is a humorous pun here, because one of the meanings of the word πνεῦμα is "flatulence," which recalls the disgraceful birth of the tutor described in §2.

42 An allusion to the quick turnover of emperors on the eve of 1204.

43 The murder through poisoning closely matches the punishment of the blinded Isaac II Angelos (r. 1185–1195, 1203–1204) by Alexios V Mourtzouphlos (1204). See Niketas Choniates, *Historia*, ed. Van Dieten, 564; Angelov, *Byzantine Hellene*, 21–22.

44 The notion of "the conquest" (ἡ ἅλωσις) was evidently so ingrained in Laskaris's mind that it was unnecessary to specify Constantinople as the conquered city.

45 On this proverbial expression, see *CPG*, 2:744.2.

Wise men weave together thoughts full of philosophy also by means of jokes, thoughts addressed and spoken before the wise. Everyone sometimes cracks a joke because he is wise. For it happens that nature succumbs to nature. From where will it pick itself up and regain its force? From pleasures that arise before and after the belly's gluttony, from the lapses of the soul that bring not pleasure but shame and disaster?[46] Nobody would say this unless afflicted with illness in his mind, but he will sink in deepest despondency, which is debilitating and harmful for the soul. For some outrageous things are wont to happen due to despondency.[47] So nature has invented knowledge as the best road; through it [knowledge] nature has brought forth a method. The method has introduced forms <of style>[48] by means of multiple division. With the forms, humor has also arisen as a part, so to say, of the very passions of the soul. For sadness and fear and joy and other such things are passions of the soul. Has not nature introduced, by means of knowledge, joy for the purpose of relaxation among those who live philosophically in virtue? Therefore we will receive gratitude from certain wise men for bestowing this dictum[49] on the later generations and will consider their enjoyment to be a sort of reward.

Every wise man tends to approach the joy of the wise as his own joy, just as the slaves of folly are eager to cut to pieces the wise when establishing their folly; they [the slaves of folly] intend to harm the offspring of Hermes[50] and ennoble the seeds of their own resistance. As for me, however, who have kept company with the former [the wise] and have kept attendance at their gates for a long time, I am following them once again. I take delight in their joy, join in their pain, and stand fully on

---

46 The question marks in the two sentences here reflect Georgiopoulou's edition, "Theodore II Dukas Laskaris," 303–4.

47 Despondency (ἀκηδία) was considered one of the eight main sins or sinful thoughts. See Evagrios Pontikos, *Praktikos* 6, 12, ed. Guillaumont and Guillaumont, 2:508, 520–27; John Klimakos, *Ladder of Divine Ascent* 13, in PG 88:857–61.

48 The passage is puzzling. The Greek words for "method" (τρόπος) and "forms" (ἰδέαι) allude to rhetorical theory. *On Types of Style* (Περὶ ἰδεῶν) was one of the treatises of the rhetorical corpus of Hermogenes (in *Opera*, ed. Rabe, 213–413).

49 The dictum (λόγιον) seems to be the proposition above that "wise men weave together thoughts full of philosophy also by means of jokes."

50 Hermes was believed in Byzantium to be the divine inventor of rhetoric. See John Doxapatres, *Prolegomena* to Aphthonius, *Progymnasmata*, in Rabe, *Prolegomenon Sylloge*, 90. See Th. L., *Ep.* 172.5–8 (p. 225), where Laskaris describes his mind paying a visit to Hermes during the process of writing.

their side, so that if it is tolerable to the learned craft of orators that I should keep away from the satire and praise the wise, I would do so with much joy. But I will refrain lest some scoffer take this as an occasion for a satire against me; and I will draw my account back to the beginning and say what I started saying, so that by setting the project under certain limits we may proceed toward loftier themes, as is my custom—toward the growth of knowledge and enjoyment by the wise. This is what we will do indeed.

10. There we were: that fellow and I, the tutor and the receiver of tuition. The one was in love with philosophy, the other embraced folly. The one desired to pursue virtue, but the other one was after debauchery. The one boasted of his greatness, the other one was mercenary. Because these qualities are incompatible, the tutor tutored in incompatible fashion as well. As he did not inflict on me what pleased him, but fired his deadly missiles against, so to speak, a blank wall and saw them all shattered, he went completely berserk. The adulterer was always lurking in hiding, was collecting his venom to pour on my head, and was as if accusing me of outrageous actions. What can I say or utter? He said that I was carrying out every impious deed, abominable by the standards of virtue, not consonant with faith, unrelated to trustful devotion, far removed from good sense, divorced from the main virtues if these are taken singly—and I do not know for what profit this was. What could be worse than to gossip against me to my parents and masters, and to concoct stories and bring them to their notice? He had never heard the Lord's saying: *A father will not give his son a snake instead of a fish or a scorpion instead of an egg.*[51] But being sick in his soul like the victim of snakebite, moved by some satanic poison and pricked on by the sting of his own viper-like wickedness, he did not see this—for he was both spiteful and lusted after power. He often threw me into the fire and pushed me into water in the manner of the boy who had suffered this from Satan before Christ cured him.[52] My Lord accomplished no less in my case than in that one, yet he did so by *sternly warning him*[53] when it pleased his foresight and by speaking the words, *be silent and get out of him.*[54] The Satan

---

51 Cf. Matt. 7:10; Luke 11:11–12.

52 Cf. Matt. 17:14–18. The reference is to the gospel story of the healing of a boy with a demon.

53 Mark 1:43. The quotation derives from the gospel story of the cleansing of the leper.

54 Mark 1:25–26; Luke 4:35. This quote (its echo continues in the following sentence) comes from the healing of the man with an unclean spirit at Capernaum.

departed after throwing me into many convulsions.[55] I will speak about all this in the right order, but now I will say what is necessary, and after making a separate chapter out of our common life, I will turn to this as a continuation.

11. A long time went on while he poured this ridicule on me, brought condemnation on me in countless ways, and hence, one may say, consumed me. He incited my servants to vilify me and bellowed threats at the outsiders, for he saw their attachment to me and to everyone around me. It was as if some gangrenous poison was spreading through his counsel. There was nothing I could do, for he possessed many defenses. But because fire sometimes bursts out even if someone puts it *under a bushel*[56] and because every current of air rises even if there is wind against it, and because breath is indispensable to all living creatures, I was also elevated in due course thanks to the providence of God and kept my mind focused, as was right to do.

Knowing that philosophy is superior to everything in life and that thanks to wisdom everything came into being from God,[57] and since I had heard that wisdom is a designation of God and that Solomon boldly cries out that *the Lord of all fell in love with her*,[58] owing to all this, I became completely enamored of philosophy and was so ecstatic about her in my mind that it seemed as if I could see her in the flesh. Therefore, I began to pursue letters and that dog was furious; the grace of Christ grew and he was annoyed and angry; the good bore its fruit in me and he stepped up the fight. All the more he grew mad, all the more I advanced in my studies; and all the more he tried to tear them asunder, all the more they came together. In fact, all the more he covered me with his foolishness, all the more I made my way into theoretical investigations. As I progressed rapidly in the study of syllogistic logic (I keep quiet about the preceding disciplines lest I appear to be boasting),[59] I wanted to construct and draw conclusions properly. But this man, who was as limited as a dot, as broad as a line, and as deep as a flat surface, resisted and tried to persuade me to worship Folly as my lady, which he held up as the crown on his head. Conversing with me in this way, he was tripping me up, for

---

55 Cf. Mark 1:25–26; Luke 4:35.
56 Cf. Matt. 5:15; Mark 4:21; Luke 11:33.
57 Possibly inspired by Ps. 103:24; Ecclus. 1:9.
58 Wisd. of Sol. 8:3.
59 The comment is somewhat insincere in light of Laskaris's description in §13 of his studies of rhetoric, composition, and poetry before he proceeded to syllogistic logic.

Satire of His Tutor

he was of a most argumentative type and was ecstatic when he tripped someone. Losing hope as to how he could strike an alliance, he complained and suffered like the evil spirits of former times. Anyone who saw him would have said that he was a ram butting in the middle of a flock and a bull kicking about in a herd—for as a man of bad character he was often in such a state. He boasted of his horsemanship by imagining himself to be a young Nestor, even though at that time he could not press down with the weight even of a Scythian saddle on any horse he was mounting.[60] But why do I have to announce the deeds of that fellow and not give the account more quickly lest I pollute even the air itself with his preposterous deeds? I am going to carry on nonetheless.

12. When that fellow saw me pursuing philosophy, he was furious and warmed up his poison. I think he had learned magical arts long ago when in the past he had dwelt on a mountain of the Bulgarian territories called Haimos,[61] which separates the region of Thrace from them. Defiled by the spells originating from this place, he was completely possessed by evil spirits and so he deeply dyed his gray hair. By mixing up the dung of different animals and smearing it, he faked youth with the dye. If someone saw him, he would have said he was the god of the Mendesians,[62] to judge by his beard and the color of his hair. For by mixing the soot of smoke with the white of his beard, he blended one color with another, and they gave his beard a blue tint. Even the intellect of Aristotle in *On Colors* has failed to capture this knowledge.[63] Someone <who saw him> would have called him the god of the Mendesians because of the fragrance of his strangely concocted perfume and because of the length of his white hair—for in both ways he possessed the right characteristics. Thanks to these, he wanted his word to be trusted and wanted to turn the most nonsyllogistical propositions about me into syllogisms! For he made

---

60 On the tutor's small stature, see §3. The light "Scythian saddle" was evidently the saddle used by the Mongols. On the author's familiarity with the Mongol style of horse riding, see Th. L., *Ep.* 179.26 (p. 230).

61 That is, the Balkan Mountains.

62 That is, the god Pan worshipped by the Egyptians, half-goat and half-man. See Herodotus, *Histories* 2.46; Strabo, *Geography* 17.1.40. See also John Argyropoulos, *Katablattas*, ed. Canivet and Oikonomides, 65.525, for a parallel in invective imagery.

63 The passage should be added to other pieces of evidence about men in Byzantium dyeing their hair. See John Zonaras's commentary on canon 96 of the Quinisext Council (691/92) in Rhalles and Potles, Σύνταγμα, 2:534. The pseudo-Aristotelian treatise *On Colors* formed part of the Aristotelian corpus circulating in the Middle Ages.

syllogisms and drew conclusions not about money, nor about possessions, nor about the beauty of pearls and stones, so that his victory would have marked slight progress and his defeat would have marked a setback—and therefore even I would have had to subject myself in strict discipline to him, since he was my tutor—but by the sight of his beard and his monkey-like walk, he strove to deceive me and draw me away from philosophy, the divine gift, the most beautiful thing truly beloved by God. Knowing him to be a trickster, I ignored him as a fool and attached myself to philosophy, as was right, led on by the nautical custom "from the oar to the tiller."[64]

13. As I progressed from syllogisms to mathematics and hence to superior knowledge (earlier I had become well acquainted with physics and, above all, prose composition and rhetoric, thus studying poetry as well), I rose to higher subjects, even though that fellow was furious. What are these [higher subjects]? And why am I becoming like the simplest individual and pointlessly keeping company with a man who is not good? For him, it was naturally fitting to brag about himself; but in my case, humility exalts[65] me and truth does not deprive me of knowledge. So whither shall I turn and whence can I steer the course of my account toward the satire, so as to denounce the tutor by leaving all this as my repayment? From no other starting point and no other path than from that fellow's insult on philosophy and his wickedness and evil plotting. For what worse thing could he do (and he would hardly have achieved it in my case), since he was hindering me from studying philosophy?

There was a man[66] possessed by the muse of Homer as well as that of Socrates, who knew the divine mathematics and God-inspired logic of Plato and Aristotle and, in addition, natural science and verbal subtlety, and was believed to know the philosophy of Pythagoras, and the study of the elements by Euclid and Theon,[67] as well as the fine arithmetic of Idiophantes,[68] the harmonics of Claudius, the

---

64 The expression seems to be proverbial.
65 Cf. Matt. 23:12; Luke 14:11, 18:14.
66 That is, Nikephoros Blemmydes. See above, pp. 17–18.
67 Theon of Smyrna (fl. 100 CE) was a mathematician, astronomer, and theoretician of music who authored *On Mathematics Useful for the Understanding of Plato*. Laskaris cites or refers to him on several occasions. See below, p. 74, n. 76; *Representation of the World, or Life*, §12, p. 153, n. 97; *Oration on Hellenism*, §7, p. 182, n. 29.
68 That is, Diophantos. See above, p. 60, n. 8.

astronomy of Ptolemy,[69] and the movements of the visible stars. My tutor greatly envied him, largely because he saw that the latter was teaching me these things. He liked to pull me away from philosophy and was eager to be lovestruck and chase women with lustful desire; and he banged his staff[70] without restraint, imitating a depiction of Hermes not in an allegorical way, but in appearance and roughness, so to say, being unlike him in another respect.[71] For he also paired up his lady friends with the servants, and he separated them off sometimes and went to bed with the ladies to perform shameful acts.

Where were the thunderbolts, where were the whirlwinds, where were the lurid lightnings that should have burned this intense person? Where were the storms and hail? People who were carnal and earthly did not care then, but now angelic beings[72] are stirring his soul. Even though Cerberus has destroyed his body, he still remains hungry. For how could this mouse provide sufficient food for that dog?

14. The foul fellow saw me making progress in philosophy—let me say that I also studied in an excellent manner the military rules, lest the listener should criticize my present account—and he remained stunned. But since he was cunning, he schemed against my teacher in order to provoke ridicule and insults and suchlike against him. The latter man, whose attitude toward me was of a friend and mentor, took all that as if suffered by someone else. For truly a friend knows how to die on behalf of a friend. But you, the son of Lucifer,[73] the offspring of wickedness, the embryo of stupidity, even if you are dead in soul and body, I will still address you

---

69 Claudius and Ptolemy are one and the same author, Claudius Ptolemy (second century CE), who wrote the *Harmonics* and the *Almagest*.

70 The author uses the rare Greek verb βακλίζω (to cudgel; LSJ, s.v.), with racy innuendo.

71 The allegory of Hermes is already employed above (see §9 and n. 50): Hermes as the god of rhetoric and composition. Here, the author alludes to the ambiguity of figure of Hermes in ancient myth and literature: a thief, a trickster, and a conveyor of the souls of the dead to the underworld. One of the attributes of Hermes was his staff (*caduceus*).

72 "Angelic beings" (οἱ νοητοί): a flash-forward to the tutor's death (§§25–26). The adjective νοητός could refer to spiritual beings, both angelic and demonic. According to a common belief, two kinds of angels, benevolent and wicked ones, appeared at the moment of death and passed (at that time or later) a provisional judgment on the soul. See Marinis, *Death and the Afterlife in Byzantium*, 11–23.

73 The ἑωσφόρος, or morning star, can refer to Satan as it does below in §22. See Lampe, s.v.

as if you were a living man. Why did you wish to separate me from philosophy or from God? For it is the same thing for someone to be deprived of wisdom as to be deprived of God. Turn the argument around! How does it look? Is it not the same to be deprived of God and be deprived of wisdom? You wished to deprive me of both God and wisdom, because the privation from the one thing destroys the unity with the other. How did you ignore <the definition of philosophy as> *assimilation to God as far as is humanly possible*?[74] For if you had wanted to do God's work as far as it is attainable, you would have liked philosophy; but since you carried out deeds of darkness, you considered it abominable. For philosophy is *assimilation to God as far as is humanly possible*. But for what reason did you overlook that philosophy is *knowledge of things existent as existent*?[75] Or do you not know that the person who knows things existent as they are by nature also comes to know God who is beyond things existent? It is from them that he progresses in his mind toward lofty heights. For the person who knows that being exists would know also the one beyond the existent. Having knowledge of him not in his essence, but in his kingship and might, and likewise in his indefinability, he would assimilate to him as far as is possible. What greater bliss is there for the human being than to be assimilated to God? No one else would be judged rightly worthy of this but the foremost philosopher who is skilled in music too. For according to Plato, the *philosopher is skilled in music, but the bad person is unmusical*.[76] But you are bad

---

74 This is the first of the six "canonical" definitions of philosophy cited by the author. The *prolegomena philosophiae* composed in the late antique school in Alexandria discuss these definitions and their origins. See, for example, David, *Prolegomena*, ed. Busse, 20–26; trans. Gertz, 103–9. For the continual influence of these definitions in Laskaris's circle, see Nikephoros Blemmydes, *Epitome logica* 4, in PG 142:720–24. See also Duffy, "Hellenic Philosophy in Byzantium," 140–43. The definition *assimilation to God as far as humanly possible* derives from Plato, *Theaetetus* 176b (cf. *Republic* 613b). See David, *Prolegomena*, ed. Busse, 26.19–26, trans. Gertz, 109; Nikephoros Blemmydes, *Epitome logica* 4, in PG 142:724.

75 This (second) definition of philosophy (γνῶσις τῶν ὄντων ᾗ ὄντα, or γνῶσις τῶν ὄντων καθὸ ὄντα in Laskaris's version), along with two other definitions (see below, nn. 79 and 82), is attributed to Pythagoras by David, *Prolegomena*, ed. Busse, 25.26–26.13, trans. Gertz, 108–9; Nikephoros Blemmydes, *Epitome logica* 4, in PG 142:724. It can be translated differently as "knowledge of beings qua beings" (the most common and literal translation), "knowledge of things existent as existent," "knowledge of things as they really are," and "knowledge of reality as it is."

76 The quotation is from Theon of Smyrna, *On Mathematics Useful for Reading Plato*, ed. Hiller, 11.8–9. The idea goes back to Plato, *Sophist* 253b–c, 259e.

as well as unmusical. If the person traversing the knowledge of things existent comes to know, as far as is possible, God, who is beyond the things existent, perhaps one could say that he understands also inferior things. But if he understands these things well, no one would say that he avoids the craft of shoemaking. Thus, if you wanted to educate me in a technical subject, you ought to have allowed me in this case, too, to study philosophy. For handicrafts, too, are from among the things existent.

15. How do you construe that philosophy is called *practice of death*?[77] Is it in the sense that it is, in fact, a teacher of good things, or that it is an incitement to pleasures? Do not shun the first interpretation. But I know well you could not bring yourself to hear the talk of death when you were alive. So how could you practice it? I am convinced that now you are suitably chastised in Pluto's land and have learned the importance of the practice of death. How came it that you did not pursue philosophy, so as to be compelled to engage in the practice of death? Had you done so, you would have escaped the tribunals that condemn you.

Hearing that philosophy is *art of arts and science of sciences*,[78] how did you, the teacher of what would profit me, strive that I remain unskilled and ignorant? But you can say you wished to teach me some particular subject. Do learn, too, what is an unassailable principle. Out of necessity, both the species and the particular result from the genus. The whole would never result from the species or from the particular; but in its part that lies in the species, it will result from every species, and again in its part that lies in the particular, it will result from the particular. For the union consists of either the whole with the whole, or the part with the part, or the edge with the edge. If you understand, take notice; but if not, then stay dead once more. Indeed, you should have known on account of this that philosophy is the universal knowledge of things existent and of every art and science, and that if I am wholly united with the whole, I would be united with the particular within that whole. In this case, then, what you wished to teach me would never have escaped

---

[77] This (third) definition of philosophy derives from Plato, *Phaedo* 81a. See David, *Prolegomena*, ed. Busse, 26.13–19, trans. Gertz, 109; Nikephoros Blemmydes, *Epitome logica* 4, in PG 142:724.

[78] This (fourth) definition of philosophy is attributed to Aristotle's *Metaphysics* by David, *Prolegomena*, ed. Busse, 26.26–28, trans. Gertz, 109; Nikephoros Blemmydes, *Epitome logica* 4, in PG 142:724. It is derived from the second chapter of first book of the *Metaphysics*, 982a32–b8, without being a literal quotation from Aristotle.

me, because you would have joined through your instruction my entire self to the whole body of the science and art of all sciences and arts. For if like things are mixed with like, all their parts enclose through the union their extremities. So the boundaries of both will include the parts of both, even if the parts do not happen to be alike. Then certainly, if you had allowed the rules, arguments, and ways of philosophy to be united with me, the particular <instruction>—should at least you have wished what you wished to teach me—would never have gone past me.

When you saw the full extent of your folly, because I was naturally suited for this thing [philosophy], and when you heard that philosophy was reputed to be *knowledge of things divine and human*,[79] what made you to like to drag me away from the divine, or rather to turn me into something completely beastly—and so you raged at the sight of my advance in philosophy? Perhaps someone who does not know divine things is more human, and he will sometimes look upward, glimpse a glimmer, and may see the light by chance. But someone deprived of any human features, who is completely beastly and serves his belly and its worst impulses, when would he rise above placement among the brute beasts and when would he be ranked in the category of the rational? When can he detach himself from the former and be conjoined with things divine? For life is easily cut short. Moral achievement is difficult. And who can therefore enjoy a share in it? But in your misanthropy you wanted to deprive me of both things [*the divine and the human*], so as to send and dispatch me, in one way and another, to your most evil ways and hence sing your victory song, having made me ridiculous just like you. Yet, by the hand of the Lord, *my enemy*, namely you, *did not rejoice over me*[80]— or rather over truth. Having survived, I will both live on and exult each day as I *trample upon the venomous snakes.*[81]

16. Because you learned in some circles that philosophy was *love of wisdom*,[82] why did you want me to live unphilosophically? I think for no other reason except to separate me from God—for *he also fell in love with her*,[83] whereas his enemy loved the opposite—and to join me to the devil. What madness! What

---

79 This (fifth) definition of philosophy is attributed to Pythagoras.
80 Cf. Ps. 29:2.
81 Cf. Luke 10:19.
82 This (sixth) definition of philosophy is attributed to Pythagoras.
83 Cf. Wisd. of Sol. 8:3.

derangement! What inhuman hatred! What perversity! Therefore, I wished to call as my witnesses the entire earth, all knowledge, all philosophy, and every form of education to observe a teacher of folly and a student yearning for philosophy, the adversaries cohabiting and the broken conjoined, the unrelated coexisting and the incongruous associated. And they [knowledge, philosophy, and education] will perhaps mock or lament this situation, or they will give themselves over to bitter joy because they cannot endure the horror. Let someone with a keener insight say that the divine has been propitiated and let him, so to speak, commiserate with those things and with me, and I will thus have some consolation.

"But what is the profit for you," one of my friends shouts out in a rather philosophical way, "to have great fear seize you, and when you become excited on the occasion of the death of this insect,[84] will you derive any benefit unless you present the anguish caused by such notorious combination? Do let it [the notorious combination] depart to suitable characters and may you not present the universe in lamentation for this piece of scrap! For this beast has his own badness as a fitting butt of jokes and has put on display his shameful and filthy misdeeds, which make him both ridiculous and imbecile." Persuaded in this way by the speaker, I abandon my goal and proceed following my earlier words to address that fellow [the tutor] about philosophy, which loathed him. I beg no one to listen to my words carelessly. For I am convinced that the listener will profit, the attentive person will find great pleasure, and every learned man will be much excited about the love of letters. For virtue is produced from the satire of wicked men. Just as the product of the bee is extracted from certain plants, although they are not perfectly good, so knowledge could, as I think, be derived now even from this demon of Poseidon.[85]

17. Having said all this to other individuals, or rather after I broadcast my account in public, I am now turning this account toward you, whose lot is to be chosen as subject of the satire, and urge you to learn as much as possible about the great need for philosophy. I do not gain grace from a graceless man. I do not draw learning or understanding from an empty individual and do not receive the

---

84 That is, the tutor.

85 The "demon of Poseidon" defies easy identification. The allusion may be to Poseidon's son Polyphemus, the man-eating cyclops who detained Odysseus and his companions, and was eventually blinded by Odysseus (*Odyssey* 9). Notably, Eustathios of Thessaloniki, *Commentary on the Iliad*, ed. Van der Valk, 1: 225.25–27, uses the word δαίμονες in reference to Poseidon's sons: the cyclops Polyphemus and the Aloadae Otus and Ephialtes.

fruit of reason from a fool. But I expose the evil in you and drive you who are more bitter than the suffering of death toward being shamed for your actions—even if you make your example one of envy, which will actually give benefit to sensible people. For as you know, you were envious about everyone. If I will give you only part of my account, it is still fruitful and philosophical for others, because it demonstrates to what end you were controlling me while I was studying philosophy: me, the son of rulers, who was about to rule through the Holy Spirit, a caretaker of many people, a protector of cities, a solace of the populace, and a midpoint of the state and co-decision-maker.[86] For if someone dragged into the law courts must be well trained and gifted in speaking, how much more is it necessary for the ruler of the people to be capable of making flowing speeches that are, I ought to say, clear to understand and adorned from every direction with virtue? What good judgment should he have, what critical sense, what magnificence and talent? What generosity in his gifts, so as to avoid mercenary spirit in receiving? What cheerfulness, directness, constancy, and everything else along with the fitting sequel of his actions? He will not accomplish any of this without philosophy.

18. For all these reasons, and many more, I had to study philosophy, even if you devised many tricks. <I had to study philosophy> because it is *knowledge of things existent as existent*, so that through close contact with philosophy I might refute every deceit along with wrong opinion and attach myself to the truly existent. <I had to study philosophy,> so that through its being *knowledge of things divine and human* I might recognize the things divine as separated from the earthly ones owing to their incompatibility, and from there I might contemplate the former things and direct there my attitude with all my strength. For the man who considers these things would never carry out shameful deeds. <I had to study philosophy> because it is *practice of death*, so that by remembering death continually, I might follow the precepts of the Best Tutor[87]—and not your precepts, you, the all-impious one—by whose memory I am pushed toward good things and distance myself from bad ones. What greater good is there in the world than the good arising from such conduct? <I had to study philosophy> because it is *assimilation to God as far as is humanly possible*, so that, because the subjects should imitate the

---

[86] A noteworthy general description of the duties of Laskaris as an uncrowned coemperor.

[87] That is, God.

ruler, I might somehow resemble the First Principle, the one transcending every principle, who is really without beginning and without end, and so that, since any work of that one is holy and good, I might perhaps live by acting uprightly and devoutly as much as possible, resembling the Principle as is right. Everyone with a mind cleansed from impurity understands what kind of blessing this is.

<I had to study philosophy> because it is *art of arts and science of sciences*, so that by God's providence and by following nature serving the divine command, I, who am the summit of things in human life, might have the complete knowledge of the first science—that is, royal science.[88] For from here gaze the wise and the ignorant person, the craftsman and the soldier, the wrongdoer and the just man, the one who is judged and the judge, the winner and the vanquished, the diligent and the lazy, the rich and the poor, households, villages, cities, and the world: in a word, all the people. Compile a work regarding what kind of man the person whose lot it is to rule should be![89] On account of all of this, I absolutely had to be a philosopher, for, in my opinion, rulers should have scientific knowledge and do nothing without it. <I had to study philosophy> because it is *love of wisdom*, so that I might through it [the love of wisdom] practice philosophy not crudely and in vain, but with great desire, love, and affection. For to labor for knowledge crudely and not with all one's soul is not proper to genuine philosophers, but belongs to those who dabble in it against their conscience—so nobody would ever call them philosophers, no matter what they do. What is done by force is uncertain, whereas all is easy and straightforward for the willing devotee. Therefore, as I had a loving attitude toward it [philosophy], I received my reward, with which I have been adorned above a sapphire stone, precious pearls, and all ornaments; and because I have been called a friend of wisdom, I will have no one to resist me.

19. As for you, do engage in discussion with me in a more logical way: demolish the points advanced and gather what you wish in your own propositions. But if that is impossible because you, being a dead man, do not have a body and organs of speech, and so you lack ability, do entrust the dispute to another like-minded person and a partner in your folly. For what great achievement is it for profit to

---

88 Originally derived from Plato, the concept of "royal science" (βασιλικὴ ἐπιστήμη) was used in late antiquity and Byzantium to refer to the expert knowledge of statesmanship and good imperial government. See Angelov, "Classifications of Political Philosophy," 35–45.

89 Laskaris rhetorically urges the tutor to compose an admonitory text on kingship, such as Blemmydes' *Imperial Statue*.

succumb to lack of profit, necessity to impossibility, and reason to foolishness! Therefore people who make demands for him must be of such kind—namely, equally gifted in folly and relatives of nothingness. What they construct will thus become stable, with firmest foundations and unshakable![90] Do make use of someone like that as your defender. But if knowledge has been implanted in you thanks to the suffering in Hades—things seem to become clearer to those who experience its punishment—transmit this knowledge to him [your defender], so that you render the company most learned. For when the flesh has melted away, when matter no longer exists, and when the soul can see without blurring, all that is finest comes together in the human being. When I say "the finest," I mean the truthful, and when I say "the human being," I mean the person with knowledge of the human condition. But as you did not live well, you lacked the recognition of being among the living. Now that you have suffered this, you are, in my opinion, exclusively human, because with the dissolution of matter, you have come to understand what is true. By your death, you have escaped oblivion and materiality. Whether you ever had intelligence, I do not know. I know, however, that you have been chained with fetters in Hades, as *with bit and bridle*.[91] Therefore, if immoderation and folly have left you, do assist the person intent on fighting on your behalf. But if you are again overcome by foolishness, give up the fight. As I know well that you have piled paralysis on paralysis, I am letting you off now from this conversation;[92] but I will not grow tired of denouncing you either now or at other times—and especially now when I have a like-minded audience of proponents of philosophy, which you hated.

After saying all this against that[93] rabid dog, I curb the flow of words addressed to him, conduct it to the earlier channel, and derive subject matter from the unshapely man in <human> shape[94] and occasions for literary work from the greatest fool ever. No one will give thanks to that fellow, but to the grace-giving

90 An ironic statement.
91 Ps. 31:9.
92 The end of the "conversation" (διάλεξις) signals that the author switches from direct address as announced in §17, with verbs in the second-person singular, to a description of the tutor and narration of his death.
93 The word ἐκεῖνος, used multiple times in §19, can be interpreted both as a demonstrative pronoun ("that rabid dog") and as an allusion to the tutor's passing ("the late rabid dog").
94 A translation preserving the word play of the phrase ἐξ τοῦ ἀνειδέου σὺν εἴδει.

Satire of His Tutor

God. May that fellow receive the punishment of his false belief, but let others receive pleasure and benefit from this. Therefore, as a friend of learning, I present to my friends and fellow learned men this satire worthy of the tutor, as if it were a delicacy from the imperial dining table.

20. He looked down upon me with a raised eyebrow and thought that whatever he foolishly said or did to be model images of virtue and culture, but he hated the good things that he saw I profited[95] from others and considered them to be, as one might say, his own demise. Oddly, the insatiable man who possessed so much mercenary spirit and voraciousness unlike anyone else—and thus received by every means what was mine and what came from me—could not get enough but planned again and again to greedily devour money and philosophy along with me. Neither tyrants nor men of power nor *the kings of this earth*[96] have seized philosophy when she fled, nor did they suppress her by force when she was condemning them. For everyone, regardless of country and lineage, embraces her through purity of virtue, earnestness of desire, and pursuit of learning. At times, she is seen as weak in the eyes of others; but when they try to dominate her, she becomes accustomed to residing in the regions beyond the peaks of the Caucasus Mountains, the solar orbits, and all the areas of the starless sphere. So he was tyrannizing over me and the money[97] for some time, but he could not lay a constraint on her [philosophy]. For how could he? Nor was he deemed worthy of seeing her, for he had foolishness as his blinders on both sides.

Living with such meanest spirit, he did not have the test of his conscience but had unsound judgment as his counselor, from which every day he got marks of bruises and acts of intemperance and insatiable greed, and managed to make futile even the Lord's own words. On feast days, he covered his head under a red-dyed woolen hat that was different from all others (this was contrary to propriety, or rather occurred with God's consent).[98] Although there were thousands of other

---

95 Perhaps ὀνεῖσθαι (from ὀνίνημι) rather than ὠνεῖσθαι (from ὠνέομαι), as in the manuscripts and the edition—an emendation proposed by Joseph Munitiz. In any case, the allusion to payments to the tutor in this passage is worth noting.

96 Cf. Pss. 2:2, 101:16, 109:5, 137:14, 148:11.

97 This is the second mention of money, which suggests that the tutor was generously remunerated.

98 Headgear was an important attribute of holding a court title in Byzantium after the eleventh century. See Macrides, Munitiz, and Angelov, *Pseudo-Kodinos*, 322, n. 23, 324.

people like him who wore refined clothing, he—being more womanly at heart than anyone else—built up the hat taller, ignoring that no one *of his age can add a single cubit to his span*[99] and furthermore that this saying belongs to the Lord. As he made the hat two cubits high, he seemed double-headed when he wore it, or rather seemed like a crocodile peeping out from some hole. He was also accustomed to have shoes prepared for him that raised him from the floor, so in some people's eyes his head gave away his falsehood, but for others it was the soles on his feet. For he was a complete fraud. As for what was in between, there is no need to speak of it, because it was nothing else but what separated his hat and his shoes. If this should be called a body, let it be called so. In addition, that giant and Cronus put on a garment that was not undignified in its craftsmanship, but became entirely undignified because he draped it around himself. He gaped at the entrance to the palace like a rodent in mousehole that had escaped the doom of a field mouse. When I saw all this, I felt shame at the weirdness. He was a great cause for laughter in both body and soul, but I was putting up with him and awaiting the opportunity of my coming of age.

21. After much time passed, I obtained ability from him but cannot call this philosophy, for parents are known from their children. I was advancing just as was expected, but he clothed himself in the dust of slander like some snake. Biting from both sides with feet and head, he was fighting against the two of us, both the teacher and the pupil.[100] As much as he brought trials and rebukes upon us, so much the more—seven times over—did we gleam like gold. For the testing of men is prone to augment their virtue. So he was setting in motion all sorts of stratagems against us, but God directed our power. What need is there for me to describe his plots, his slanders, his libels, his insults, and everything else that would have moved even a creature made of stone if rushing in like manner against it? He threw all that on our heads like a heavy stone. When he saw that we were unbreakable in our reasoning and friendship, he *lit the furnace*[101] of his soul against us—this ancient Nebuchadnezzar and new Bel of an imaginary Belshazzar,[102] this giant of a blockhead by his self-aggrandizement and a Thersites in stature by his compressed

---

99 Matt. 6:27; Luke 12:25.

100 That is, Blemmydes and Laskaris.

101 Cf. Dan. 3:19.

102 The comparisons are inspired by stories told in the Book of Daniel. Nebuchadnezzar orders the execution of the three youths in the fiery furnace (Dan. 3). The pagan god Bel

size, this tail of Chimera,[103] this venomous monster of the spring, this great evil and greater evil and wholly evil and truly evil, this birdbrain by his intelligence,[104] this frog by his croaks, this swine in his whole lifestyle, this dry ebb, this sea disaster off Thule,[105] this sacred precinct of shamefulness, this house of debauchery, this climax of sexual pleasures, this enemy of prudence, this beginning, middle, and end of everything disgusting, this son of Mohammed by the great roundness of his shape,[106] this font of evil, this Satan himself. However, God—the great eye, the guardian of all that breathes, the architect of the heaven and the earth,[107] the God of the living and the dead,[108] the Lord of all that is, and was and is to come, and the King and God of the material and the immaterial, of the perceptible and the imperceptible—he did not allow us to fall into his furnace, but guarded and saved us from it, while consigning him very soon to damnation—for death obliterates the maliciousness of any soul.

22. Having recounted, as was necessary, the deeds of this fellow against us, I am now going ahead to recount the details of his death, leaving to others to reveal his evil designs against his servants, his crimes in condemning God's servants,[109] his adulterous and lewd impulses, his insatiable gluttony, his slovenliness in housekeeping, his libels against strangers, his tardiness in performing services to the imperial majesties, his uninspired and ineffective advice-giving, his acts of

---

with insatiable appetite is featured in the addition to the Book of Daniel known as "Bel and the Dragon" (Dan. 14:1–22). King Belshazzar and his feast are described in Dan. 5.

103 The tail of the monster Chimera had the shape of a snake, according to *Iliad* 6.180–81.

104 Literally "a storm petrel in his intellectual grasp" (ὁ κέπφος τῇ γνώσει). The storm petrel, a seabird reputed to feed on sea foam, referred proverbially to foolish people. See *Souda*, kappa 1347 (ed. Adler, 3:96).

105 A mythical uninhabitable island in the far north. The reference to a "sea disaster" (θαλάσσης πάθημα) is puzzling. Laskaris may have in mind stories about the unnavigable sea around Thule derived from the ancient geographer Pythias of Massalia, as reported by Strabo, *Geography* 2.4.1, and retold in the twelfth century by John Tzetzes, *Allegories from the Verse Chronicle*, ed. Hunger, 22.133–39, 24.206–7.

106 Either a proverb or reference to a real person.

107 Cf. Pss. 123:8, 133:3.

108 Cf. Acts 10:42; Rom. 14:9.

109 The phrase ὑποτελεταὶ θεοῦ may refer to clergymen. The rare word ὑποτελετής can also mean a taxpayer (see *LBG*, s.v.).

cowardice in wartime and dissensions in peacetime (these, I certainly think, were for keeping his own peace), the magnitude of his sloth, his usuriousness in gold, his disrespect for the saints, the filthiness of his actions, his openness to bribery (whenever he passed a judgment), the foolishness of his speech, the unsoundness of his frame of mind, his tongue-tied attitude toward saying a good thing and quickness in harming a person (the devil, in a way, resided on his tongue), his lack of compassion, his misanthropy, his shadiness, his underhandedness, his lawlessness and disdain for the law, his atheism. For he did not know if there was a God at all. Every judgment is subject to God as to a master, and consequently so are the punishments and retributions due for these [character faults]. If he had recognized what a judgment was, he would have recognized who is the Judge. But since the unjust judge does not know the Judge, therefore he was ignoring his [God's] judgments. What an utterly foul fellow! How *the son of lawlessness*[110] pulled his power-loving mind away from divine nature in imitation of Lucifer! However, let others speak of such matters truthfully, since they saw them more accurately.

As for me, after I compare him to persons of his like mind, I am going to turn my account to recounting the sort of disgraceful death that happened to befall that fellow, because it was quite ridiculous. I cannot easily find evil persons with whom to compare him. For inasmuch as he allowed evil to infect others, being entirely its full embodiment, who would be a person of this kind, even if he might be used for a comparison? As the particular is less than the universal, evil was inherent in him in the same way. Everything in him was like in a storage vessel, whereas in anyone else it was like in a small cup. I will not be out of my depth if I compare the part with the whole contrary to scientific knowledge. This comparison could perhaps be considered scientific in reference to quality. For as regards the equal division into parts, the number six can be compared to twice twelve, except not quantitatively.[111] This utterly evil person can likewise be brought to comparison as regards some point of resemblance, given that a spoonful of sea water is similar in quality with the ocean, but would not be similar in quantity. I cannot liken him to the greatest individuals—for how can one find high-standing individuals who are fools? It is from among people similar in mind and nature that I can take up a

---

110 Ps. 88:23.

111 Yet another digression (a learned one in this case) characteristic of Laskaris's stream-of-consciousness style.

Satire of His Tutor

comparison that serves him. If I am going to deal with this by force, I will have an excuse. For everything about to be recounted is going to be true.

23. Now, first, I can match him bodily with Thersites[112] of old, unless somehow I will find great incompatibility with him. For even if the one resembles the other in height, still he is more undignified in his limbs, more unsightly in his shape, and worse in his manners and speech. In terms of personality <I can match him> with the savagery of Echetos.[113] Even if I am comparing a private citizen to a tyrant, their common conduct makes my comparison not inappropriate, for they both thought and acted similarly. For *such as was the speech* of the one, *so was the life* of the other; and *such as were the doings* of the one, so of the other.[114] The life of both men was likewise full of murder. In terms of avarice <I can match him> with Perseus[115] of Macedon. Imitating the latter's conduct he was burying the gold. Indeed, I think coins were placed with him in the grave because of his darling avarice. He had the malady of avarice no less than Navatos,[116] although he shunned his alleged virginity, being an expert in accepting and rejecting. For he should have accepted the latter [virginity] and rejected the former [avarice]. However, that person [Navatos] welcomed the latter [virginity] and he [the tutor] rejected it, but he [the tutor] utterly desired the former [avarice], which Navatos practiced in an unbridled fashion: in both aspects he fell into disaster! <I can match him> with Judas in his lack of faith, something that he had in equal magnitude.

---

112 An allusion to Thersites has already been made in §3 (see p. 62, n. 16), and Thersites is also mentioned by name in §21.

113 The Epirote king Echetos is made notorious for his cruelty in *Odyssey* 18, and he is used as an example by Blem., *Imperial Statue* 52 (p. 58). See also *Representation of the World, or Life*, §11.

114 Based on a saying attributed to Socrates and cited in commentaries on rhetorical theory: ὁ Σωκράτης εἰώθει λέγειν, οἷος ὁ βίος, τοιοῦτος καὶ ὁ λόγος, οἷος ὁ λόγος, τοιαῦται καὶ αἱ πράξεις καὶ ἀναστρέφων τὰ αὐτὰ ἔλεγεν. See Syrianus, *In Hermogenem commentaria* 1, ed. Rabe, 77.7–10; John Sikeliotes, *Commentary on Hermogenes, On Ideas*, in Walz, *Rhetores Graeci*, 6:395.3–5.

115 Perseus (r. 179–168 BCE), the last king of Macedon before the Roman conquest, is given as an example of avarice by Blem., *Imperial Statue* 74 (pp. 64–66).

116 That is, Novatian, a third-century theologian who was condemned as a heretic. There were proverbial sayings in Byzantium about his arrogance, misanthropy, and, as this passage suggests, avarice. See Strömberg, *Greek Proverbs*, 18; Anna Komnene, *Alexias* 6.12.7, 10.7.1, ed. Reinsch and Kambylis, 1:196.36–37, 301.64–65.

But why is it fitting to compare him to humans? What kind of similarity is there and why is it fitting to do so, when that fellow was a human-shaped animal, or rather, an utter beast? It is with animals that his comparison is most apt, something that I absentmindedly overlooked, but will now bring forward as I think of it. He certainly resembled *a stallion* in his lust, because he *neighed* uncontrollably *for his neighbors' wives*,[117] a lion's whelp in plundering,[118] a deer in his soul, a fox in cunning, an ape in unsightliness, an Indian ant in lust for gold,[119] a raven in gluttony, a seabird in his frame of mind,[120] a fish in speechlessness, a dog in impertinence, a camel in swiftness, an elephant in agility, a donkey in musical ability, a bear in social skills, a wild boar in gravitas, a jackal's skin in the smoothness of his manners; as for frankness of opinion, he resembled a leopard's skin. I want to compare this fellow also to the sweet scent of the dung beetle. Through the scent of his deeds, he resembled the reek of brimstone[121] and the fragrance of a corpse. The quality of these lifeless things pulls me away like a counterweight and pushes me to compare him with it—I mean the hardness of hail, the coldness of snow, and the difficulties of stones to move.

After I have fittingly compared him with all these, I can compare him truly and most naturally with the devil; and I can compare him for his conduct, mind, and deeds. I believe everyone will admit this, even if he is not a friend of learning or of learned men. For even an adversary has respect for the truth. But what excellence! What manly virtue! What combination of the finest qualities![122] If this [combination] was not such and not so great by its initial formation, he [the devil] would not have given so many graces to the person celebrated here. He [the devil] assembled along with these also qualities beyond these to give a shape and form to the man—this is why he bestowed on him such graces.

24. But what punishment must I suffer from a most loquacious rhetorician, one versed in spinning language and dwelling among the Muses—first, because I

---

[117] Cf. Jer. 5:8.

[118] Cf. Ps. 103:21.

[119] The fabulous gold-digging animal of India is mentioned by Herodotus, *Histories* 3.102–5, and Strabo, *Geography* 15.1.44.

[120] Literally, "with the prudence of a storm petrel (κέπφος)." On the negative characteristics assigned to this bird, see above, n. 104.

[121] Cf. *Iliad* 14.415.

[122] The three exclamations are full of irony.

have extended my words in the comparisons of this lump, an insensitive and empty character, and second, because I have forgotten his death, which perhaps contains an intricate story that delights and profits my audience? Nonetheless, even if I have been punished, the sentence and punishment did not come from Themis.[123] For a soldier corrects another soldier, a general another general, a scholar another scholar, a craftsman another craftsman, an artisan another artisan, a farmer another farmer, and a rhetorician another rhetorician. So I fear with good reason the descendants of Demosthenes and Hermogenes, and am already refraining from making comparisons lest I suffer the misfortune of the poor timekeeper.[124] I am going to proceed to what I planned to recount about his most unseemly death. My narration will start from the time of our stay in Nicaea. It goes like this.

25. While we were residing in Nicaea, a city that I love—as I imagine do all good-hearted people, for even its name holds a sign of victory[125]—we were occupied with the matters arising at that time. I mean the matters of the marriage feasts and the court celebrations, matters that for me were royal and involved my father.[126] Their fame, glory, splendor, and all the other acts of excellence have escaped the notice only of the dumb and the simple-minded. When we had finished the joyful festivities, the time came for an expedition, and the emperor with his army and together with me set off for the region of Prousa. When the heavenly Dog Star moves about in the visible sky, before which Virgo aligned with the Big Dipper passes through,[127] it was at that time that we set off for that place. But this senile man was struck down by some illness, the result of the aberrant flow of the humors, which were railing at the prolongation of his old age and sought to minister to his demise. He continued to dally in the city in order to take care

---

123 That is, a verdict by the goddess of justice.

124 Literally, "the misfortune of the man who does not know to speak in relation to the water clock" (τοῦ μὴ λαλεῖν πρὸς ὕδωρ εἰδότος πάθημα). This proverbial expression was based on the failure of speakers at the law court to keep to the time allowed by the water clock. See Plato, *Theaetetus* 201b2; Anna Komnene, *Alexias* 14.4.5, ed. Reinsch and Kambylis, 1:440.10.

125 A wordplay on Nicaea (Νίκαια) as the city of victory (νίκη).

126 The events in question were the celebrations for the marriage of Laskaris's father, John III Vatatzes, to Constanza (renamed as Anna in Nicaea), the daughter of Emperor Frederick II.

127 The heliacal rising of the Dog Star (Sirius) occurs during the hottest day of the summer. See the discussion in Angelov, *Byzantine Hellene*, 332.

of himself, but also to indulge further in sexual pleasures at the end of his life, so that these become fitting travel provisions for his departure. For he yearned to add crowning debaucheries to his debaucheries and add fuel to his offenses through more offenses.

He did this and remained in Nicaea, while we stayed in the area of Mysia.[128] I will rightly call the stay there an introduction to God's excellence in order for God to show me secretly, as if in some curtained space, the separation from that fellow (under whom I had suffered unbearably) and possibly to lift in advance my spirits which that fellow had tried in all sorts of ways to dash. God changed this illness from unwellness to a full disease, and the man in need of medical attention became really ill. When some angelic messenger[129] told us the utterly good news, we sang hymns to God, just as Moses[130] did over the victory against the foreign tribes. While we tarried in the place, the illness weakened him. Wasting him greatly, it forced him to leave Nicaea and overcame the doomed man, as expected. When the beastly fellow reached us, the cultivated ones, he was a skeleton, so to speak. What a great sight it was! *The mountains were leveled by force*[131] and *the tops of the hills brought low*[132] by an illness slight in strength and by the established order of nature. When we saw him, we felt uncustomary joy, for we had never conversed with him without sorrow. After staying with us for about a week, he set off for Thrakesion,[133] carrying the illness upon his head and maybe also intending to arrange for some errand on our behalf. I put off describing what he did to us while being away from us.

That fellow went off to where he wanted. God who separated us from him granted besides that we would no longer be subjected to him. One could describe most figuratively the day of separation as a day gold-blossoming in its joy, a day clothed as if in a robe of bright clarity, a day shining like the sun, a bride adorned

128 Mysia is an ancient region of Asia Minor west of Bithynia.

129 The author plays on the double meaning of the word ἄγγελος as "angel" and "messenger."

130 Exod. 15:1: the victory hymn on the flight from Egypt.

131 Cf. Hab. 3:6.

132 Cf. Isa. 40:4.

133 A large theme, or province, in the southern part of the Nicaean realm centered on Smyrna, Nymphaion, and Ephesos. On its location and administration, see Angold, *A Byzantine Government in Exile*, 246–48.

Satire of His Tutor

as in a bridal chamber, an abundance of good things that streamed, so to say, into broad and big channels of sweetness, a day as if announcing *a gospel of joy*,[134] an angel from heaven to the mortals, virtue itself, exultation itself, rejoicing itself. Everyone should consider this not figuratively but assign it truly to that day, because it removed the devil common to the whole world from us as well as from the entire earth. When the man had gone to the regions of Asia where we were privately residing at that time, he wasted away, even as he fought through physical means to sustain his disease-stricken body with gluttonous meals, drinks, and a variety of foodstuffs. Just as a loose string cannot produce a sound and the tuner fails in his expert craft once the cord is broken, in this way also nothing material functions at the time of the soul's separation from the body, no matter how much someone tries his methods—for it is from here [from materiality] that the body gets the structure of its human frame. Once the human frame departs from its physical boundaries, at the time when the all-seeing eye determines, its servant remains motionless, by which it shows . . .[135]

∼

. . . unnecessary to exult in one's mind about someone's suffering. When he began to utter that sweetest saying that makes a proclamation,[136] the impious man passed away.

26. How great is the power of God! The *dew* of exultation poured into my soul, more than the dew *flowing down upon Mount Sion*.[137] After shedding a few tears in a public capacity and paying lip service[138] by saying a word of sorrow, I departed with great joy. But shortly thereafter, after a few moments had passed, I arrived at the desired state of mind. O what was my joy then! Rejoicing daily in this way, I learned the events at that fellow's death. They were as follows. As the disease

---

134 Cf. Luke 2:10.

135 Here there is a large lacuna in all surviving manuscripts. A note in Parisinus gr. 3048 (*Diktyon* 52693), which was copied by Michael Souliardos in 1486, mentions "folios" missing. The copyist left in this place an empty folio. According to Astruc, "La tradition manuscrite," 397–98, it is impossible to determine the length of the lacuna.

136 It is likely that there was a scriptural saying in the immediately preceding paragraph, which has been lost.

137 Ps. 132:3.

138 Literally, "with the tips of my lips," a set expression indicating superficiality.

overwhelmed him, both gaining control of the parameters of his vital powers and diverting the flow of the humors forever owing to their faulty condition, his flesh in the end fell apart. Even so, he refused to obey death. His pulse went on from the first down until the last combination of pulsations and from that pulsation until the end: the pulses proceeded quickly and feebly in the manner of ants.[139] Then he called for the best doctors and inquired about death. At the first examination, they understood his dark destiny and wrote him off. It was early in the morning. But he once again struggled like a crab to remain alive, although his vital energy was going away. At their second examination, they tested the pulse and found that it was already disappearing. When he asked to be informed, they mentioned again the failure of his health. Being persuaded <regarding his imminent death> contrary to his conscience, he did not break into tears in order to make penance but contrived once more something against me.

He knew we were approaching the area where he was staying. This messenger of doom sent messengers to call and summon us to his side, ostensibly so that we might grant him forgiveness. But this did not happen. He disclosed his scheme to the receiver of his soul,[140] who was quite like him, a scheme we accurately learned of from others in the end. As he wanted badly to heap another evil onto the evils he had done me earlier, he could think of nothing else in his final moments but to inflict an additional wound upon me. Since he knew my mind's disposition toward him, he planned that while I approached him in tears, he would mercilessly bite[141] my foot like a dog in order to imprint on me this seal of evil deeds and so I would appear to many to be lamenting him with tears of pain. But he failed in his evil

---

139 The description is based on Galenic medical theory. The combination of the pulsations (συζυγία τῶν σφυγμῶν) refers to compound pulses arising from twenty-seven combinations, called συζυγίαι, of quantity of the diastole (e.g., long-narrow-high pulse or long-wide-high pulse). See Galen, *On the Different Kinds of Pulse*, ed. Kühn, 504–6, 543, 617; Galen, *Synopsis on the Pulse* 25, ed. Kühn, 515; Theophilos Protospatharios, *On the Pulse*, ed. Ermerins, 17–21. An "ant-like" pulse (κατὰ μύρμηκα), which was also expressed in Galenic medical theory with the verb μυρμηκίζω, refers to an anomalous weak pulse. See Galen, *On the Different Kinds of Pulse*, ed. Kühn, 553, 555; Galen, *Synopsis on the Pulse* 22, ed. Kühn, 507–8; Theophilos Protospatharios, *On the Pulse*, ed. Ermerins, 47.

140 Probably the author means the devil rather than a confessor at the tutor's deathbed.

141 The biting should be interpreted metaphorically rather than literally. The image fits with earlier comparisons of the tutor to an insect (§16), a snake (§21), and a dog (§§19, 23).

scheme. For God had foresight, and before we arrived, he had left the company of the living.

He then granted most people to be left in peace from him. But he had deceived the rather simple-minded through the homonymy,[142] conveying peace in his communications with everyone. He also asked for peace whenever he moved his tongue. Whether he asked for peace seeing the horde of demons on earth in order to then find rest there to their joy, or whether, bereft of the peace of the angels, he was asking for peace underground, I have no knowledge. However, he kept asking. It seems to me <he did so> in order to become a truest servant of the demons by secretly showing it [the underground peace] to them, to shackle himself to their hands, and to be led off to the underworld. This is what he did. In his very last moment he kept plotting away confidently, while suffering and doing these things. He breathed his last having lived throughout his life with every kind of lawlessness, injustice, sin, misanthropy, wickedness, insatiate greed, debauchery, slander, calumny, irreverence, and unbelief.

27. *Blessed is God*[143] who did all this, turned it into profit, and *brought us out of darkness into light.*[144] He accomplished all this and was our benefactor, showing oftentimes and abundantly to everyone the all-powerful might of his right hand. Let no one suppose that I am by nature inhumane, because I have produced this description. For this is not a description of my conduct, nor have I produced it out of malice. But God knows that I was defending philosophy, which that fellow despised. In addition, <I produced the description> because I judged that making evil known is a virtue for the individual bringing it into the light (for the simple-minded person flees when obstacles are in plain sight, but falls into a trap if they are somehow hidden under other things) and because the denouncer of wicked deeds extols as divine those actions which are not. This is the method and this is the subject about which I spoke, being urged to speak out by philosophy. In God's name, I entrust to the readers themselves to fill in whatever I may have left out. Let that [the present work] be taken as mine, but the latter [a possible longer work] belong to mightier authors. As for the rest, should they find their hesitation to be an impediment out

---

142 The puzzling "homonymy" (ὁμωνυμία) may allude to the peaceable-sounding name of the tutor. Alternatively, the author may be referring to the ambiguity of his invocations of peace (the peace among the demons, as is explained further). See above, p. 19.

143 2 Cor. 1:3; Eph. 1:3.

144 Cf. 1 Pet. 2:9.

of weakness, let them at least publicize this [the present work] with great fanfare among the future generations. For this fellow was absolutely the worst. This is what I ask wholeheartedly of everyone. To the devil that has disappeared, I say the following: "You, wretch, you could not bear to hear the name of philosophy, but you had no power to do any harm against her. She, for her part, because she is humane, offers on behalf of philosophers everywhere this gift to you, an inalienable legacy, fitting and everlasting."

2

Memorial Discourse on Emperor Frederick II

A Memorial Discourse on the emperor of the Germans, lord Frederick, by the same Theodore Doukas Laskaris, the son of the most exalted emperor, lord John Doukas.

1. Today it is my duty to give a brief speech about a man who was a ruler and a general. Rulership always suffers gravely, more so than a sick body onerously bearing its disease, in its destiny to be the subject of reproach, as speculations ridicule it with unfair and excessive words. Gratitude and liking will never come to follow even those who are good, but, for all the others, ingratitude and dislike will ever grow from one surge of blame to another.

Many words indeed have been spoken in praise of those virtues, so to call them, which occur among *speechless animals*,[1] and of the progress of the natural achievements[2] found, too, among these unreasoning creatures, even if nature does everything in accordance with reason. But even as such, they are celebrated since they represent true gain and virtue for our profit. No word, of course, is said

---

1 The praise of "speechless animals" (ἄλογα ζῷα) is mentioned in Hermogenes' chapter on the encomium in his *Progymnasmata*, no. 7, in *Opera*, ed. Rabe, 17.5. In this sentence Theodore makes a pun on the words ἄλογος ("speechless" as well as "unreasoning," "irrational") and λόγος.

2 The so-called natural virtues (ἀρεταὶ φυσικαί), common to humans and animals, are the lowest scale of virtues in the late Neoplatonic system. See O'Meara, *Platonopolis*, 46; Michael Psellos, *De omnifaria doctrina* 67.1–2, ed. Westerink, 44; John Italos, *Questiones quodlibetales* 63, ed. Joannou, 87.

about the bastardly acts[3] of evil and the misfortunes that naturally occur among unreasoning creatures. I see the opposite among humans. As regards the progress and virtue of the reasoning animals, oblivion among the general public brushes aside and wipes out their deeds. There is a continuous and unbroken memory in all humankind of whatever particular faults and slips there are of the unsound and unfitting sort. Faultfinding, as if it were inherent by nature among the reasoning animals, always drags down leadership. Muddying the thoughts and confusing the intellect and the thinking faculties, faultfinding treacherously incites and arms the tongue against fellow reasoning animals and makes the sufferer bellow more loudly than a herd of ox-deer,[4] who emit in a deranged fashion their ignoble and undignified voice during birth pangs and mating, leading to their ridicule by the animals with souls and minds like theirs.

2. Harsh criticism,[5] then, is launched with such force as to overtop the summit—that is, the chief person who is the ruler and general—and it desires to touch, if it were possible, the vault of heaven itself. The man seized by this passion, who lacks rational judgment and fancies himself to be beyond any blame, directs every harsh criticism against the ruler. It is indeed a very strange wonder how unpleasant things gain more ground when good things are altered, dimmed as it were, and made to vanish. And the campaigns and good deeds of generals, their wise counsels and acts of endurance, their toils and travails, their food deprivation and contempt for freezing weather, the extension of boundaries and the terrifying of enemies, the prizes of victory and the domination over foreign peoples, the crushing defeats of adversaries, and everything that accompanies and most becomes a general, all this is defeated by the basest things: namely, oblivion and blame. Harsh criticisms of the ruler are easily found, but praises of virtue are cast away

---

3 Literally, "aborted deeds of evil" (τῶν τῆς κακίας ἀμβλωμάτων). The author seems to use the word ἄμβλωμα (aborted child) with the meaning of νόθος (illegitimately born child). See above, *Satire of His Tutor*, §7, p. 65 and n. 32.

4 The ox-deer (ταυρέλαφος) was an exotic animal in India and Ethiopia described by Kosmas Indikopleustes, *Christian Topography* 11.3, ed. Wolska-Conus, 3:319.

5 The word used repeatedly throughout the work is ψόγος. It is translated as "harsh criticism," but it also means "invective" as a literary composition. See above, p. 20.

to the Cynosarges.[6] Consigned to exile are the achievements of peace, prosperity, guardianship of the laws, the equally balanced and proportionate weighing of the scales of justice, compassion, benevolence, admonition, kindness, discernment, and whatever else is proper to a ruler. But the opposite things are spoken about more and more openly and become public owing to the greedy and mercenary attachment to shameful matters, which establishes the harsh criticism against the ruler. When in a short while a wicked opportunity emerges among wicked people, the good things are concealed through oblivion and place for ridicule is given to shameful things. It is as though the former ones, the noble things, are sent to the grave, but the abominable ones are exalted into a monument of contempt.

What is strangest is that if the ruler knowingly considers his lot, he tolerates the harsh criticism and scares away the evil. And he indeed notices this: namely, that if some other fellow general[7] has been changed for the worse by time, fortune, doom or whatever accidental change, he [the fellow general] endures the wounds or stigmas and the bruises of the community's ill will; but if he [the fellow general] has done something good and glorious, he has added nothing to the glory of his name.

If very lenient[8] or considerate individuals make a decision, it is partial and truly much removed from the right rationale and purpose. For when two things have been and still are combined, each one remains distinct both in separation and in mixture.[9] In one kind of decision, the weight of the nearby balance exerts force—the decision truly of a ruler—for the weight, role, and honor of the ruler is the decision by which benefit is weighed in the balance and measured out for the

6 On this Greek proverb, see *CPG*, 1:398.6–17, 2:76.16–77.2. In antiquity, the Cynosarges was a temple of Heracles outside the walls of Athens that was frequented by illegitimate children.

7 The "fellow general" (ὁμοστρατηγός) may allude to the emperor Frederick II, whose death occasioned this work.

8 The "very lenient individuals" (οἱ φιλανθρωπότεροι) follow the principle of *philanthropia*—clemency, leniency, and humane application of the law, especially punitive law. On the concept, see Hunger, "Philanthropia." Philanthropy was an imperial virtue in Byzantium. Laskaris disapproves of it here, but he still lists it among the nineteen virtues of the ruler in *On What Is Unclear and a Testimony That the Author Is Ignorant of Philosophy*, §12.

9 A philosophical digression characteristic of Laskaris's style. The implication is that *philanthropia* ("clemency," "leniency") and justice are two different principles, even when a judge combines them or tries to follow both.

subjects. But the other and slavish decision entails one thing only, to fulfill what is wished for.[10] Certainly, truth is a weapon for close combat, which honorably takes pride of place on the ruler's tongue.[11] As the intellect of the sovereign mixes truth with the justice meted out to the populace, he cuts out the unrestrained condition. As he cuts and restricts in order to save the polity allotted to him and so that truth would take part in its government, he sows the seeds of envy. For wherever there is a trial, the *worst* is cut down at the roots from *the better* with the axe of *decision*.[12] Hence, together with the judgment and the pruning, stuff that forms part of the envy for things good arises as if spontaneously, and hence the ruler receives a far greater share of blame than *kindness for kindness*,[13] as someone has said. Thus, as the mind of the ruler who is in charge strives for the health and salvation of the polity, it draws hatred from among the foolish.

3. But what an insanity! Or rather, to speak more truthfully, alas, what a satanic assault! For the filthy army of demons will not cease to envy the *chosen things* [of God].[14] Indeed, considering what is good and well done to be utterly weak, and comparing it to dreams, is an attitude deriving from the Envier[15] himself, which takes possession of surly souls sharing in his inclination. Glorifying shameful things that covet and cling to the earthly realm is an attitude that his perversity in the flight from goodness has produced among the wicked. Yet, a ruler and general, who plans, acts, and occasionally hesitates (for in the right moment even inaction is action), carries out everything on behalf of the people and the realm.

---

10 "The other and slavish decision," in contrast to the "decision truly of a ruler" in the previous sentence, corresponds to the decision of lenient and considerate individuals mentioned at the beginning of the paragraph.

11 On "truth" as one of the main virtues of the ruler, see below, *On What Is Unclear and a Testimony That the Author Is Ignorant of Philosophy*, §12, p. 169 and n. 50.

12 The comment ἀξίνῃ ῥιζοτομεῖται διακρίσεως τὸ χεῖρον ἀπὸ τοῦ κρείττονος is an echo from Blem., *Imperial Statue* 14 (p. 48): ὀξεῖα τομὴ διακρίσεως, διαιροῦσα τὸ κρεῖττον εὐθὺς ἐκ τοῦ χείρονος.

13 Cf. Sophocles, *Ajax* 522: χάρις χάριν γάρ ἐστιν ἡ τίκτουσ' ἀεί (it is kindness that always begets kindness). The line from Sophocles was used as a maxim in Byzantium. It was excerpted in the tenth-century *Souda* (chi 118 [ed. Adler, 4:789]), and in the twelfth century Nikephoros Basilakes composed a rhetorical exercise based on it (*Progymnasmata*, ed. Pignani, 104–9).

14 Matt. 22:14; Col. 3:12; Titus 1:1; Rom. 8:33.

15 The devil.

Therefore, what kind of punishment will those who have received benefaction from him and who slander him not suffer, if indeed not a punishment in human fashion for the time being, but in divine manner at the time of retribution?[16]

When the polity is prospering and the realm is made grander and greater, and furthermore, when good order and peace incompatible with bandit attacks (fully incompatible as they are) are present in the cities, what goodness, then, would not be stored up in the ruler endowed with a mind through which he can arrange for peace and prosperity even in uncivilized areas? For this is a property of the philosophical and pure mind of the ruler, just as the Stagirite[17]—who gives primacy to philosophy and in a way legislates that royal highness should be obedient to it—declares that peace comes to the communities when these two unique things are united in one. For royal excellence mixed with philosophy, as well as the royal dignity clothed in philosophical grandeur and hence highly decorated and glorified, adorns the divine leader of the people as its unique adornment. For kings have for long been called *leaders of the people*.[18]

4. But we should return to the earlier point and resume our speech. For it is not always worthwhile to engage in theory and return to the things recounted with all possible means. When we add one argument to another and find that one inquiry depends on another inquiry—someone would perhaps say that the arguments and considerations are interlinked—we will never come to the end of our subject. Because their wishes—those of the ruler and the subjects—are at variance, it is utterly necessary either that the designs of all people be fulfilled and the ruler be honored, which is preposterous (for if such absurdity occurs, *the molars* of a multitude of most shameless *whelps*[19] will tear apart the realm), or that the ruler should incur hatred in administering the steadfast balance of the scales. The second possibility is preferable, and indeed this kind of hatred is better than dishonorable and useless honor, so to call it. O good hatred! For as long as the realm is preserved and the natural good freely moves about in it, the words of detractors,

---

16 Cf. Isa. 61:2, 63:4.

17 Aristotle.

18 "Leaders of the people" (κοσμήτορες λαοῦ) derives from the *Iliad* 1.16, 375, etc. The literal meaning of κοσμήτορες is "adorners." The Homeric designation drew the attention of Blem., *Imperial Statue* 49 (p. 58), 77 (p. 66). This and the previous sentence feature a notable wordplay in the phrases θεῖον κοσμήτορα, κόσμον ἐξαίρετον, and κοσμήτορες λαοῦ.

19 Joel 1:6.

or rather of people who do not think bravely, would not harm the most illustrious name of the ruler. Thus all rulers, if they are installed for the *preservation* of the realm,[20] should carry on their shoulders heavy burdens and blame, even if with pain and certainly with perseverance, and should not be worried. Much more than a rain flooding the woodlands of the earth, harsh criticism of the ruler softens his soul for the benefit of the subjects, as long as it [the soul] is intelligent and thinking. The ruler thus should not protest against his suffering, but should be strengthened by Providence from on high, and should be strengthened further in this way from within himself, and perform things for the preservation of the common good, and deem nothing more important than that, even if blame would fully turn him into a monument of evil. These remarks are what truth allows us to say.

5. Because liability to err follows the mortal kind and oblivion of good actions follows on death, what noble thing would someone get from praise? None, unless he is in the happy possession of a famous name on account of his trophies. Even though he does all things for the community and bequeaths everything to it—for we can possess nothing once we leave this world—he himself endures all the hardships, but he has gained no profit by leaving behind noble and good things to the citizens and the country folk. Since all these people are blinded by oblivion and lack of judgment, *good things* become for them *obscured*.[21] It would be a great and grand thing if someone with a pure sense of purpose who has scrutinized the subject will lament their lack of judgment![22] The multitude in a way despises what is carried out on behalf of the people for the preservation of virtue, even if the things <carried out> are burdensome for the ruler, even if they are hard to accomplish, because the multitude is unaware that, evidently, through those efforts it is preserved and perseveres. So it parades and proclaims things unworthy of mention, but consigns to oblivion and the grave, and obscures, the other things, all of them good, which are done for its preservation.

What pleasing thing could someone do? Nothing indeed. For the nonexistent is akin to nonexistent just as the existent is to existent—in the manner of nonbeing and being, I mean. And so useless things are akin to useless people and bad things

20 The expression εἰς συντήρησιν καθίστανται τῆς ἀρχῆς resembles the phraseology of Blem., *Imperial Statue* 4 (p. 44): εἰς συντήρησιν τῆς ὁλότητος. The latter phrase is quoted verbatim in the description of royal virtues in *On What Is Unclear*, §12, p. 170 and n. 58.

21 Cf. Wisd. of Sol. 4:12.

22 The statement is intended as irony.

to all foolish people. Indeed, making harsh criticism belongs to all useless people, even if it inappropriately attacks a useful man. The natural and best praise for the ruler and general is that he carries out what brings safety to the multitude, even if all foul people will grind their teeth at him; everything else must be left aside, or rather, to say it more correctly, must be banished. If the good man bears the insults of shameless people also after his death, he will not be blackened in his soul in the manner he will be in his decaying body. Whatever the truth might be, it becomes known, if not to the foolish and unbridled individuals then certainly to those capable of thinking, and all the more to nature herself and to reality. If sometimes oblivion might conceal good things, it does not conceal the name. When the name is mentioned in harsh criticism of its bearer, do not the local trophies[23] stand by in his defense? Do not those trophies that survive aid the realm significantly, while those that are gone with the ruler's departure from life give room rapidly to wrongdoers of the realm? Will they not multiply the praise and commemoration of the ruler? For the parts of the realm that are harmed and endangered will of necessity speak the truth, for the enemy, too, respects virtue.

6. All these things being so, after the shortsighted people have busied themselves with impertinent matters—for harsh criticism, as shown above, is their petty craft for their entire lives and they occupy their hands with nothing else—and since the ruler and general struggles for the common good, justice will put truth and falsehood on the balance, and will assign to each of them appropriate gifts.[24] The gifts of justice will never be obliterated, but will truly endure as one's most cherished private belonging. For the *gift of God* is indeed by nature *irrevocable*,[25] but the flawed words of mortals are inconstant and very deceptive.

All this has rightly been put together in a very brief speech and reveals truthfully the characteristics of the subjects and the ruler.

---

23 The laconic phrase "the local trophies" (κατὰ τόπους τὰ τρόπαια) should probably be interpreted inclusively and metaphorically—a reference to victories, the expanding frontiers of the realm, and other military accomplishments, including the construction and strengthening of fortifications in local areas (a Nicaean policy).

24 "Gifts" (δόματα): perhaps inspired by Eph. 4:8 (ἔδωκεν δόματα τοῖς ἀνθρώποις), which is indebted to Ps. 67:19.

25 Cf. Rom. 11:29.

3

Moral Pieces Describing the Inconstancy of Life

Moral Pieces Describing the Inconstancy of Life composed during the period of mourning for the passing of the ever-remembered and blessed empress, lady Elena, his wife, by the same Theodore Doukas Laskaris, the son of the most exalted emperor of the Romans, lord John Doukas, before the embassy of the marquis Berthold of Hohenburg to the same most exalted emperor.

1. Nothing dispels despondency other than the soul's knowledge of the characteristics of its nature. Nothing strengthens afresh the perceptive powers of the soul other than realizing that dust is akin to dust.[1] Nothing drives away the most frequent storms of sorrow other than recalling God to one's mind and the fact that even though we are, and have been created, mortal, we will never see anything happening to our harm, but rather everything will happen for our salvation through the Spirit. For God exists, and if so, there is also providence and retribution. But I would also say that there is judgment even before the arrival of the Just Judge and his decision. I name the judicial instruments, calling them judgment and discerning decision. As God presides on high over many cherubic and seraphic hosts who bear witness to this as his servants and slaves, there is nothing equal to God. For the *first intellects*[2] stand like slaves beside him, through whom nature regains strength after distancing herself from him by whatever lapses she wishes

---

1 Cf. Gen. 3:19; Ps. 102:14.

2 The "first intellects" (οἱ πρῶτοι νόες) are the angels, according to pseudo-Dionysios, *Celestial Hierarchy* 6–7, ed. Heil, 26–32, who is indebted to Proclus, *Theologia platonica* 3.21, ed. Saffrey and Westerink, 3:75.14–16.

to commit. Through him nature is virtuous and through him nature was created and persists, even if she hastens to come to an end owing to her composite character. So then the soul, being composite, turns from one path to another and from one place, shape, and sign into other sets of forms and shapes, and is unsettled as she goes in a circle,[3] and harms herself when turning occasionally to pleasure and living in profligacy. Being corrupted one thousand times, the soul therefore ruins her eye[4] as she is slackened by pleasure[5] and as she spurns the dignity of immateriality. For this reason, after absorbing into herself the corruptions of the moment—and because she corrupts herself with corruption out of her own will—the soul nears destruction and revolves in circles imitating the inconstancy of time. For the obscure tendency of the moment, the waywardness of fortune, the slackening of the soul, and the change of circumstances impart nonexistence to things appearing to exist and beset the cheerful traveler with the bitterness of sorrow. Deceptive life, alas! O nonexistence! No man profits in anything if he does not profit with a view to profiting him [God] who profits in all things. But who will do anything? No one can do anything really. Who will struggle with the inconstant flow? For the lives of mortals are like the impulse of time, the flow of a river current, and the movement of a breeze. For all of these resemble one another and ever flow inconstantly and make their way with no constancy whatsoever.

2. Large is the sea of life and hard to cross, because the man who powerlessly sails on it is utterly unable to find harbor. For he is constantly disturbed by the motion of the winds. According to Homer, *mortals are weaker than everything*,[6] because they have in themselves continuous misfortunes. For they are in every way weaker than everything, because everything in humankind has come to be nothing at all. For as everything in humankind is turned upside down and altered, the inconstancy of the affairs of life becomes evident, because also the properties of the soul, being changed, depart from their prior relationships and do not remember

---

3 For the notion of the circular motion of the soul, see Plato, *Timaeus* 43a–d, 47d; pseudo-Dionysios, *On the Divine Names* 4.9 (PG 3:705). See also MacDonald, *History of the Concept of Mind*, 51–52.

4 The concept of an "eye of the soul" originates from Plato, *Republic* 518c, 533d, and is commonly found in Christian and Byzantine theological writing.

5 In §2 Laskaris contrasts the slackening or weakening of his soul by pleasure to its hardening through virtue.

6 Homer, *Odyssey* 8.169, 18.130.

anything they cherished. For food, luxury, comfort, servants, honor, pomp, and everything else mortal nature is accustomed to value are of no benefit and use; none of them is for the sake of virtue and edification. The soul hardens and enjoys none of these things since they have no permanence. For they disappear with time and are considered to be nothing on account of fortune, because when they pass away unexpectedly, they bring sorrow rather than joy. Wretched nature, what will you do? You have been allotted a mixed composition beyond comprehension, you have earned a noble name in that you are called rational. You abound in rational thoughts and have such a divine spirit, but lo and behold, you are unluckier even than senseless objects when you incur these horrible corruptions caused by time. For time flows, lives pass, customs slip away. The future is unpredictable, no one sees it, everyone is deluded: the possessors because they have no possessions, those who weep and those who laugh, the playful and the diligent. Medicines are ineffective, the disease of corruption grows with the passage of time, the ship is wrecked, its equipment is destroyed, the soul at the helm falls asleep, the sail is torn asunder through carelessness, the rudder is tossed overboard, the wind is adverse, the sun sets, night advances, the storm intensifies, the burden is great, the journey is long, time is short, the future is unclear, everything is terrible, danger is near, perdition is inevitable. For as the ship of life is fully destroyed with the passage of time, everything in it is dispersed and perishes.

3. Journeying on the heights of happiness, I received there at the hands of fortune the experience of time's inconstancy. Dwelling on account of this on the peaks of grief, I learned that there are things valued by mortals but destroyed by time and leaving behind no glory in them in the end. Sailing across the sea of life, I was taught its inconstancy. After experiencing all this and turning my eyes all around with my spiritual strength and observing everything, I see everything void of existence, matters worthy of lamentation rather than joy. I praise the lament of Heraclitus[7] rather than the kingdom of Sesostris and his ostentatious chariot.[8]

---

7 Heraclitus was known in antiquity as the weeping philosopher. Lucian, for example, contrasted him to the laughing Democritus in *Creeds for Sale*.

8 According to Diodorus of Sicily, *Bibliotheca* 1.58.1–2, ed. Bertrac, 118.7–21, the mythical Egyptian king Sesostris had the habit of yoking to his chariot four subject kings instead of horses. In an elaboration of the story popular in Byzantium and reported by Blemmydes, one of the harnessed kings stared at the revolving wheel of the chariot, comparing it to the inconstancy of fortune. Sesostris then released the kings from their yoke. See, for example,

I marvel at the turning of the wheel <of fortune> rather than at Croesus's wealth. I exalt the simplicity of Carinus[9] rather than the novel devices of the wonder-worker.[10] For what is considered to exist of the things that are unappreciated and nonexistent is nothing. Since mortals who are dying bequeath what they appreciate to people who do not appreciate it, all things are indeed appreciated and none of them has constancy. Alas, what is this then? What is the passage of time? What is the inevitability of fate? What is exaltation before ruin? What is dishonor after ruin? What is greed? On whose behalf are battles fought? In what do troubles lie? Why is there diligence? For what reason are there dissensions? What constitutes a theft? Wherefore is there money? Where is fame? What is its benefit? The servants are empty-handed, nobody is a helper, nobody is a guard, nobody will be able to be an ally. The former things are before death, but the latter are after. Even if the former are unprofitable, people covet them with passion. Reason focuses on the latter things, the former perish. They bring lamentation; truly everything is utterly destroyed by the corruption of time. Therefore, traveling lightheartedly and being unaware of how easily mortals slip, I saw and learned just now what I suffered from. Even though I should, even before suffering, have understood what I did not control through having no experience of suffering, I fully blocked the entryways of the spirit and reason with the softness and smoothness of pleasure, and allowed no room for receiving the fine details of knowledge. In so doing, or rather suffering at all times, I remained incurable.

4. *Walking in a broad space*,[11] I was journeying unaware of perdition, planting a seed in the earth from which a fruit never grew, not living a virtuous life, and running a course far distant from the true path. For even if I thought I possessed something, nothing I had was permanent for me, but these things were far from

---

Theophanes, *Chronographia*, ed. de Boor, 1:273.14–25; Theophylaktos Simokattes, *Historiae* 6.11, ed. de Boor and Wirth, 243.10–244.15; Blem., *Imperial Statue* 53–55 (pp. 58–60).

9 According to a story told by Synesios of Cyrene in *On Kingship* 16, ed. Lamoureux, 116–17, the emperor Carinus (r. 283–285) impressed the Persians, his enemies, by his plain clothes, coarse food, and bald head so much that they thought him invincible. A succinct version of the anecdote is reported by Michael Psellos, *Historia syntomos* 53, ed. Aerts 34.

10 It is unclear which "wonder-worker" is meant here.

11 Ps. 118:45.

me by nature, even though mixed in me by convention.¹² For the inconstancy of the moment and the corruptive force of circumstances—as well as the fact that the attachment of the nonexistent to the existent amounts to nothing—destroy what is thought to be mine. Alas, what a terrible situation! A situation quite unfamiliar to me earlier! Who will achieve anything by applying his craft and, after piecing together the parts of inconstancy, will impart stability and a share of existence to them? God indeed created incorruptible what is now corruptible, but *the vessels of honor and incorruptibility*,¹³ infected with evil and subjected to separation from virtue, undergo the suffering of decay and dishonor—that is, they vanish through dissolution caused by death. For the blooming life of worldly affairs drags the unreasoning part of the soul to the intemperance of pleasure and a total perdition of the soul. For when human nature is impelled by habit toward pleasure in the manner of a *horse and a mule*,¹⁴ it clearly has no comprehension of virtue, because once having broken the bridle and bit of reason through earlier disobedience, it is pushed over the cliff, not conscious of its fall. Thus nature suffers, thus people follow suit on account of nature, thus I too am blinded in my mind as though by nature itself, thus time goes by, thus affairs change, thus evil gains ground, thus things considered to exist have truly no kinship with things that exist, thus instances of passing away become abundant, thus inconstant things disappear under the force of time. Therefore the person who has suffered and has been chastened moves beyond the flow and corruption of time and passing away. But the careless person revolves on the wheel without any stability, because everything mortal follows diminution rather than being.

5. The opinion of the crowd prefers to look at what humankind should not look at and abhors what it should rather enjoy. For the earthly component that weighs down heavily on the crowd's opinion leads it to its earthly kin. When this occurs, the observer is lulled and wallows in corruption, taking pleasure in matter. And so the parts of the spirit that are following their sovereign perish powerlessly, as they fail to rush toward the virtue of the good. For what earthly thing will anyone measure in the balance with virtue? Nothing at all, since there is not anything

---

12 On nature (φύσις) vs. convention (θέσις) as principles of association discussed at length in Laskaris's treatise *Natural Communion*, see above, p. 53.
13 Rom. 9:21.
14 Ps. 31:9.

whose being virtue does not ordain, and because a thing reigning not through virtue, if it governs over matters it should not, presides fortuitously without purpose. To be honored on account of virtue with the happy lot of honoring the parts of honor is nothing but a benefaction of God. For this reason everyone ought to embrace virtue. For what is everything else? Temporary pleasure, weakness of reason, effeminacy of the soul, aberration of the intellect, instigation of evil, invitation of pain, continuous sorrow, lamentation about the final moments, groans of the companions, even if these are to no avail, *thoughts of many hearts*,[15] coals glowing like an echo's diminishing sound, ill-timed repentance, message of misfortune. A story of sorrow is terrible for those who tell it and is unspeakable for those who hear it. Everything is lament, everything is melody resounding with ululation. Jeremiah lamented[16] and *Jesus wept*[17] and prayed for things that without exception are caused by erring human nature. These and similar matters utterly persuade me, too, to weep today, for I suffered something that my mind did not grasp, my vision did not expect to see, and fortune acting on her own brought along. So I mourn and weep in my mind and soul, because human affairs have come to be worthy of lamentation as inconstant, nonexistent, useless, and having nothing that is unrelated to sorrow, while everything is corrupted and rushes toward the missile of the catapult.[18]

6. Some people previously admired imperial glory and others yearned for riches and the pleasures of luxury, but most people yearn for everything—some for the heights of glory, others for the joy of money, and yet others for the easy and untroubled life of luxury. I am amazed at the opinions of the crowd and at the reasons why it has come to admire what has no share in anything admirable. Amazed therefore at what admirers should not admire, I have come to marvel at nature's creation. As I marvel at nature's creation, I examine things in which I find nothing worthy of admiration because they are also subject to passing away. For they are altered over time and changed by way of misfortunes and are not far distant from the nonexistent. Hence I have come to wonder at passing away as it dissolves the

---

15 Matt. 15:19; Mark 7:21; Luke 2:35, 9:47, 24:38.

16 The five songs of lamentation in the Old Testament are attributed to Jeremiah.

17 John 11:35.

18 "Catapult" (σφενδόνη): on this meaning, see the tenth-century military treatise by "Heron of Byzantium" 44.39, ed. Sullivan, 90. See also Laskaris's use of this word in his *Oration on Hellenism*, §22, p. 190, below.

bond between soul and body. I have come to wonder at insatiate greed that gives rise to lapses from virtue. I have come to wonder at life's deception, through which people created to exist are as though nonexistent and therefore are nonexistent. I have come to wonder at all these things not because they are admirable in value but as something unusual, extraordinary, and far from necessary. Every soul must therefore wonder at the inconstancy of human affairs, so that by wondering at their inconstancy it may attain the constancy of virtue. Because most people wish to be virtuous for their own profit[19] (for being virtuous on account of the natural good is achieved solely by a man assimilated to God), for this reason also those who explain the *knowledge of things existent*[20] marvel at time as well as at the corruptions and changes caused by time, laying it down as a law that none of them has constancy, and that the decisions of a philosophical soul are steadfast. They laid down much the same also about the acts of fortune, comparing it to the passage of time. In this they did not miss the mark, but rendered the copy most truthfully after its prototype. Therefore there is nothing more unstable than fortune, more changeable than time, and more liable to err than the nature of mortals. So while being corrupted in their deceptive relationship among themselves, mortals are corrupted with regard to virtue.

7. One must always remember the sweep of circumstances, the change of times, and the constancy of life's inconstancy. For if we kept these things in mind as intelligent creatures, we would never cause pain to the soul, as we would think uniformly and truthfully, and we would both recognize and shun deception under its fallacious shape. For the nature of human affairs is colored with different dyes, in which harmful things are also sweet (*a honey, so to speak, flowing into the throat*[21]), yet they cause the soul unbearable affliction, because in this the soul will acquire a deprivation of both what it lacks and what it has rather than acquiring the delight of joy. For looking intemperately at the nonexistent brings harm; harm brings corruption, which in turn leads to perdition. But what is more unfortunate than perdition? For it is fully impossible for nonbeing to be more nonexistent

---

19 On the juxtaposition of "profit" and "the natural good," see below, the *Oration on Friendship and Politics*, §§3–5.

20 That is, the philosophers. One of the six definitions of philosophy in the late antique *prolegomena philosophiae* is "knowledge of things existent as existent." See above, *Satire of His Tutor*, §14, p. 74, n. 75.

21 Ecclus. 49:1.

than nonbeing, since both are nonexistent by nature. Therefore one should keep in mind things existent rather than nonexistent. I will say it again: everyone must consider all things to be nothing, on the grounds that nothing truly has constancy, because through time, fortune, the force of circumstances, the change of the season, the advent of decay, or some other way all parts of everything are transformed from what is supposedly existing to what clearly does not exist. For this reason, O humankind, we should turn our gaze to the existent by dragging away our spiritual eyes, so to speak, from attachment to things believed to be, because there is not anything that is not part of nonbeing, should it not be gazing upon the existent. For each thing that was is united with similar things, and the thing that assumes being in its parts[22] is nonbeing. Time, luxury, livelihoods, wealth, glory, servants, children, parents, flesh, sinews, bones, humors, and all that is of the flesh are destroyed, having nothing constant, as they are parts of matter and corruption.

8. By necessity the compacted thing alters with the seasons and through the impulses and forces of time. The altered thing is transformed from what it was into what it was not. What is transformed is transformed from what it was into what it was not by diminution. What has been diminished comes close to corruption.[23] The thing subject to corruption is truly nonexistent. For coming-to-be cannot happen naturally except when a compacted thing is dissolved, because the latter was produced from something that was not. For "to be" and "not to be" signify the terms of being and nonbeing, something that they call "existence" and "nonexistence." The thing both compacted and changed is not truly existent. For the thing compacted and changed (the former from nonexistence into being and the latter from what was considered existent into nonbeing) reveals inconstancy and false appearance. Therefore everything in the coming-to-be of things human is nonexistent except for the soul alone. Honors, glorifications, luxuries, and everything that the nature of mortals produces through desire are truly nothing. For this reason everything nonexistent imitates the force of time and the changes in the atmosphere. For seasonal rain, snowfall, the appearance of hail, blasts of wind, freezing frost, droughts caused by the sun's fire and by the conjunction of the stars,

---

22 Indebted to Aristotle, *On Generation and Corruption* 321b10–322a4. See also Nikephoros Blemmydes, *Epitome physica* 6, in PG 142:1080.

23 "Alteration," "diminution," and "destruction" are three of the six types of motion described in Aristotle, *Categories* 15a13–33. See also Nikephoros Blemmydes, *Epitome logica* 21, in PG 142:840.

dry spells as a result of the absence of moisture, rising exhalations, and a myriad of other things that are no better than fortune and resemble its calamities transform the fine nature of the air. O the inconstancy of nonexistence! Praise be to the constancy of existence! Nonexistence will never dominate being, but will be led into obedience because it is its slave. Therefore we must not be slaves of our fellow slaves—I mean, of time and life's pleasures, since they are nonexistent and our fellow slaves. We ought to fit ourselves to virtue, so that through virtue we may be joined to existence.

9. Intelligent people should be amazed at the alterations of time, the changes in life, and the transformation of thoughts not as things unexpected and unusual with respect to the good, but as things amazing in their own right and impulse, because they have a self-drive toward the worse and none of them is directed toward stability. Hence it is highly astonishing when admirers are admiring what should not be admired. Therefore, those things that are worthy of amazement are admired among all people as extraordinary spectacles, for they indeed distract the mind with their unexpected character. For the glitter of a precious stone distracts the senses because it is shiny and costly, and as on a scale[24] draws toward its possessor the abundant value it has. In the same manner the alterations of time, the changes in life, and the transformation of thoughts necessarily provoke wonder through their shifts. Meanwhile the steadiness of mortal minds is shaken. O change! O turnaround! O transformation! Everything races toward diminution, and the diminished thing races toward disappearance and darkness. What is worse than a dark thing? Hence the soul is darkened even if it is bright by nature. For kin takes delight in kin, but what is incompatible and dissimilar brings about discord. Thus everything passes away, thus everything runs after time, thus all the affairs of mortals flow inconstantly. Therefore every noble soul keeps to intellectual rather than corruptible things. For nobility is measured not by blood but by the way of virtue, simplicity of conduct, and purification for the purpose of apprehending and uniting with the existent.[25] Thus is the soul honored, thus also it becomes firm, and

---

24 "Scale" (καθέλκυσις): the only other occurrence outside Laskaris (see below *On What Is Unclear and a Testimony That the Author Is Ignorant of Philosophy*, §13, p. 173, n. 62) traceable through the TLG is in the scholia on Aeschylus's *Persians* 437, where ῥοπῇ is glossed as ἐν βάρει, ἐν καθελκύσει.

25 On nobility as a moral category in opposition to nobility of blood, see below, *Representation of the World, or Life*, §8, pp. 147–48.

pulls itself away from the temporal and worldly corruption of life, attains a better state, and takes intellectual delight in forever contemplating divine ideas.

10. What is this then? Time passes, lives become extinct, and the human race goes along with the flow. The manifestation of the nonexistent is in the dissolution of things thought to exist, just as the lack of light demonstrates darkness. A distancing from the existent is, on the other hand, the fall of a soul not having divine illumination, the corruption of the things of life (because by nature they belong to corruption, not incorruptibility), and the absolute aberrancy of everything not of the intellect. For stability belongs to no other than the contemplator of God. It is therefore better to conspire with the constant to distance oneself from nonexistent things. For the nonexistent things, the distancing is like nothing happening, because they are thought to exist and be good while they are not good. So this should be espoused now, this should be accessible to all people, this distances the soul from corruptible things and brings her essence toward full completeness of the incorruptible by purification through virtue, this checks the force of evil, this breaks the impulses of the soul's animal powers, this gives everything good to the good. For nothing else can implant virtue in the soul but her association with other good souls. For bad company spoils good plans. Therefore the advice of bad people leads *toward the path to hell*,[26] brings perdition, and causes shameful ruin, while it does not provide at all the praise of virtue to the one who aspires to it. What an amazing thing! I will say it again. What is this then? Everything already belongs to corruption, everything rushes toward diminution, everything is carried along by the passing of the seasons. Therefore decay generated by the formation of the elements in the body[27] produces separation between matter and intellect, and causes the former to remain near its kin, while making the latter rise toward the realm of the Lord so that it renders to it a suitable servant's tribute. For this can occur only if decay began previously. That is why decay corrupts, but virtue solidifies. Passing away is thus frightful for easygoing and lax people like me; but for others who are steady and good, it is virtue that is awe-inspiring and passing away desirable,

---

26 Cf. Prov. 2:18.

27 The transformation of the elements during generation and passing away is an argument made by Aristotle in the second book of his *On Generation and Corruption* (e.g., 334a16–334b31). See also Nikephoros Blemmydes, *Epitome physica* 4, in PG 142:1084–85.

since it is through dissolution caused by it that they reach the end of their toils and acquire the recompense of rewards.

11. If there is nature, there is a beginning of motion. If there were no beginning of motion, nature would have had no beginning. If it had no beginning, the thing without beginning is not nature. For nature is the beginning of motion and rest.[28] Indeed, if there is nature, it had a beginning also. If it had a beginning, it would come to rest in order to make truly manifest what nature is—namely, the beginning of motion and rest. When nature itself has begun to act, all things in and for the sake of it blossom, being in a state of generation and growth. But when nature contracts, comes to rest, and totally disappears, its pretty and attractive features become withered and unattractive, being replaced with things that are nonexistent, truly falling into decay and becoming humbled. Indeed, everything subject to generation and passing away brings exceeding despondency and ill-repute in regard to the soul rather than ephemeral joy and a fleetingly brief period of pleasure. This is why human nature both blossoms and fades away over time, differing in no way from grass, the foliage of plants, and the withering of a flower. For even as human nature presides in matters of high and greatest distinction, rules over the souls of fellow slaves (or, so to speak, over their life-giving capacities), measures out for them its gifts, and assumes, so to speak, a mask of independence, it is unexpectedly reinstated as a slave by death and finds no aid in any helper. Where is money? Where is the abundance of livelihood? Where is the company of soulmates? Where is the height and majesty of glory? Where is the help from those who have received benefactions or the assistance of recipients of charity? Where are the hands to defend against murderers or the strength-giving muscles? Where is the protection of servants? Where is the friendly return of favor by friends? Where is the helpful obedience of children or the power of parents to help their children? All are unprofitable, all are in vain, all are far removed from the goal of assistance. So the human being, once born, faces corruption; but once dead he rather faces incorruptibility, revolving in a circle and having a good share in life's corruption. Therefore circumstances that change and reverse with the passage of time carry along with them the human being as well, who blossoms temporarily but is by nature quick to wither away. In this wise, being wounded through

---

[28] Aristotle, *Physics* 200b–202b. See also Nikephoros Blemmydes, *Epitome physica* 7, in PG 142:1089.

his fall from his original state of long ago, the human being is easily overcome at the hands of corruption, for he is both the end and substance of corruption.

12. I was born in the light of day and in a worldly valley. I was brought up in pleasure like an innocent lamb.[29] Living thus in luxury, enjoying myself and benefiting from the greatest good fortune, I gave no heed to misfortune, but taking delight, so to speak, in my own soul, I was running the course of my life replete with all goodness. For what good thing did I not fully have at my disposal? With what objects of desire was I not richly endowed? I filled my heart completely and abundantly with everything. I felt utmost joy in my soul and in my soulmate—for speech cannot call her[30] by any other name than "a like soul" and "a sharer of my life." O terrible calamity! What can I say? I am torn apart in my soul. What shall I utter as I pour out the sound of my voice in my loss?[31] What shall I cry out as I articulate unintelligible and ill-omened sounds? I am really absolutely shaken, even if someone should say that the constitution of the soul is brave. An abundance of people have received my benefaction, but I wander about powerlessly, suffering this affliction. An inconsolable misfortune has seized me. A worm presses on my bones, causing their joints to dissolve. A chimera of thoughts burns me up. A hydra of reflections—a many-shaped and many-headed monster—tears my soul with its teeth. A viper of pain is devouring my entrails. Sorrow, a veritable dragon, consumes me. A basilisk[32] of suffering enslaves the imperial character of my free spirit. Instead of stepping on top, I am trampled underfoot. Instead of crushing, I am crushed to pieces. Instead of raising my head because of great virtues and happiness, I am hapless. Now I have suffered a misfortune that indeed surpasses all misfortune. Woe to me, woe to me! The springtime of my soul has died. I am shipwrecked and have given up hope of deliverance. Everything falls to corruption. For when my life comes to an end, the bond of my soul and body has by necessity been loosened. Even if someone should say that the bond is thought to continue, this will not be so. For once the soul has been released, the intellect transformed, the eyes of love blinded but in a perceptible way (for this could in no way happen in the realm of the intellect), and all spiritual powers changed, would

29 Cf. Lev. 1:10; Jer. 11:19.
30 That is, Elena, the deceased wife of Laskaris.
31 Cf. Prov. 10:24, 13:1, 13:15; Pss. of Sol. 9:5, 17:22.
32 That is, a poisonous reptile. On the basilisk, see Ps. 90:13; Isa. 59:5. Note the play on words.

any other bodily part or limb be left unaffected in the body? Surely none. Indeed, the body is thought to be dead for some time before being fully consigned to decay. My essence, bodily constitution, and frame are considered now to be among the living, but they occupy the land of the dead. My eyes, shed your tears! My chest, be broken up! My heart, accept dissolution! My arms, be torn out as your shoulder joints are broken all along! My legs, suffer dissolution through injury to the sinews! My tongue, slow down or be dead in truth! My ears and senses of smell and touch and all my organs of perception, be turned to stone! And you, my whole body with its inner and outer parts, gain the suffering of death, dwell in Hades together with your soulmate in order to share her pain. For a bond of incomparable love made us happier than all people, but the thieving and cruel hand of Hades cut the bond mercilessly. What should I suffer? I will ask nothing but the end of my life. This cannot happen in any other way but by descending into the abodes of death and accepting the punishment of Hades and the affliction of diminution, because I have been deprived of my life, my soul's spirit and heart's substance, and the salvation of my life, both spiritual and corporal.

4

Oration on Friendship and Politics

By the same Theodore Doukas Laskaris, the son of the emperor, lord John Doukas, to lord George Mouzalon, who asked how subjects[1] should conduct themselves vis-à-vis their lords and lords vis-à-vis their subjects.

1. Alexander, king of the Greeks, fellow soldier and commander of the Macedonians, a ruler of the former [the Greeks], but fighting as a comrade-in-arms with the latter [the Macedonians], set up many and different blazing trophies of virtue in the world: victories over enemies, conquests of lands, utter destructions of peoples. He famously brought entire cities of almost the entire world[2] under his lawful rule. In this way, he makes the fame of the Greeks and the Macedonians known until today and, as I think, their fame will always continue to be well known. Together with all these greatest achievements that surpass, so to speak, even human nature itself, he thought one thing more special than anything else and is much more honored for it by everyone than for the many trophies of his famous campaign. This thing

---

1 The Greek word used throughout the oration is δοῦλος. In most cases, I have translated it as "subject," but occasionally, depending on the context, I have preferred "servant." The author has in mind sometimes imperial subjects and sometimes the emperor's (and any powerful lord's) servants, companions, and associates. The δοῦλος is bound by ties of friendship (φιλία) with a socially superior individual: a "lord" (κύριος), "master" (δεσπότης), "potentate" (ἡγεμών), "ruler" (ἄρχων), and the "emperor" (βασιλεύς) himself. I have been consistent in the translation of these five words, which are not necessarily interchangeable. In §7, the author refers to multiple potentates (ἡγεμόνες). I have translated as "lord" and "lady" the unofficial honorific titles κυρός and κυρά in the manuscript heading. See Introduction, p. 12.

2 Reading πόλεις ὅλας ὁλοκλήρου κόσμου σχεδόν instead of πόλεις ὅλας ὁλοκλήρους κόσμου σχεδόν as in the MSS and the edition.

is the following. Like the five senses through which the full comprehension of the knowable rises up to interact with the leading faculty—the discerning power of reason—he considered five friends of the royal and sovereign head worthy of his friendship and honored them.[3] The men were his soulmates, like-minded and well balanced, with inclinations of their minds equal to his pure reason.[4] For even if they differed from his Ares-like temperament, they carried out the Hermes-like[5] wishes of his head with all diligence and to the greatest extent possible. He called them friends, exalted them in glory, adorned them with his care, and honored them in every way, unceasingly, perpetually, unchangeably, splendidly, and manifestly as worthy friends of his. Therefore, he is praised and admired for this great honor done to his friends rather than for the greatness of his achievement and his divinity. For their minds, which agreed fivefold and united with the reasoning of his mind and carried out intelligently his conceptual goals, requested the subjects to march from the borders of Thrace all the way to Africa together with their lord. O amicable lord and subjects well-disposed to their lord and loyally joined with him! O intelligent head and divine limbs attached to it harmoniously in the best fashion! O beautiful and good concert! O divine harmony fashioned by virtues, a harmony that does not resound with its beat in order to charm souls, but persuades everyone to draw delight and joy from another kind of clapping of hands out of astonishment at its achievements!

---

3 On Alexander and his companions as paragons of friendship, see above, pp. 28–29.

4 "Pure reason" (εἰλικρινὴς διάνοια) goes back to Plato, *Phaedo* 66a, and to early Christian authors.

5 Laskaris seems to envisage here Hermes as the god of invention and the originator of secret philosophical knowledge (as in the Hermetic corpus). Elsewhere he also presents Hermes as the inventor of rhetoric. See above, *Satire of His Tutor*, §9, p. 68, n. 50.

Oration on Friendship and Politics

2. They [Alexander and his five friends] indeed became like model pictures[6] of virtues in the world by the gift of nature[7] and by the indissoluble union and unbreakable bond of their relationship.[8] For those who preside at lofty thrones and oversee in the manner of kings people lying under their feet come to resemble him [Alexander] by imitation and make many gifts flow frequently, watering like *an early and late rain*[9] the hearts of their servants and friends. People who have eradicated beforehand every weed from the field of their pure devotion[10] regularly give most beneficial fruits of truthfulness to the bosom of their esteemed and revered head. With what in the world can the friendship and loyalty of a true servant be weighed in the balance? With money? With fortunes? With possessions? Or with the excessive and useless-looking display of things of every kind? For the end of all these is ruin, and sorrow caused by their absence presses down the soul of their owner. For deprivation of a thing possessed causes grief to its possessor.

But since the relationship of friendship is threefold,[11] it is in three ways that it inspires the sincere good deeds of anyone who possesses any of its parts. Three rivers flow from friendship. One river gives pleasure through its taste to the bodily organs of sensation. Another river is finer on the whole and clear, and the other

---

6 The expression "model pictures" (ἀρχέτυποι πίνακες) is found in the opening of Gregory of Nazianzus's funeral oration for his brother Basil of Caesarea as well as among several middle and late Byzantine learned authors—always as part of an art metaphor referring to the process of imitation. A treatise on rhetoric datable to Laskaris's times considers the funeral oration to be an exemplary piece. Laskaris himself shared with George Mouzalon a manuscript containing Gregory's works. See Gregory of Nazianzus, *Oration 43 (Funeral Oration for Basil of Caesarea)*, ed. Bernardi, 117.8; pseudo-Gregory of Corinth, *On the Four Parts of the Perfect Speech*, ed. Hörandner, 105.87–88 (and see 117 for the suggested date); Th. L., *Ep.* 172 (p. 225). A version of the same expression (πρωτότυποι πίνακες), which I have translated identically, appears at the end (§10).

7 For the same expression, "gift of nature" (φιλοτιμία φύσεως), see Gregory of Nazianzus, *Oration 31* 10.23, ed. Gallay, 294; Th. L., *Ep.* 8.4 (p. 11), 65.14 (p. 94).

8 "Relationship" (σχέσις): the first appearance of this frequently used word, which has been translated as "relationship," "attachment," and more rarely as "attitude" and "possession." See above, p. 45.

9 Deut. 11:14; Jer. 5:24; Hosea 6:3; Joel 2:23; Zech. 10:1.

10 "Devotion" (ὑπόληψις): on the meaning of this word, see above, p. 45.

11 See above pp. 29–30 on the three types of friendship, a categorization inspired by book 8 of Aristotle's *Nicomachean Ethics*.

is purest and unmixed with any material mix and clear in itself, flowing smoothly and carrying a true stream with which only people of sound and sincere nature can be filled abundantly. This entire river is intellectual and spiritual. For whoever has a friendly attitude toward something on the grounds of the natural good and beauty, he has drunk from the stream of the true river in the manner of a friend. But the man who delights in the current of the other river, who is fully pleased in his mind with it and who has a relationship of friendship for the sake of profit, he is inclined much more toward material things and is distanced from the first river farther than earth is from heaven. As for the man who falls into the third river and takes full delight in its material, filthy, and muddy pleasure—a man of earth and flesh—he is distanced from the second river as far as Tartarus from earth.

3. According to this model analogy, the relationship of friendship is divided into three: for the sake of pleasure, profit, and the natural good.[12] But while it is divided into three, it fulfills as a whole the desires of every devotee to friendship, for the friend enjoys the good fortune of receiving his portion and is always truly delighted with what he receives through the relationship. Certainly, a man is utterly of earth and flesh if he takes delight in material things, and he is an utterly hedonistic lover with regard to what he loves. The friend for the sake of profit is more exalted and immaterial, for people solely devoted to pleasure are prisoners far removed from immateriality. The person concerned with his share of benefit and advantage, who has a friendly attitude in view of this share, is a spiritual and more exalted man. For it is toward the profit that he looks. But divine and exalted is the man who because of the natural good itself, which is more perfect and exalted than earthly things, approaches the most perfect plenitude of goodness, being uplifted in a way that befits God. For the person who has a weakness for pleasure is dragged down by the thing that pleases him; he loves because he is forced to love. The man who values the for-profit exchange between the thing given and received—for the exchange is one of profit and of a concrete thing—is amicably disposed toward his partner in receiving. The man who is both upright and good, who is above every earthly matter and uncorrupted, who is full of all truthfulness, who is a holiest treasury of every justice—he does not set his eye on any pleasure, he does not consider its sweetness, he does not enjoy the illusions and appearances

---

12 First introduced here, the concept of "the natural good" (τὸ φύσει καλόν), literally "the good by nature," is described in detail in §4.

that come from it. But neither does he concern himself at all with any profit unless this is mainly directed toward what is principally good by nature. Certainly, he looks exclusively toward the existent and what is truly and principally good and beautiful, through which and in which he finds his foundation and support.

4. For all these reasons, it is better to honor and love emperors rather than all friends, brothers, and relatives. For the triple assemblage of friendship is truly combined in them. In them there is pleasure. In them there is profit. In them there is the natural good and uprightness. For what kind of pleasure does not dwell among the emperors? Who is the person whose sole desire is some profit, who would not obtain it among the emperors? Which man, delighted in the natural good for its own sake and solely for its being the natural good, will not wish to have the emperors as his first and unsurpassed friends? For through them, the state of peace among the people is granted by God. Through them, the fame of the fatherland has arisen. Through them, everyone holds on to his own possessions and escapes the clutches of fierce enemies. Through them, by their toils and labors, the frequent plundering raids of enemies are warded off. Through them, the boundaries are extended. Through them, the host of enemies flees. Through them, the migrants from among the brethren are honored in every way and every place.[13] For even the enemies respect and honor the ruler's virtue and therefore respect the captive brethren. Through them, foreign people draw their sword for the protection of the population of our compatriots.[14] Through them, there is good order in the cities, peace among the common people, calm among the subjects, restraining of the shameless, inspiration of the upright, crushing of the wicked, good deeds of the crafty, the settlement of territories, establishment of government, justice among all people, moderation in passions, the virtue of practical wisdom, courage in the face of enemies, and, simply put, establishment of all the good and beautiful things in the world. All these are naturally good and beautiful, and the overseer of all of them after God is none other than the potentate himself. Therefore,

13 Particularly relevant to the empire of Nicaea as an "empire in exile."
14 "The population of our compatriots" is a translation of ὁ ὁμόφυλος λαός, literally "the people of the same stock." Laskaris seems to envisage foreign alliances as well as the role of the emperor of Nicaea in intervening on behalf of Greek-speaking Orthodox populations living under the Latins and the Seljuk Turks. The word λαός, often used by Laskaris in his writings, appears in a notable way in his *Oration on Hellenism*, §5, p. 179, in the phrase "the Greek people" (ὁ Ἑλληνικός λαός).

let those who wish to adhere amicably to the natural good obey amicably the ruler over good things, loyally in every matter, and honorably. For what is more exalted than the natural good and what is more dignified than the imperial office? What is truly more divine than the dignity of an emperor, ruler, and potentate? What is truly more lovable than natural excellence? Nothing indeed, and nothing indeed is greater in goodness than the ruler's dignity. Let the man who wishes in his soul to be virtuous with regard to natural goodness be attached amicably to the ruler as the real head of the entire structure of the populace, because he is manifestly the image of God.

5. But let the person whose entire concern is profit obey the ruler, so that he may gain his friendship and draw to himself his goodwill, and he will forthwith gain all sorts of advantages, resembling a limb that is abundantly supplied from the head—namely, the emperor. Therefore, let the man who is engaged in some affair for the sake of profit be united with the master and emperor by friendship and affection. Let him give and take, so that he may draw profit, give benefit in return, and gain what he needs, and he will earn in all sorts of ways the abundant beneficence of his master. Because he loves the best exchange, let him give what is wanted from him and let him receive things difficult to obtain. Let him, first, deliberately give the finest mode of discernment and hence let him receive the finest love. Let him give the rhythm of his sincerity and let him receive genuine membership in the <master's> household.[15] Let him give the most pleasant aspect of his character and let him take delight joyfully in the things of his master. Let him give the steadfastness of his patience and let him receive the honor of a sure seat together with his lord. Let him give the constancy of his frank speech in his contribution to the affairs of his lord and let him receive the words of his lord's frank confidence: *Well done, my good and faithful servant!*[16] Let him give the veracity of his tongue, through which alone all pollution of evil is washed away, and let him receive all the more the shining of his master's goodwill. Let him give the truthfulness of his enthusiasm and he will receive the generosity of his master pouring like a river. Let him give *labor and toil*,[17] and let him rest full-heartedly at the bosom of

---

15 The word οἰκειότης, translated here as "membership in the household," also has the historically concrete meaning of the status of *oikeios*, a quasi-official epithet designating a high-status individual in the emperor's household. See Verpeaux, "Les οἰκεῖοι."

16 Matt. 25:21, 23.

17 1 Thess. 2:9.

his master like a genuine child. Let him give the warmth of his heart, and let him receive the fervor of free speech in order to draw the goodwill of his master. Let him give the zeal of his heart as he renders his lord the services required and fit for a master, and let him be seated in a like manner with him in every honor. Let him give every inclination of his heart without restraint according to the impulses of his master's heart, and let him receive every inclination of the master's true goodwill. Let him grant his every wish to his lord, and let him receive the thoughts of his master's heart.

But let him never conceal from his lord any questions he may have, and he will have hidden knowledge of the secrets of his master. Let him give his every word to the full range of arguments of his lord and he will receive the constant love of his lord for the words he poured and let out of his mouth. Let him grant every knowledge of his eyes to his master's ears and his master will *guard him like the pupil of his eye*.[18] Let him give the breezes entering his spiral hole [his ear] and he will receive the right ear of his lord in the judgment of his inappropriate deeds.[19] Let him give and bind the sandals of his immoderate attachment to pleasure with the manacles of love for his lord and let him receive the *sandals on his feet*[20] of the peace of his master. Let him give the tranquility of his soul's habits in the inquiries by his lord and he will receive in humility the reward of his master's beneficence. Let him give the simplest response, one that does not pursue curiosity, to the wishes of his lord and let him receive a joyful gift, one loved even by God himself, *for God* loves *the cheerful giver*.[21] Let him give the lock of his tongue well sealed by the hands of his lord and let him receive scope for true freedom in his speech in his lord's presence. Let him grant the depth of his knowledge to the depth of his master's knowledge and let him draw in abundance the lordly secrets gushing out from his master's heart, warmed by true friendship and benevolence.

---

18 Deut. 32:10; Ps. 16:8.

19 According to the *Treasury* of Theognostos, a thirteenth-century florilegium, Alexander the Great had reserved one of his ears for the accuser and the other for the defender during trials at his tribunal. See Theognostos, *Treasury* 19, ed. Munitiz, 199.70–80. The author implies that the emperor's friend will be given special treatment. According to Exod. 29:20 and Lev. 8:24, the right ear was the one anointed by God.

20 Luke 15:22.

21 Cf. Prov. 22:8a. This is a nearly verbatim quotation, with the verb ἀγαπᾶ replacing εὐλογεῖ found in the Septuagint.

Let him give full-hearted acknowledgment on behalf of his master, and let him be acknowledged before his fellow subjects—in a transient and earthly fashion in this world, but I believe also by Christ in the kingdom of heaven.[22] Let him give the eagerness of his body and let him receive the good cheer of his master's soul. Let him give his entire mind to conceive what the mind of his master enjoys and let him receive legitimate recognition of a material kind from his lord. Let him give every inclination, let him give every impulse, let him give every attitude coming from the warmth and impulse of his heart, and let him receive from his lord every goodness, cheer, benevolence, gift, benefaction, and everything that is good. Let him give the end of everything good and the origin, source, root, and cause of everything that is noble and precious—his sincere and pure, holiest, most honored, most dignified, and truly divine devotion—and let him receive all the money, all the affairs, all the properties, all the works, every possession of his master, every knowledge, and every beneficence and cheerfulness of his lord. On account of all these good things, let the man who wishes to embrace friendship for the sake of profit become a friend of his lord far more than of all other people.

6. On the other hand, if someone has a predilection for something owing to his joyous pursuit of pleasure and wants to have a peaceful and friendly share in and inside the thing that stirs his impulse, let him prefer to spend time in quietude with the overseeing sovereign[23] as his friend. For every abundance of pleasure is found at the imperial court. Let the lover of pleasure submit quietly to the emperor and he will draw every stream of pleasure to himself. Does he love money? Who else will empty out a gold-streaming river for his household servant other than his benevolent lord? Does he love properties? Who else will appoint him as a lawgiver[24] of many cities other than his benevolent lord? Is he a lover of food and luxury and does he consequently use his wealth for all these things? If he wishes, let him sate himself with their enjoyment. Is he excited about the clothes of people softened <by pleasure> and does he feminize his manhood by his attachment to such things? All these are to be found in the residences of emperors. Does he find enjoyment in songs that echo out harmoniously thanks to soul-enchanting

---

22 See Matt. 3:2, one of the many mentions in Matthew's gospel of βασιλεία τῶν οὐρανῶν.

23 I see no reason for the omission of the word ἡγεμόνα in τὸν ἔφορον ἡγεμόνα, as suggested by the modern editor.

24 A possible echo from Ps. 9:21.

Oration on Friendship and Politics

music? When he hears in the imperial court *the voice of the trumpet*,[25] let him pay homage to pleasure, flinging himself completely prostrate on the ground.

But if he is in love with the exercise of the hunt and accurately shoots the deer, the bear, and the panther, if he knows how to draw the sharp sword and how to use it against the chest of the wild boar, if he delights in hunting wild and savage animals, spending a night hidden in a wood, if he prides himself and rejoices in the accuracy of his archery and in the prowess of his swordsmanship, all the more let him serve as a companion to his lord.[26] In this way, if his prowess has been praised, the servant would share in the praise of his master and will have the pleasure of being praised by his lord. Is he an excellent horseman, riding swiftly and turning elegantly? Does he handle a lance with vigor and wield a shield with dexterity and skill? Does he set his ankles in motion as if they were wings on his horse? Does he jump like no one else? Does he run with strength and display his body flying in midair, as might be said, through his swiftness and agility? These things, if ever found, are beloved by everyone. Let a person who has these [abilities] establish friendly relations with his master, so that he may win praises and gather prizes from his master's hand. Hence he will gain truest pleasure when his master honors him, his fellow subjects extol him, and, simply put, all people acclaim him.

For there is another obviously true point. When a servant draws laudatory pronouncements from the master in addition to his master's goodwill, then all his fellow servants come to honor and revere him; and not only his relatives and those inclined to be his friends do exactly as described, but even his enemies automatically become once again his friends. Equally in the opposite case, when the lord's stern eyes gaze at one of his servants, then his companions, relatives, friends, and brothers turn to hate and speak ill of him in the manner of enemies. Therefore, the wish of every servant needs to slavishly follow the wishes of the master, just as a sea current follows the prevailing winds, victory follows the victorious general, happiness follows success, the pilot at the prow follows the tide, and the chariot follows the dexterity of the charioteer. To sum up, everything that is naturally performed

---

25 Dan. 3:5, 7, 10.

26 There is a sudden switch here from the emperor to the figure of the lord (κύριος) and master (δεσπότης). I have accordingly translated the word δοῦλος as "servant" for the reminder of §6.

follows naturally the order of nature. For it is by following nature and through the lordly power of the Creator that the ruler governs over his fellow subjects.

7. According to the above patterns, it is paramount by the laws of nature that a subject's every wish follows the thinking of the emperor; it is from there that the subject will gain pleasure, collect what is to his liking, and sate himself with what gives him enjoyment. For how much pleasure will the subject who sits in council alongside his lord gain when the rumor of this is bruited everywhere, spreading by word of mouth the master's favor toward him, making much of him in specific detail, and trumpeting the constancy of his outspoken speech, the purity of his affection, the robustness of his status as member of the household, the discreet exercise of his freedom, the high honor of his glory, the inner drive of his courage, the unmixed quality of his devotion, his unquestioned independence in undertaking works and actions, the true fervor in his role as go-between,[27] the assistance given by him to the needy, his just verdict on wronged people, the efficiency of his utterly free speech, his lord's immediate fulfillment of his desired plan, his precedence over his fellow subjects, his ceaseless communication with his master, his unspeakable gladness, the continual summons for him arriving hourly from his lord's lips—"Summon for me," for such are the latter's words, "my loyal and longed-for subject!"—and above all, the heartfelt and pure affection of his lord, thanks to which all these things naturally follow. How great will be the pleasure felt by the subject! How great the joy! How great the rejoicing when his name is pronounced everywhere and by all with praise! Truly, all these things make up the most supreme kind of pleasure. Because pleasure, profit, and the natural good are the product and fruit of a royal root and because the subject who loyally attaches himself to the royal root rejoices in all these things, it is paramount that all be friends of their lord rather than of friends, parents, and brothers. It is from here that pleasure, profit, the natural good gush forth like rivers. Therefore, one should befriend the potentates above all others, so that one may profit from all these

---

27 The "role of go-between" (μεσιτεία) alludes to the *mesazon* (μεσάζων), the chief minister of the emperor. His position is sometimes referred to as παραδυναστεύων (see below, *Representation of the Word, or Life*, §13, p. 154, n. 103) and sometimes as μεσιτεύων. The fourteenth-century ceremonial book of pseudo-Kodinos designates the *mesazon*'s post as μεσιτίκιον. See Beck, "Der byzantinische 'Ministerpräsident,'" 319, 337; pseudo-Kodinos, ed. Macrides, Munitiz, and Angelov, 84.3.

Oration on Friendship and Politics

things, and because he who loves the potentate comes to love the first potentate.[28] But he who loves the first potentate and who honors and reveres the one appointed by his grace will truly gain all sorts of benefactions from God himself. For all these reasons, the subjects ought to keep their lords as their friends.

8. But since we have mentioned above that famous hero [Alexander] and along with him the persons who were his friends, it is necessary to speak truthfully about them. Otherwise it may seem to the foolish that his relationship with them was something fortuitous and unimportant. For in all truth, that famous great master who had true friends, being himself truthful, lavished goodness on his truest servants. So he both gave and took back, for he had also given and received earlier.[29] After giving his friendship, he gathered the service and friendship from the servants and friends. Their gifts to Alexander the Great are the following: spotless fidelity, unsullied affection, faultless devotion, servile loyalty, heartfelt kindness, dominant affection, contempt for the flesh, service with earnestness or indeed with enthusiasm, avoidance of tardiness in meeting his needs as required from them (although his needs of pleasure were not many, except for victory in battle and care for culture), their true like-mindedness with him, their courage in his wars, their bold spirit in hardships, their expert and hearty encouragement in a crisis, their unity of thought in their decision-making regarding the arrangement of the army in a battle line of war, their disinterest in money out of love of him—for he drove out of his way anything to do with money.

To put it simply and briefly, everything and nothing was theirs. For everything supporting his honor, his will, his attitude, his desire, and his purpose belonged to them, no matter whether fears or alarms, sorrows or friendships, deprivation of family or exile from the fatherland, contempt for the body or thought of pleasure. Those who were feeding many thus did not ever suffer hunger; they were famished, however, for fleshly pleasure owing to certain assignments given by their lord that prevented them from partaking of pleasure. As for all these assignments,

---

28 "The first potentate" (ὁ πρῶτος ἡγεμών) is ambiguous. Is Laskaris referring to the emperor or to God? The former possibility seems more likely, both because of the mention of "potentates" in the plural earlier in the sentence (see also the reference to "potentates" in §9 below) and because the following sentence explicitly uses the word "God" (θεός). "The one appointed by his grace" (ὁ κατὰ χάριν) would then be the chief minister, which is the duty that Mouzalon himself came to occupy during Laskaris's reign.

29 The puzzling sentence seems to imply multiple episodes of reciprocal exchange.

even though harsh, difficult in nature, and alien because human nature inclines to material things, the friends still treasured them as their own in their hearts, carried them out, and healed their lord's soul.[30] But they abandoned all that had to do with enjoyment, good fortune, nourishment, luxury, new praise, glory, the untroubled nature of pleasure, and all that titillates the senses and weakens the devotion—as things entirely foreign and hostile to them.

For all these reasons, that noble person [Alexander] treated them [his friends] as if they were sense organs of his semidivine body. Indeed, he in a way adopted them to serve him as his sight, hearing, smell, taste, and touch, and they carried out his wishes to the full. So he distinguished these prudent men appropriately, honored them with an escort, lavished money on them, and set them above all others by the dignity conferred. He set his own goodwill as an imperial belt[31] around them, robed them with splendor in the bright garment of his personal affection, adorned in a true fashion the head of their pure devotion with the crown of his heartfelt inclination and choice, and in his indulgence made them reign together with him, lavishing his kindness on them as their master. That was how the brave men worked and received rewards. They drew royal goodwill to themselves by their labor, effort, and zeal for virtue.

9. For all these reasons, being turned together with his own servants into a statue made of virtues, the master represents the ruler and the ruled. But turn your gaze, all potentates and servants, toward this beautiful statue![32] Get an imprint of its virtues, draw qualities, learn the loyalty of a servant, learn the goodwill of a

---

30 Healing the soul is a concept found in Plato (e.g., *Laches* 185e) that entered Greek theology.

31 The Greek word for "imperial belt" is διάδημα, which traditionally means "crown." In the later Byzantine period, however, the word refers to a ceremonial belt (*loros*) draped around and attached to the official attire of the emperor. See Macrides, Munitiz, and Angelov, *Pseudo-Kodinos*, 12, 137, n. 353.

32 The statue (ἀγαλματουργία) made of virtues seems to echo the notion of an "imperial statue" (βασιλικὸς ἀνδριάς), the title of Blemmydes' mirror of princes. Interestingly, according to the ε recension of the Byzantine *Alexander Romance*, Alexander was depicted in the company of a few select friends in statues in Alexandria. Thus, it is said that a statue of Alexander and three of his friends (Philip the doctor, Seleuces, and Antiochos) was placed on a tower at the eastern gate in the urban walls of Alexandria and another statue was set up in his funerary monument in the city. See *Alexander Romance*, ε recension 24, 34, 46, ed. Trumpf, 87.10–88.4, 124.8–10, 178.5–10.

Oration on Friendship and Politics

master, behold a friendly master and servants who are friends of their master, and imitate the finest and most beautiful reciprocity of the image! For what draws a subject close to his own lord? Nothing else except the pure plenitude of his trustful devotion. And what convinces a servant to give himself body and soul to his master's wishes except the purity of the lord's affection? It is thanks to this that masters enjoy the company of true servants. It is thanks to this that servants give up even their own lives on behalf of their master. But I will also say something even more unusual. The love of true servants surpasses that of many and great blood relatives. For all these reasons, the friendship of a master and the goodwill of the servant raise their affection up to the vault of heaven, as they are intermingled and completely mixed in their reciprocal relationship, as they cut off unbecoming attitudes within them, and as they are genuinely mixed in the master and his friend. O good and cheerful friendship! O servant's goodwill and trustful devotion! For the highest [friendship] mingled and united with the highest [goodwill] has broken the most shameful pits of depravity[33] and has raised up the best virtue, that of love, even if the latter had been plunged into the mire of sin,[34] by purging love of any mistrust and disrespect; and it summons up the forces of friendship—I mean justice and practical wisdom—for the *recovery* of the lost imperial *drachma*[35] of love and trustful devotion, and rejoices with them in the splendid chamber of the mind—the capacity for judgment—while taking delight in divine thoughts.

Since you, however, who savor and hear today this speech of ours need—for the confirmation of your progress, instruction, friendship, loyalty as servants, and trustful devotion—to walk in wisdom as intelligent men, taking delight as it were in this good lesson, I say the following, and do listen to my words: Love your lord[36] and walk lovingly in his footsteps.[37] Embrace trustful devotion. Be fully united with him in affection. Be convinced of the master's preeminence and the servant's subservience. Recognize the one who is appointed and the one who appoints. Recognize like sheep the shepherd. Be blind to pleasure and purify your

---

33 For the expression βάραθρα τῆς κακίας, found mostly in ecclesiastical authors, see John Chrysostom, in PG 47:330, 376, 407.

34 An allusion to the Fall of Adam and Eve. On its role in Laskaris's thought, see Angelov, *Byzantine Hellene*, 191; *Moral Pieces*, §§ 4, 11, above.

35 See the parable of the lost coin in Luke 15:8–10.

36 Cf. Deut. 6:5; Matt. 22:37; Mark 12:30; Luke 10:27.

37 Cf. Mic. 4:2.

eyes from all prejudice. Let each of you love the lord even more than your own flesh, for *he lays down his life*[38] for you. But do strive to lay down your lives for him, for he would have offered both body and soul on behalf of the most insignificant one among you. Dash down falsehood along with heartlessness and untrustworthiness, as if they were the Babylonian infants, upon the hardest rock of truth,[39] friendship, and trustful devotion. Conceive in your minds the truth and give birth to an offspring of friendship brightly ensouled with trustful devotion. Shine like stars and you will truly attract with the gleaming brightness of your spotless purity the inner intellectual sight of your lord. For if you devote all these properly to your lord—soul, body, speech, knowledge, flesh, spirit, fame, wealth, honor, peace, calm, goodwill, and love—he will grant all his possessions without discrimination to you as his true sons, friends, and subjects.

10. I have written all this in this oration out of love for you, my beloved and loyal child, both as model pictures of virtues and because of your excellent request. Your shrewd mind sought nothing unprofitable, but something superior and surpassing everything: tell me if you remember what the request was. If you ask, I will say it. But I know you are urging me, so I will immediately say what request came from you. The request was: "How should subjects serve their masters everywhere and how should they fall in with their wishes in a worthy manner?" That was, if you remember, what you said. Behold and accept the fruits. Should the fashioning of the oration appear fitting to you and to others, glory be to God the Skillful Worker.[40] Should this not be so, *the corrector of the wise*[41] will render powerless the opinions of those who are evil and will make us wise through the activity of the Spirit.

---

38 John 10:11, 13:37–38, 15:13.
39 Cf. Ps. 136:8–9.
40 "Skillful worker" (τεχνεργάτης) is a new coinage and a designation for God in the spirit of the neologisms in Laskaris's treatise *On the Divine Names*.
41 Wisd. of Sol. 7:15.

5

Representation of the World, or Life

(*Explanation of the World*, book 3)

Dedications

Dedicatory Letter to George Mouzalon (Ep. 187)
Another letter to the same *protosebastos, protovestiarios,* and *megas stratopedarches,* lord George Mouzalon.

There are two kinds of components in the world, or rather in the universe, based on which the world has taken shape: matter and immateriality. We have long been accustomed to present to you the more precious parts of both. Hence, having rightly offered material delights, wealth, pleasure, luxury together with nourishment, and many material things, we are offering you this discourse, an immaterial one, which speaks loudly about matter and immateriality, depicting in it a sort of representation of the world, or life. After you receive it as your special honor, do persuade us, being a shrewd and guileless man, to bring you other discourses, because we have brought you many earlier. Pray after receiving this work that we will bring you these kinds of ornaments countless times, my child Mouzalon, my breath and sensation, life and support, who are made manifestly powerful by my commands.

Dedicatory Preface to Explanation of the World

Festa, p. 97 *Explanation of the World* by the wisest *autokrator* Theodore Doukas Laskaris, the son of the most exalted great emperor of the Romans, lord John Doukas, written before the full completeness[1] of his imperial rule, addressed to George Mouzalon, on whom the same wisest emperor bestowed brotherly status after the full completeness of his imperial rule, and this wisest *autokrator* considered him worthy of being called his brother,[2] promoted him to the dignity of *protosebastos*[3] and *protovestiarios*,[4] and honored him as *megas stratopedarches*[5] by creating this dignity for the first time.

Festa, p. 98 Asking questions is important, Mouzalon, because through the method of inquiry we come to possess in this way what we lack by nature. This is a primary argument of philosophy from long ago. If the questions are especially and exceedingly about the most excellent and precious subjects, they are certainly well-posed. Aware that asking questions is a good thing, nature knows that asking about goodness is very

---

1 "Full completeness" (ἐντελέχεια): this Aristotelian term, which means "actuality," "complete reality" in philosophical contexts, fascinated Laskaris. Some titles of the edited collections of his works, which were prepared during the period 1254–1258, refer to his accession in November 1254 as the sole emperor as ἐντελέχεια τῆς βασιλείας. Translatable as "full completeness of his imperial rule," the phrase points to the end of his coemperorship and the onset of his independent rule on the death of the senior emperor, John III Vatatzes. See Agapitos and Angelov, "Six Essays," 62; Angelov, *Byzantine Hellene*, 83.

2 The brotherly status of George Mouzalon is attested in Laskaris's letters to him after his accession. See below, p. 131, n. 6. Laskaris followed a practice of his father, John III Vatatzes, who had designated his chief minister Demetrios Komnenos Tornikes as his "brother" in official documents. See George Akropolites, *History* 49, ed. Heisenberg and Wirth, 1:90.20–23; trans. Macrides, *George Akropolites*, 250, 254, n. 19.

3 Laskaris granted the three titles of *protosebastos*, *protovestiarios*, and *megas stratopedarches* to George Mouzalon on Christmas 1255 at Lampsakos. See Akropolites, *History* 60, ed. Heisenberg and Wirth, 1:124.1–7. The honorific dignity of *protosebastos* ranked thirteenth in the fourteenth-century court hierarchy, according to the ceremonial book of pseudo-Kodinos. For this title and the titles mentioned in the following two notes, see *Pseudo-Kodinos*, ed. Macrides, Munitiz, and Angelov, 455 (table).

4 The household office of *protovestiarios* (keeper of the emperor's wardrobe) ranked sixth in the court hierarchy of pseudo-Kodinos in the fourteenth century.

5 The military office of *megas stratopedarches* was still in existence in the middle of the fourteenth century, when its holder was responsible for provisioning the army; it ranked tenth in the court hierarchy of pseudo-Kodinos.

much and certainly excellent. So you did well to ask: both because you are asking questions and also because you asked about superior subjects. What I call "superior" are, in my opinion, the universal matters. We will not be ungrateful, having conferred adoption on you,[6] but will give instead of *an egg*, the pearl of knowledge, and *instead of fish*,[7] a voice, or rather philosophical voices, which destroy the dumbness of ignorance and truly lead you toward a harmonious arrangement of everything. Do not neglect the arguments because of their lofty nature. We will elucidate for you as much as possible their meaning in this complete treatise on the world, which we will entrust to you as much as it is in our power. God the Perfecter of the best deeds will fittingly bring the study to an end.

There are two good things in it: a clarification of important matters and a praise of God. As regards the former [clarification], virtue is furnished through experience, because knowledge and great learning lead toward virtue the soul's eye, which is cleansed by them alone, while being darkened by deceptive deeds. The latter [praise of God] arises because anyone examining the things in the universe surely comes to examine at the same time that God is the maker of the universe. As he examines, he discovers. As he discovers, he ascribes to him [God] greatness, being moved by amazement at his great deeds. Salvation of the soul is introduced based on these two best things. Therefore, we will not hesitate to entrust to you what is best. The study of the treatise will be for your rational nature a foundation of virtue in the future, and the treatise will persevere unto the ages of ages under God's watch.

Festa, p. 99

First, we will teach you about the union and the separation of the particular and simple elements and about their properties and in what way they are united and in what way they are not, and about the many other things said in the book.[8]

---

6 References to adoption are found in Laskaris's letters to Mouzalon. See Th. L., *Ep.* 165.1 (p. 221), 210.14 (p. 262). They do not necessarily signify legal adoption, however, and can be understood metaphorically. Laskaris often calls Mouzalon "son," signaling a close relationship and difference in age. See Th. L., *Ep.* 150.1 (p. 214), 151.8 (p. 215), 152.3 (p. 215), 164.1 (p. 221), etc. After his accession as the sole emperor in 1254, he began to call Mouzalon his "brother." See Th. L., *Ep.* 214.45 (p. 266).

7 Luke 11:11–12.

8 The word λόγος is translated as "book" rather than "discourse" or "oration" whenever the author is describing the four constituent parts of the collection. The reference here is to book 1 of *Explanation of the World*, titled *On the Elements* and edited by Festa, "Κοσμικὴ

Then, <we will teach> about the heaven and its movement, shape, and other matters.[9] Afterward I paint a sort of "representation of the world, and life,"[10] in which I will speak distinctly about everything. Next I will discuss philosophically that I do not know anything anyhow and in any way. I will do it this way for the following reason: namely, because I ought to speak about the elements before heaven; for the heaven is an element, even if a different one, which is divine and unmixed, according to the doctrine of Aristotle. I should speak about them [the elements] before the rest, because the composition is divided into three sections: what contains, what is contained, and what connects in itself the container and the contained. What lies above is the book *On Heaven*, which holds the content. What lies below is the book *On the Elements*, which is held as content. What connects both of them is the book painting the representation of the world, and life, which is integrative. It is necessary to start earlier with the account of the contained, because it is down below, then to recount the features of what contains, because it is high above, and next move to the things lying in between because of their integrative quality. For the extremities are prior to the middle, insofar as something measurable is called "a middle" and "an extremity." If someone speaks of a middle, he speaks in relation to the extremities; if he speaks of an extremity, he does so in relation to the middle. We have now begun to speak about things that are bound together and are mutually binding. Therefore, we determined that it was necessary to speak earlier about what needs binding and then about what binds together. We call the entire treatise *Explanation of the World*, because it talks openly about everything.

In the three sections, the discussion is about the things high above and down below, and about bonds of union. In the last section, the goal is rather theological,[11] in that I say that I do not know anything. For Socrates in his great knowledge beyond the rest said he knew nothing and so earned top ranking among all people.

Festa, p. 100

Δήλωσις," (1897–98). A few sentences below, the author also uses the word τμῆμα (section) to refer to the four parts of the collection.

9 This is book 2 of *Explanation of the World*, titled *On Heaven* and edited by Festa, "Κοσμικὴ Δήλωσις" (1899).

10 Interestingly, the treatise is called here and once again below "representation of the world, and life," while both the dedicatory letter to Mouzalon and the manuscript heading name it "representation of the world, or life."

11 The reference is to negative or apophatic theology, in which Laskaris had special interest. See Angelov, *Byzantine Hellene*, 197–98.

Therefore, I am entrusting to you the treatise on the elements, both the particular and the universal; the demonstration of every movement and shape of heaven, of the good and worst incidents; in the third book, <I entrust to you> an explanation of the universe and the many varieties of life, from which you will richly derive the greatest concepts in your mind. In the last book, I say that I do not know anything. I reveal at the same time in this book that I do not know anything philosophical. For I am a philosopher and am not ashamed.[12]

I composed these books for the great benefit of many: first, for your own special benefit and that of your people; then, for the profit of people receiving the gift through you. Addressing you, I write first concerning the elements, then concerning heaven, and next concerning all things in the *Representation of the World, or Life*. Lastly, I write about no one having knowledge of anything. By pretending that I say these things about me, I elevate them to the level of theology. After assembling the books about all matters under one single purpose, I call the collection *Explanation of the World*.

I judge it necessary for your pure intellect to have this knowledge. For it is good to store the treasures in a fine vessel in order to preserve them undamaged and distribute them, when they are opened at the right moment, among those people who request them and who are determined to be worthy. Accept, therefore, the tome, gather its usefulness and importance in your mind, and give back the loving affection of your goodwill. Since we have nourished and raised you, since we have instructed you through bodily training, we are nourishing you in a similar way also spiritually, as you now see, because we very clearly know that you are sound in intellect and have a formidable mind, firm thinking, excellent standing, correct reasoning, dignified conduct, most approachable character, pure way of thinking, firm habit of mind, stable constitution of the soul, prudent way of reflection, well-sounding speech, cultured life, trustful devotion and pure love toward us, and thousands of other exceptional things that owing to the surfeit of words we will not say, as though by rhetorical omission. We believe with confidence that you will prefer this to any other of our favors, although you have received, you are receiving, and you will receive countless and greatest favors in the future. Through this one, you will multiply your goodwill, even though, as you know, we have granted

Festa, p. 101

---

12 The same phrase οὐκ ἐπαισχύνομαι found in a Pauline letter (2 Tim. 1:12) may be the inspiration here.

you the status of an adopted son. You will reveal to your formidable mind what has been revealed in the books. We implore in the name of God that you make progress in the future in your good deeds.

Representation of the World, or Life

Festa, p. 21   1. After having frequently examined what lies in nature and is inferior to nature,[13] as was my custom, I came to see nothing stable, except that there was an instability in particular things and an all-encompassing stability derived from God. I therefore left to everyone else the stability of things unstable insofar as it is stability, but devoted myself to the examination that Plato, too, long ago called "divine fire,"[14] because it exposes hidden things. I felt in this some divine and providential feeling beyond the power of reason.

Because I am convinced that it is right for you to gain knowledge of this treatise,[15] I will not deprive you of it, George Mouzalon, who are most prominent among all my friends, but I wish to present you with this best repayment—for your own benefit and owing to my affection for you. When you get hold of the treatise may you multiply the gift as a sharp-witted man. For you are mighty, you are so great, and you stand apart from those born long ago, according to my opinion,

---

13 Laskaris refers here to his *Natural Communion*, a philosophical work in six books, which explores two principles of association in the universe, nature and convention. See above, p. 53, n. 94.

14 One wonders where, if at all, Laskaris read about Plato calling his philosophical inquiry "divine fire" (θεῖον πῦρ). There is perhaps a distant echo from late antique Neoplatonism. In his *Commentary on Plato's Timaeus* 2 (ed. Diehl, 43–44), while discussing the creation of heaven (*Timaeus* 40a), Proclus speaks of a pure and celestial divine fire. However, Byzantine authors used the expression "divine fire" in many other contexts, usually in reference to the fire of divine punishment. The allusion appears to be to contemporary judicial ordeals by red-hot iron, which were known in Byzantium as "holy fire" (ἅγιον πῦρ). See George Pachymeres, *History* 1.12, ed. Failler, 1:55.5. They were described by the thirteenth-century archbishop and high ecclesiastical judge Demetrios Chomatenos (*Demetrii Chomateni Ponemata Diaphora*, no. 97, ed. Prinzing, 303.12–14) as "revealing hidden things," which is similar to the phraseology here. On the phenomenon of the judicial ordeal by red-hot iron in the states of Epiros and Nicaea, see Macrides, "Trial by Ordeal."

15 Here and elsewhere Laskaris calls the work a "treatise" (πραγματεία), but he also designates it as an "oration" (λόγος) in §§1, 2, 4, 8, 10, and 14 and a "composition" (συγγραφή) in §4.

if indeed my <opinion> is acceptable to learned people.[16] The oration is called *Representation of the World, or Life*. Receive it unhesitatingly.

2. But who can strain his eyes? Who can comprehend the divine? Who can be purified? Who can extract himself from what drags him down? For a nature that is all-powerful has been gaping at shameful things. I will say it again. Clay follows the potter, food the cook, and those aboard a ship follow their helmsman for no reason other than nature. But whoever rises up and turns his gaze from things down below possesses a vast amount as a consequence.[17] Philosophy hides herself, her admirers are useless, and the person who chooses her at once faces the resistance of many. I have obeyed only her since my early youth and cannot bear to hide the veritable truth in the depths of my mind.

Because I have been nourished in philosophy from long ago, as many people have recognized, I am determined that it is right for you too to know the things in life. I am also determined that as long as I live in my mortal body you should be the prominent guardian of all my written works. The oration is long, but I will display no rhetorical skill.[18] If perhaps after resisting I will display[19] <rhetorical skill> under compulsion, how much <of that skill> will I reveal if I surrender to style subjects that lie beyond the power of reason? In this sphere [style], there is rhetorical skill but no figures, rules, definitions, and principles of scientific knowledge and the other matters that, as it seems to me, have not eluded scientific experts. For truth—and I myself alongside it—hold judgments, not opinions, especially regarding the terrible instability of circumstances and choices, which is witnessed in the flakes and flurries of snow as well as the showers of hail, for all these are swept away by the wind because they are not solid.

Festa, p. 22

Do accept this oration and treasure it in your heart, you who yearn for my words more than you love yourself. Everything in it is as follows and let no one suggest that reason investigates, while the greedy eye turns from one thing to another.

---

16 The youth of Mouzalon, who was younger than the author, is a theme found both in the dedicatory letter to the treatise and in the dedicatory preface to the collection *Explanation of the World*.

17 A sudden twist of thought characteristic of Laskaris's style. The literary feature is particularly prominent in this work.

18 The word δεινότης is translated here "rhetorical skill," but it can mean more narrowly "force," as one of the seven rhetorical virtues discussed by Hermogenes, *On Types of Style*.

19 As per the manuscript reading δείξω.

For I write not to *ridicule by name*,[20] nor do I write an encomium, but I philosophize and cry out: "O man, lift up your eyes and observe!" The light bearer has risen and, after crossing the horizon, it has been elevated on high; the stars have disappeared. Life is going on: the market people go to the market, those in trials are occupied with the trials, those in lawsuits occupied with the lawsuits, and those working in the palace are busy in the palace. Law is hence common for those who wish to live by the law. In the world it is as in a single city, where somewhere there are groans, somewhere outpouring <of words and emotions>, somewhere dancing, somewhere blessings and purifications, somewhere thefts and lawsuits, and the other things that living people encounter, with the law ruling supreme for those wishing to be governed by the law. Experience suffices as an infallible and solid witness of what has been said. But for me experience does not suffice only as experience, but as elucidation of many arguments.

Festa, p. 23

3. Therefore, adopting a stentorian voice, I say the following: "The person who judges took his seat, and who is judged? The one who gives or the one who receives the judgment?" It seems to me that the former person, the giver, will also receive, but the latter who rightfully receives will give as much as he can in order to *deliver his soul*.[21] Once again I say: is this possession or deprivation? What is the principle of the things in nature? If the Stagirite[22] listened to what has been said, he would have assigned to *the positive* as a common principle also *the privative*,[23] the former [the positive] because the judge is receiving[24] and the latter [the privative] because

---

20 For this quotation from Hermogenes, *On Issues* 11 (in *Opera*, ed. Rabe, 88.11–14), see above, *Satire of His Tutor*, §1, p. 60, n. 9.

21 Isa. 44:20.

22 Namely, Aristotle.

23 The terminology here (στέρησις, ἕξις) is indebted to Aristotle, *Categories* 12a26–13a36, and is translated accordingly.

24 Laskaris alludes here to corruption among the judges, which was also the topic of an essay written toward the end of his life. See Agapitos and Angelov, "Six Essays," 44–45 (Essay 4), 70–71 (commentary). The reprehensible judicial practices are not clear. The author may have in mind outright corruption or may be targeting the customary fees collected by judges (*sportulae*, Lat.; *ektagiatika*, Gr.), which the early and middle Byzantine emperors strove to either ban or regulate. See the discussion by Chitwood, *Byzantine Legal Culture*, 53–60.

the rightfully entitled person is being deprived. Already we have a first confirmation of the proposition.[25]

But you, most excellent assembly, do make a contribution of better confirmations, because for a wise man wisdom is the origin of many topics for discussion.[26] The principles have suffered in turn; the covetousness characteristic of deprivation harms the power of possession, and possession brings into being the nonbeing of deprivation. As I said, when the principles have suffered this, instability gets hold of the things around them. Lo and behold the resulting absurdities! For once one thing has been allowed, many things follow. Hence the planter of seeds plows the land at the rising of the Pleiades,[27] but when he looks for the harvest in the wintertime, he would not fill his bosom.[28] There is a right occasion for things in this life, which is responsible for harvests and words.

It is now timely that I should speak concerning my own words and deeds.[29] The reaper of the crops[30] did not have his hands full and the collector of sheaves did not fill his bosom,[31] because everything carried out naturally receives a natural completion; but what is contrary to nature from the outset brings about shameful results contrary to nature. For when the winter comes, the general prepares the weapons as necessary, strengthens the fortresses, builds walls around the strongholds, empties the fields of provisions, arranges the battle order, trains the troops, and collects the baggage of war weapons, so that he can make the campaign suitable for the spring after having made the appropriate arrangements and so that he can proceed well toward action. But the one who does contrariwise spoils the

---

25 That is, the confirmation (κατασκευή) of the "instability in things particular" (§1) and the "instability of circumstances and choices" (§2). The terms κατασκευή and ἀνασκευή refer to school compositions of "confirmation" and "refutation" of propositions. See Hermogenes, *Progymnasmata*, no. 5, in *Opera*, ed. Rabe, 11; Aphthonius, *Progymnasmata*, no. 6, ed. Rabe, 13–16.

26 "Origin of many subjects for discussion" (ἀφορμὴ πολλῶν ἀφορμῶν): wordplay on the meanings of the word ἀφορμή.

27 That is, at an inappropriate time. According to Hesiod, *Works and Days* 383–84, the farmer should start harvesting during the heliacal rising of the Pleiades.

28 Cf. Ps. 128:7.

29 A cryptic remark: it is unclear what words and deeds Laskaris has in mind. The following sentence, which is equally cryptic, probably refers to the author himself.

30 An example of a future participle (ὁ ἀμήσων) that does not convey tense or intent.

31 Another echo from Ps. 128:7.

Festa, p. 24 troops, leaves the soldier without honor, and empties the fortresses when a time for battle and not for dallying has come. Who will raise in wintertime the mast of his ship in the seas and take a grip of the ship's tiller? The timing truly exposes the ignorance of the person who does so. In a little while, laments will be heard in the homes of the sailors and no one will be able to put the situation right. But a good captain has considered the season and has protected the ship from the storm. For to be tossed by the waves is equal to destruction, because most people are fainthearted.

The best things are all those done according to nature. The others are aborted, sometimes causing fear with their excess, sometimes arousing laughter with their inadequacy. For my part, when I come to think of foolish talk, I find Xerxes to be frightening and the Assyrian Sardanapalus to be deficient: the former because of his covetousness and the latter because of his secretiveness.[32] I admire Philip, greatly esteem Cyrus, and praise others who lived at that time in the same fashion.[33] What is done according to nature is prone to attract acclaim, but the other to repel praises. Who has lived in the best manner? It is the person who led his life according to nature. Who has been blessed in his undertakings? It is the man who pursued knowledge. But the man who attends to temporary profit and neglects the bliss <of pursuing knowledge> has experienced pleasure for a while but has failed to gain acclaim.

4. I have said much about praise and blame. As for those people who consider reason to be the overall goal of the treatise, my initial words will have been said in truth.[34] And if someone criticizes me for promising to describe the instability

---

32 On Xerxes and Sardanapalus as negative examples, see Blem., *Imperial Statue* 23–25 (p. 50: Sardanapalus), 137–40 (p. 88: Xerxes). Blemmydes indeed describes Xerxes as covetous. The secretiveness (παρυπόκρυψις) of Sardanapalus seems to be related to his life of pleasure, effeminacy, and decadence—all legendary features of Sardanapalus reported by Blemmydes.

33 Blem., *Imperial Statue* 21 (p. 50), 210 (p. 114), gives Cyrus and Philip of Macedon as ancient examples of, respectively, chaste and just kings.

34 In the introductory paragraph (§1), the composition of the treatise is described as an experience "beyond the power of reason" (ὑπὲρ λογισμούς), which explains the reference here to things said in the beginning. A similar idea also appears in §2, where the subject matter is again said to lie "beyond the power of reason" (ὑπεράνω τῶν λογισμῶν). Clearly, ὁ λόγος in the present sentence means "reason," although the word can also refer to the composition itself as "an oration" (see below, p. 139, n. 37).

Representation of the World, or Life 139

of the world's affairs, yet digressing to a different subject, and therefore taunts me that I deserve laughter, I myself will burst out laughing. The rhetorician conveying this comparison and example to other rhetoricians has ridiculed in advance his own insensitivity.

Unstable things are unstable in two ways: some in actions and others by their origins, each furnishing an example for the other. The failure of a law leads to the correction of the law, and the soundness of a law leads to failure of legal things. For not every law is also true law, because what everyone performs is not utterly unfailing.[35]

Festa, p. 25

As for me, by connecting the mentioned patterns with good and bad things in nature, I display through this composition the inconstancy and craftiness[36] of mortals. Whoever might be intelligent and deft will pluck the fruits and, having listened to one kind of thing, will turn his mind toward another. Just as the reflection in mirrors carries the knowledge of the shapes to the mind, with the spirit obtaining this knowledge, so it will happen with words: the mind grasps what lies in darkness and transfers it to the light of truth. The principal subject in what is related here is life. The things in life follow in sequence. The oration is a confirmation of the proposition of the treatise.[37] Its object is the lack of order in the world. Its knowledge is a philosophical knowledge. Its virtue is goodness, and whoever wants to proceed let him advance without fear by these means.

What can I say? I will say it again. What order is there in the world? Plato spoke well, yet no philosopher is a king, because no king is a philosopher.[38] Consider

---

35 The pessimistic view of the law has two aspects: first, there are lapsed or flawed laws in need of correction, and second, the conduct of individuals contributes to the failure of legal order. The "law" (νόμος) seems to encompass not only codified law but also usage and custom.

36 The Greek word πολύτροπον used here makes the reader think of Odysseus in the *Odyssey*.

37 The translation of λόγος as "oration" in the phrase κατασκευὴ δὲ τῆς πραγματείας ὁ λόγος makes sense in the context, but see above, p. 138, n. 34. On the meaning of κατασκευή as a rhetorical term, see above, p. 137, n. 25.

38 Echoes of Plato's dictum (*Republic* 473d) are common in Byzantine panegyrical and admonitory texts addressed to the emperor. Laskaris consistently presents himself (e.g., §§2, 12 in this work) as a nursling of philosophy, yet strikingly states here that "no king is a philosopher." One can account for the tension in various ways: the understanding of philosophy here as Christian perfection and ascetic life (on this, see Dölger, "Zur Bedeutung"); the

that Plato spoke about a philosopher and a king, about the philosopher-king and the reigning philosopher, and where and how one reigns and acts philosophically. The latter [the reigning philosopher] rules over passions, but the former [the philosopher-king] rules over royal subjects governed by someone nourished in philosophy. So it is rare for someone to rule over passions or be a philosopher.

After I had already exposed disorder and instability among the judges, I bought order among the grandees but was led astray about the officials.[39] Investigating private affairs, I saw from the beginning what is truly inappropriate for them and saw from the end what was not fitting for the beginning. Do consider those who take away and those who seize with *guiltless hands*[40] the tribute of blood.[41] The eagle tests bastard eaglets by setting their pupils toward the sun.[42] The prophet proclaims, *it is impossible to hide injustice from God.*[43] Where are those who do wicked things, those who act contrary to nature, the polluted ones? For behold, *this is a jealous God*[44] and *a Lord powerful in strength.*[45]

Festa, p. 26

5. For his part, Isaiah, who gazes at this \<earthly\> Jerusalem, calls it a *garden-watcher's hut*[46] due to the apostasy of the surrounding nations. This home of the

---

tradition of contrasting the king and the monk-philosopher based on John Chrysostom's influential comparison (see John Chrysostom's work "Comparison between a King and a Monk," in PG 47:387–92, of which key passages entered, among other authors, the tenth-century, thematically arranged Chrysostomic collection of excerpts by Theodore Daphnopates, in PG 63:695); and most of all perhaps, the spirit of realism permeating this work.

39 The author distinguishes three kinds of powerful individuals here: "judges" (κριταί), on whose corruption he comments above in §3; "grandees" (ἄρχοντες), a fluid term that could include anyone in position of authority; and the "officials" (οἱ ἐν τέλει), who are revisited in §13 as subject to unspecified oppressive measures. The "officials" include the unjust individuals with tax-collecting power mentioned later in this paragraph.

40 Cf. Ps. 23:4.

41 Targeted are the injustices of tax collectors in the countryside. For the comparison between tax money and the subjects' blood, see George Pachymeres, *History* 1.14, 23, ed. Failler, 1:63.3–5, 97.26–29.

42 On the saying that eagles test their babies by exposing their eyes to the sun, see, for example, the poetic work by Gregory of Nazianzus, in PG 37:1516, and Kosmas of Jerusalem's commentary in *Commentary*, ed. Lozza, 335–36.

43 Cf. Jer. 16:17.

44 Deut. 6:15. Cf. Exod. 20:5.

45 Jos. 10:7; Judg. 11:1.

46 Isa. 1:8.

Representation of the World, or Life 141

prophets, the mother of all the churches, the ancient initiator of our salvation, which has nourished so many in the faith, is now filled with pollution. The prophet foresaw this, because he was exceptional among the prophets. He laments over her, but I for my part lament over the great city,[47] the well-balanced and ever-influential one.[48] And please consider, my good fellow, this to be its [Jerusalem's] characteristic feature: never did the disarray[49] of the city hold sway over *the large sections* <of the world>, in Philo's opinion,[50] just as famine did not become prevalent (this was an insult on Gaius and there was again a threat of exile for the Jews);[51] neither equality nor friendship, nor enmity and strife, became prevalent.[52]

Certainly, when Hannibal was in Africa, when Brutus was in Rome, when Alcibiades was in Sicily and went as far as Cyzicus, when Semiramis was among the Persians,[53] and at other times in other places, all of them flourished. The peak of their power was the same, and the praise by their servants was so sublime that it could flatter and sycophantically spoil each of them by lauding him like a god. Lions among the four-footed animals and ravens among the flying creatures are

---

47 The unnamed "great city" (μεγάλη πόλις) must be Constantinople. The mention of the fall of Jerusalem in the previous sentence draws attention to the parallel with Constantinople's conquest by the Latins. Constantinople was traditionally known as the "megalopolis" (μεγαλόπολις). See Niketas Choniates, *Historia*, ed. Van Dieten, 157, 256, 257, 323. Notably, Laskaris calls Nicaea "megalopolis" in his encomium in praise of the city (Th. L., *Op. rhet.*, 79.273–74).

48 The neologism ἀειρρεπής (ever-influential) is formed by analogy with composite adjectives, such as ἰσορρεπής, χαμαιρεπής, and ὀξυρεπής.

49 The Greek word is ἀταξία, literally "disorder," introduced as a theme of the treatise in §4.

50 Philo of Alexandria, *Embassy to Gaius* 48, in *Opera*, ed. Cohn and Wendland, 6:164.18, describes envy as moving along "large sections" (μεγάλας ἀποτομάς) of the inhabited world, a passage that seems to be behind Laskaris's μεγάλας ἀποκοπάς. On the author's familiarity with this work by Philo, see below his *Oration on Hellenism*, §13.

51 Gaius is better known as the emperor Gaius Caligula (r. 37–41). According to Philo, he became angry when hearing that the prospect of a famine in Judea delayed his planned journey from Rome to Alexandria. See Philo of Alexandria, *Embassy to Gaius* 248–60, in *Opera*, ed. Cohn and Wendland, 6:201–3.

52 The moral is that even after the fall of great cities, life still goes on.

53 Two of the examples can be found in Blem., *Imperial Statue* 145–47 (pp. 90–92: Hannibal), 160 (p. 98: Semiramis), even though not in the context of the rise and fall of great rulers. Brutus and Alcibiades are absent from the *Imperial Statue*.

encountered in the desert, but the perdition for kings is slanderers and flatterers in the city. Slander and flattery are simply[54] difficult weapons to fight. No one from among all the mentioned <sovereigns> ruled with the care Caesar and Alexander had in this matter. Even if some kingdom held sway over Libya or Asia (which occupies the larger part of the earth) or Europe, it did not control the human mind. Could man not dwell on earth by himself?[55]

6. Nature is weakened by what lies above and beyond nature. Frost presses hard on the flesh and the warmth of the sun dulls pain. These are opposite things.

One should know that order and disorder are the best things in life. For when one is dissolved, it establishes the other, and the other in turn builds up the former.

Many hidden things lie in the world and in life. For how many people deceive the unintelligent with humble words? And how many people who are not humble-minded seem most gentle to the gullible? For the fox sometimes has the appearance of gentleness. The deer that raises its neck feigns pride in the eyes of the rather simpleminded. Yet, seized with fear when seeing the dogs of the hunters, the latter [the deer] suddenly runs swiftly, both running for her life and abandoning any semblance of haughtiness and pride. The former [the fox] puts on an appearance, flatters in a perfect way as she walks around, lives in self-deception, and goes about as though having the shadow of someone else.

At times the masterly mind falls asleep in the undertaking of good works and the baby birds escape in their innocence through and around the fenced wall. Let those with intelligence think of them [the baby birds] as the designs of the multitude, but let the simple person think of the child birds themselves.[56] Then, what is revered rushes down in the darkness, for it is in the dark that it moves around. And what is gentle, changing into the shape of a shameful woman, moves around the fenced wall, and stretching out a foot she feels for an opening while searching for an entry and looking out for the quarry. When she finds those in the shed asleep and the quarters of the birds unguarded, she leaps through the surrounding fences, devours as much as possible, and kills the majority, as there is no limit to

---

54 A translation for καθαπλοῦ, a hapax not found in the lexica.
55 Cf. Isa. 5:8.
56 That is, the simple person is incapable of understanding the allegory. The birds (namely, the designs and inclinations of the multitude) easily fall prey to the fox in a woman's shape—that is, the dissimulating and destructive mind.

Representation of the World, or Life

her gluttony in such deeds. Thus, what is revered changes into shamelessness and what is fearful[57] and subtle into the audacity of impudence.

Having seen how an irreverent mind can do such things, I have come to marvel at impudence. The human being is more secretive in his speech than speechless animals, saying one thing while being occupied with calculations about another. Hence he legislates about justice and seeks an excess of money. On the one hand, it is good that someone can obtain money from a just source, for at the right moment he will feed the people by giving them a portion. On the other, I have judged it sacrilegious for someone to greedily appropriate a mass of wealth.[58]

7. I saw him[59] pass judgment on decorum and be ruled by shameful women. I saw <him> angrily attacking in speech, taking his words back, being reduced to silence, losing heart in fighting, and fearlessly conspiring; and when one shield was added to another shield, a helmet to helmet, and a man to man, <I saw him> carrying over the slopes and hills whatever material possessions he had and ordering that a declaration of his care for the multitude should be feigned.

Festa, p. 28

I saw another man who had the color of an Ethiopian, but in his thoughts had the appearance of an angel of light through the announcements of his expressed reason.[60]

I saw another man who sang of disasters, but derived money from what he sang.

---

57 The adjective περιδεής has the double meaning of "fearful" (as translated here) and "frightening" (as translated above at §3, p. 138), just as the adjective φοβερός in the *Moral Pieces*, §10, p. 110, is used in the same sentence with its double meaning of "frightful" and "awe-inspiring."

58 The target seems to be both unjust tax collection and the greed of private individuals.

59 The first anonymous example of deceitful behavior is that of a conspiratorial individual referred to simply as "him" (αὐτόν). The schemer may be Michael Palaiologos, the future emperor and the author's second cousin, who was suspected of disloyalty more than once in the period 1253–1258, during the reigns of both John III Vatatzes and Theodore II Laskaris. See above, p. 5. Alternatively, he may be identified with Constantine Tornikes or Alexios Strategopoulos, two generals who did not obey the emperor's orders during the military campaign against the Bulgarians in 1255. See Angelov, *Byzantine Hellene*, 154–57. Andreeva, "Polemika," 15, preferred to identify him with Blemmydes.

60 On the originally Stoic distinction between "immanent reason" (λόγος ἐνδιάθετος) and "expressed reason" (λόγος προφορικός) articulated in speech, see Nemesius, *De natura hominis* 14, ed. Morani, 71–72; trans. Sharples and Van der Eijk, 123–25, esp. 123, n. 612.

I saw another man who killed many people and who received many praises from many people for God's divine judgments about the correction of offenders.

I saw poor men considered to be rich. I saw rich men who pitied themselves.[61]

I saw those who killed some in a snare and had the condemnation assigned to others.[62]

I saw those who struggled but did not finish and handed over their agenda to people caring little about the end goals.

I have also seen <the following>: in nature, afflictions of the air and the stars as well as burning fires of the ether; in the waters, currents; in the breezes, howling sounds. <I saw> different kinds of earthquakes, changes of winds, massive snowfalls, outbreaks of showers, *the breaking up of the clouds*,[63] and all the other things.

And I <saw> more than what has been mentioned: artisans and reasoning men unappreciated by the authorities.

I saw species of birds that passed floating through the air and were attacked, as was only natural, by others.

I saw debauched people being honored. I saw handsome people being despised, flatterers holding power, dancers, male and female, and people who cause laughter by their appearance and about their opinions; I saw things too numerous to count.

<I saw> both the living and the dead as is recounted about Polydeukes.[64]

<I saw stars> that rose up and went down after their rise in order to carry the heavenly bodies somewhere around Atlas.[65]

---

61 The description again fits Michael Palaiologos, who is reported to have flaunted his lack of money when he seized the imperial office, even though he came from a prominent aristocratic family. See George Pachymeres, *History* 1.23, 25, 27, ed. Failler, 1:97.2–4, 103.1–6, 107.5–9. Andreeva, "Polemika," 16–17, has suggested that the author had in mind himself in light of his dispute with Blemmydes on taxation.

62 The murderer may have been Theodore Philes, the governor of Thessaloniki, whom Laskaris accuses of murder in a letter to George Akropolites and expresses his shock and anger at Philes' counteraccusations. See Th. L., *Ep.* 77–78 (pp. 103–6); Andreeva, "Polemika," 18; Angelov, *Byzantine Hellene*, 122–23, 368–69.

63 Pseudo-Aristotle, *De mundo* 395a15–16.

64 Castor and Polydeukes (Pollux) were heroes and half-brothers known also as the Dioscuri. Castor was mortal and Polydeukes immortal.

65 According to Greek mythology, the Titan Atlas was punished by being compelled to hold heaven on his shoulders at the western end of the world.

Representation of the World, or Life

I saw more things than those mentioned, things at whose variety the multitude is amazed. I saw breasts, robes, and silhouettes of women depicted with crenellations,[66] who attract notice to themselves—just as the Gorgon's head, with its boiling rage, brings disaster to the sailors who catch sight of her wherever she lies in wait.[67]

Festa, p. 29

I also saw many people practicing silence and others who looked on and did not comprehend. For the common custom for all people is to exchange mutual flatteries, unless someone is a philosopher.

I alone feel the pain among everyone else, even if someone else just like me has since long ago devoted himself to philosophy. What is going on here? The whole universe now utters a cry. But the listener blocks his ears with wax, so that he may sail past the cravings of the multitude, like Odysseus past Charybdis,[68] and this is his reasoning.

I call the reasoning of the multitude a "reasoning" that does not focus on good things. The ruler who alone has completely surpassed instability by his high rank is capable of overcoming the reasoning of the multitude.[69] It is right to convert the opposites into well-arranged order in accordance with justice.

But I saw in some places rulers who were ruled over, kings who were governed, and chief men who were overcome, just as illnesses of putrefaction dominate in turn, while the mostly phlegmatic illnesses are overcome—those illnesses which dominate through pleasures.[70]

---

66 The description seems inspired by an artistic work and recalls the depiction of the *tyche* of ancient cities, including Constantinople, as a woman wearing a crown in the shape of a walled city.

67 On medieval and modern Greek popular beliefs in the Gorgon, which assumed the characteristics of the Siren, see Politis, "Γοργόνα." On some Byzantine beliefs about the Gorgon, see also *Physiologus*, redactio secunda Byzantina 23, ed. Sbordone, 242–47.

68 According to book 12 of the *Odyssey*, the men of Odysseus put wax in their ears while sailing by the island of the Sirens, not between Scylla and Charybdis.

69 Laskaris sets the ruler against the multitude, as he does in the *Memorial Discourse on Emperor Frederick II*.

70 Putrefaction is a common cause of illness in Galenic medicine. The link between pleasure and illnesses of the phlegm may be explained by Galen's idea that extra phlegm was generated in the digestion of certain foods. See Siegel, *Galen's System of Physiology and Medicine*, 224. It is perhaps notable that a later treatise attributed to Galen (pseudo-Galen, *On the Humors*, ed. Kühn, 490.1–2, 492.00–493.11) locates the phlegm in the mouth, the loin

I also saw the best of goals being achieved, both the natural and those inferior to nature, and saw both excellent order and turmoil among the grandees, and saw many reported slanderous things that were leaning in another direction. For the whole universe is not one but consists of different components. Therefore, things not dishonored diverge from those someone will dishonor in speech, and the case is similar with honored things. The mockery of a bad thing announces the beauty of a good thing, and the repetition of excellent deeds denounces the foolishness of their opposites. Have the opposites been dishonored and who will place value on what is not good? The person who will hate what is not good would by all means desire what is better. But my purpose now is not to dishonor or to honor, but only to put forward what is done in life.

What will I do, however, without having crossed the ether and seen heaven? I can perceive it in my mind as circular in motion and shape. Having been chased away, will I be brought down to the netherworld and show to prospective laudators or admirers the things down below, the dread tribunals in Hades? Above all this, the requital lies in store, no matter whether I might suffer punishment or, having brought my fellow men next to the accidental, I might point toward profit in other locations and times.[71]

Festa, p. 30

8. I should now shape my oration mostly from what has been composed already in order to preserve the beautiful and flourishing shapes of thoughts and figures that are delightfully about to take on colors. I will say it again. Spring is the first season and ill people are restored to health. Experience has shown them this and has given them early confidence from the flowers blooming in the fields. The farmer sharpens his scythe, the captain at the prow equips his galley, the soldier polishes his sword, the servant stocks up what is necessary. But death is already here. People who have been philosophers in theory and in practice are joyful, but anyone who has lived profligately and unwisely is overwhelmed as he comes to his senses. For he feels a sharp sense of pain for the sweetness that he had senselessly enjoyed. That much <I will say> about those who are sick.

---

muscles, and the stomach; it also attributes specific human types (lazy, foolish, frivolous, and unsettled people) to the predominance of phlegm.

71 A particularly enigmatic statement. The "accidental" (τὸ συμβεβηκός), a term in Aristotelian logic, is understood to refer to the "nonexistent" and the "unknown" in *On What Is Unclear and a Testimony That the Author Is Ignorant of Philosophy*, §1.

But what can I say about the money collectors? They claim taxes, they demand revenues, they build up treasure with penalties and groans, they grow wealthy drawing the *irresistible water*[72] of curses and forcing iron into the souls of many. The ox tilling the land is in utter pain, for it sees that the taxpayer seeks a loan, not because he takes out the loan for enjoyment from what he has given <as security> but because he is compelled by taxation and pays up by taking <money> from others.[73]

Isaiah proclaims: *Head and tail, great and small,* and all the rest whom the Lord *took away*[74] from Judea. I offer an interpretation and say with ease: injustice has destroyed the powerful and emptied out the brains of the people. What pleasure is there? Night rushes by and people enjoying their dinner are left famished for pleasure on the following day.

People have received honors and the honorands are known by name. Trajan, who has been called "the great emperor" and "father," gave distinction to the name of paternity, and the emperor before him [Nerva] was great and ever-remembered.[75] But I also know many honorable individuals among the subjects and not a few among the taxpayers, mostly among those without pedigree, and in rare cases, as word has it, among noble people.

Having mentioned nobility, I will praise Moses and his successor Joshua. The former became the unifier, lawgiver, and best leader of a great people out of being nobody. The latter fully obeyed the lawgiver and held leadership by virtue through the choice of his superior. That nobility is excellent and beautiful which flows from the inner traits for the benefit of the external ones, not the nobility which wishes to bestow distinction on the inner traits because of the external ones. Good habits are true nobility; and the mind not wallowing in materiality is the father of most

Festa, p. 31

---

72 Ps. 123:5.

73 In the later centuries of Byzantium, the land tax is known to have been collected twice annually: in the spring (March) and in the autumn (September). See Smyrlis, *La fortune des grands monastères*, 216–17. The passage here is an additional piece of evidence and suggests that taxpayers in the countryside resorted to loans to meet their fiscal obligations in the spring before the collection of the harvest. The borrower apparently is required to give collateral guaranteeing the repayment of the loan.

74 Isa. 9:14.

75 Trajan is given as an example in Blem., *Imperial Statue* 61–64 (p. 63), where he is mentioned as Nerva's heir. Laskaris is aware that Roman emperors of the past had assumed the title "father of the fatherland" (*pater patriae*).

noble thoughts. Nobility of conduct makes famous the person who acts accordingly.[76] Purity is opposed to dishonorable persons. But there is the gluttonous eye that directs its strength to dark things, the ear open to nonsense, and the tongue repeating lies. The name "noble" is often given to a person who has these characteristics, thanks to which it deceives many sheep, drives them out of the fenced abode of truth, and mercilessly swallows all of them up.

In addition to these, I saw things carried out at the right times. The king of the Persians was called "great" in former times and Cyrus became a legend, but the innovator Xerxes is disgraced. I see before my eyes Croesus putting a question to Solon and not receiving a blessing,[77] as well as many people admonished by the turning of the wheel[78] and corrected.

But lo and behold, the spring has passed. Nature, which at first rushed into spring, has learned its lesson from what it has experienced, having been defeated by its inconstancy of purpose, and has come to regret things it had done well.

9. Lo and behold the summer. Species of crawling animals inhabit the woodlands, and flocks of birds dwell in the forests. The farmer has taken charge of the wheat field and chases away the wild beasts. The young farmhands are going to reap the crops in the field and spread out couches of wheat sheaves. Everyone, or rather all nature, is directed toward actions. There are campaigns and battles with which the leaders busy themselves. There are deferred payments and binding ties, with which the commoner is registered.[79] The former [the leader] does so by duty and the latter by his status as a commoner. The merchants turn to their sales, the ambassadors look to representations, the doctor to those who have been consumed by fever, and everyone goes about all the business that is appropriate for this time.

Festa, p. 32

The common law that weighs equally on all is that of conscience: for if someone committed some error in the spring, conscience pricks him to make a

---

76 On the author's view of nobility, see Angelov, *Imperial Ideology*, 226–34; Angelov, *Byzantine Hellene*, 67–68, 111–12.

77 According to Herodotus, *Histories* 1.30-33, when Croesus inquired from Solon whether he could be considered the happiest man on earth, he received a negative answer from the Athenian sage, who pointed to the change of fortune of rulers.

78 On the turning wheel of fortune, see above, *Moral Pieces*, §3, p. 103, with n. 8.

79 This puzzling passage seems to revisit the subject of taxation treated in the description of the spring (§8).

correction in the summer. But lo and behold: many people after an initial loss of their senses gain a second <instance of it>. What can possibly drive toward a second rebellion Maximian and Licinius,[80] who were oblivious of their first ones, in which they escaped capital punishment in great fear—and in earlier times, the individuals legitimately in power, I mean Gaius Macro and his associates[81]—other than the first and the second failure of their intention? In both cases, it was easy to turn away from their purpose: the former [Maximian and Licinius] by not insulting for a second time their benefactor and the latter [Macro and those around him] by letting the clown[82] play his unseemly tunes. Their experience, their flourishing power, and the youthful spirit of their first strike sufficed for one aborted attempt.[83] Yet, after suffering and not accepting a passive role, they are punished in a way they could sense, unjustly and justly each in each case. The *God of Gods*[84] punishes before these events, making known the most concealed of mysteries. These events occur after the prime of life and the fulfillment of pleasures.

But I have improperly chanced upon the mentioned improprieties and disgraceful things, and lawlessness has arisen together with conduct. People who at first opportunity immersed themselves in a sea of early pleasures have perhaps experienced what pleasure brings. But those who after that experience indulged and were indulged in their errors would suffer the taste of vomit,[85] since

---

80 The tetrarchic emperors Maximian (r. 286–305, 306–308, 310) and Licinius (r. 313–324) rebelled twice against senior colleagues—in 306–308, 310 and in 314, 324, respectively—before their downfall.

81 Laskaris has in mind the emperor Caligula's praetorian prefect Macro (Quintus Naevius Cordus Sutorius Macro), although he somehow conflates Caligula (Gaius Caligula) and Macro by speaking of Gaius Macro. Macro had already served the emperor Tiberius and assisted the accession of Caligula in 37, but was subsequently removed from power and committed suicide. The source may be Philo of Alexandria, *Embassy to Gaius* 32–61, in *Opera*, ed. Cohn and Wendland, 6:161–67, because the author has already cited this work above in §5.

82 The clown (γελοιαστής) is the emperor Caligula, who is said to have joined dancers and jested with mimes. See Philo of Alexandria, *Embassy to Gaius* 42–45, in *Opera*, ed. Cohn and Wendland, 6:163–64.

83 The historical example of two rebellions of Maximian and Licinius may, again, allude to the tumultuous career of the general and future emperor Michael Palaiologos. See above, p. 143, n. 59.

84 Ps. 49:1; Dan. 2:47.

85 Cf. Prov. 26:11.

humankind has experienced this after the removal of the Lawgiver's command and they [humans] have rightly interpreted the misfortune.[86]

10. After summer, autumn is already here; and after the transgression, there is no response; and after the lawless action, there is impertinence too. The blossoming of sprouting greenery has changed to decay. Lo and behold: the fruits are gone (one should think of the seasons and the fruits as corresponding to the concealment of thoughts) and the grape cluster has ripened, the vine has given its wine, and *the lofty trees*[87] have produced their seasonal fruits. Those in charge of the estates have collected in the storehouses the levies from the village elders.[88] The field has remained like a wife after childbirth. The person in charge of the estate has received and stored, and the storehouses have been filled with grain and oil.

Which wise man will consider these things and keep good guard over the impulses of the soul? When autumn has come (for it is not unseemly that I should summarize my oration), people who have misbehaved at a young age owing to inexperience in goodness and who have not collected what the summer brings forth are humiliated in old age, for when the first in a series has been destroyed, then naturally all that comes later is destroyed. The season of transition has arrived, leading to the decay of bodily strength. Woe to me! Woe to me! I am passing away. The flower is gone away, the fruit has been scattered, the atmospheric currents that bring together clouds too damp for the mind to advance have dissolved all thoughts. For I see many individuals who are lawless after their first experience and other people <who are lawless> after they have reached their prime, and before them people who were lawless from the beginning. Lo and behold: the perishing of fruits, that is, of thoughts; the falling of leaves, that is, reflections; the decay of young shoots, that is, the attempts at beginnings; the withering of tree trunks, the inconstancy of speech, the dissolution of a root, the annihilation of the intellect. Alas! The tree that has been well planted and was envied at the beginning has been brought to ruin by the devil.

---

86 The Fall of Adam and Eve.
87 Homer, *Iliad* 9.541, etc.
88 The word used for "estate" is οἶκος and for "village elders" is οἰκοδεσπόται. On these two terms, see Kaplan, *Les hommes et la terre*, 158–67, 235–38. The οἰκοδεσπόται are heads of households mentioned in thirteenth-century documents. See, for example, Miklosich and Müller, *Acta et diplomata graeca*, 4:147.

Representation of the World, or Life 151

11. For winter now enters together with autumn and the fruits that were not well ripened perish. I see Echetos and Phalaris, the former weakened after the pruning and the latter, much tested, confessing that he had not come to his senses before the pruning.[89] For in his letters to Pythagoras, sent as if to his own father, he [Phalaris] accuses himself before him.[90]

After the autumn comes winter, and I see the dog Cerberus barking justly against the unjust, <I see> judgments passed on dead people and public punishments. Coming to the teaching of my Jesus, I see the rich man turned old by pleasure and Lazarus being full of youthful vigor as a reward.[91] I see winter armed with freezing ice that follows after autumn, turning from dew to rainy winds, from moisture to snowflakes, from clouds to snowfall, from torrential rain to snow, from floods, the major symptom of moisture, to an unbearable experience of drowning. I see all this. I cry and cry and I surrender myself uncontrollably to those who lament. Someone laughed in response to the crying man and contrariwise he [the crying man] cried in return. In the eyes of the naive, the goal is all the same. In the eyes of the intelligent, the similar goal is obvious. The one wept over what the other laughed about; and the man accused of what the crying man bewailed laughed at it loudly. The laughter and the lamentation of both were about the world and what is found in the world.

Festa, p. 34

12. But lo and behold! Having leaped over the seasons in which ordinary human life has been depicted <by me> in its customary ways, I have been carried up to another, unchangeable sort of nature. I see amid the things recounted that mistress and royal lady who is honored and renowned among immortal gods and mortals. She is Lady Philosophy herself. By having served her obediently, being her humble nursling from my early days, I have learned her mysterious secrets, which are still with me. Sometimes she leads me around the peaks of Olympus and reveals to me the movement of the stars. At other times she leads me through the

---

89 Echetos, the king of Epiros in Homer's *Odyssey*, and Phalaris, an ancient tyrant of Agrigentum in Sicily, were paragons of cruelty in Byzantium. The word ἐκκοπή means "mutilation," in addition to "cutting off," "pruning," and may allude to the Homeric description of Echetos (*Odyssey* 18.85–87) as a cruel ruler who favored punishment by mutilation.

90 The reference is to spurious letter by Phalaris to Pythagoras, which circulated in antiquity and Byzantium. See Hercher, *Epistolographi Graeci*, no. 23 (pp. 413–14). See also no. 74 (p. 428).

91 Based on the parable of the rich man and Lazarus in Luke 16:19–31.

air (for Olympus is the same as the sky)⁹² and shows me *phenomena* of *pits* and *jars*, and makes me understand *torches* and the rest.⁹³ She transports me to the damp nature of water, teaches me how the phases of the moon become and constitute life experiences, and closely examines the ebb and flow of tides,⁹⁴ and hemiplegia and apoplexy, which are the equivalent to *recurvation without cure*.⁹⁵ She brings me nectar and makes me drink, or rather, giving me ambrosia and nourishing me, she brings me to the marketplaces. After she places me there intoxicated with pleasure, she urges me to consider whether there is anyone who sells in a just way⁹⁶ dishes, garments, and delightful foods and drinks. Raising me, again, with bloodied hands from the butcher's shop, she leads me to the weaver's workshop, takes me aside, and questions me, saying: "Tell me, what do you see?" Observing that I do not know these things well, she teaches me: "See how the weaver steals, but another man steals the thief's way of thinking. For someone is already talking in front of the gate, measures the silk on the scales, sees the movement of the spindle, and considers the glitter of the gold." After she explains things sufficiently for me, she takes me to the stall of the silversmith and points out to me with her finger the metals, those used for welding and those for separating. And having shown me this well, she lifts me up to the bedchambers and shows me beds made of ivory. Bringing me close to the garments, she instructs me to look at their many-colored variety that is not ignoble.

After instructing me in many things, she adds an honor to the honor and takes me into her entourage. Leading me, she holds my head with five fingers. When I ask why she does not put the other hand on my head, she teaches me, proclaiming the following: "The five are what purify the five, and unless someone is purified through the five he cannot get engaged in other things nor can they occupy him." As I find all this enigmatic, I ask for an explanation. She then says the following: "There are five mathematical disciplines and five sciences, by which the eye of

Festa, p. 35

---

92 Cf. Pseudo-Aristotle, *De mundo* 400a8.

93 Terms for different comets used by pseudo-Aristotle, *De mundo* 395b10–13.

94 Cf. Pseudo-Aristotle, *De mundo* 396a25–28.

95 Deut. 32:24. This incurable disease is mentioned as a divine punishment in the Greek Septuagint version of the Song of Moses (it is absent from the Latin Vulgate). Galenic and Byzantine medical terminology is linked here with scripture.

96 A sale made "in a just way" (δικαίως) evokes the idea and ideology of a just price (δικαία τιμή). See Laiou, "Economic Thought and Ideology," 1132–34.

the soul is purified, having been purified earlier by the five <mathematical disciplines>, and by which the eye of the soul reaches perfection."[97] On the one hand, she says that I possess thanks to her "five" and "five," and, on the other, that five are not yet completely pure. Yet she moans as she speaks.

Then I ask her to teach me, and she says, adding one moan to another:

Where are the people who open their ears, the people who are prepared to see, the people whose sense of smell is sharp, and the people whose sense of touch is delicate?[98] After the arrival of old age, time is already rough: pleasure turns to bitterness, suddenly there are misfortunes. Where now are the bastard minds? The vision of hell's punishments is frightening. Where are the devotees of silliness and singing? Let them indulge themselves, for they will lament. Let them laugh, for they will be found guilty. Let them hold sway over others, for they will be overcome by fire. Let them taste of all the pleasures, for their experience will be to be deprived of all.

As she says this and groans, she trains me in the appropriate way.

13. Lo and behold! Thanks to her [Lady Philosophy], I focus my mind on what is important by sharpening the glance of my eyes and by making my soul's spirit spin near my intellect.[99] I rise up far and descend down with all my strength, and I cause my power of reasoning to turn around in a circle. As I gaze, I see a single coherence that controls everything through a single nature, an ungraspable and invisible nature, by which existent things have come to be out of nothing and thanks to which they persevere and are sustained. Just as no one who removes the heat from the fire will expect to allow this fire to continue, who will extract and turn away nature, and make nature to still dwell in nature? Its lordship is common over all things. It has been well stipulated in this regard that *three dimensions are*

Festa, p. 36

---

[97] Theon of Smyrna, *On Mathematics Useful for Reading Plato*, ed. Hiller, 15.11–14, attributes the five cathartic mathematical disciplines to Plato and specifies them as arithmetic, geometry, stereometry, music, and astronomy. The play on numerology continues in the following sentence and in the following paragraph, where the author refers to the five senses.

[98] That is, four of the five senses: hearing, vision, smell, and touch. The only one missing is taste.

[99] On the notion of the circular motion of the soul, see above, *Moral Pieces*, §1, p. 102, n. 3.

all there is and *that which is divisible in three directions is divisible in all*.[100] The statement has been formulated for a reason—namely, because it [nature] is both a triad and a monad, being one and three: the former by nature and the latter for reasons lying above and beyond nature. For it is above and beyond nature that three derived from one is found in one, because we have known that everything ends up by nature in a different kind of thing;[101] but with respect to things that are of the same kind, if each of them ends up in being consubstantial, they lie entirely beyond nature. I am facing the air, and ether lies in the emptiness, water above the air, and earth in the water. In whatever way you may turn everything over in your mind, you will find each and every thing cyclically resulting in something else. If you divide that into parts, you will not find the situation any different after doing so. There is not otherness in that nature—or rather in this nature (for the former phrase, "in that one," signifies faraway things, but the latter, "in this one,"[102] signifies a nearby or unifying nature). But this nature faces itself and is self-enclosed and of the same origin. She is perfective and regal vis-à-vis the universe.

As in the whole body the soul is present inside it as a whole, so God is present in everything in nature—not in a confused manner, but he is fully and always present in everything. He holds the universe together. He holds sway over the ends of the earth and no one else except for him wields kingly power. The person who is emperor reigns through him, and he who is his deputy[103] tyrannizes over the officials through him. Whoever rules over any single breathing soul has received the authority for this from him. Every creation continues to exist by his wish. Like the leader in a dramatic chorus, the helmsman in a boat, and the commander

---

100 See Aristotle, *On the Heavens* 268a9–10: διὰ τὸ τὰ τρία πάντα εἶναι καὶ τὸ τρὶς πάντῃ. The philosophical passage was used in a Trinitarian context by Nikephoros Blemmydes in a theological letter to Laskaris: *Oeuvres théologiques*, ed. Stavrou, 1:350.16–18.

101 The transformation of the elements is part of Aristotelian natural philosophy. See, e.g., Aristotle, *On Generation and Corruption* 334a16–334b31.

102 "In that one" (ἐκείνῃ) refers to "that nature" (ἐκείνῃ φύσει), which can be divided into parts, in contrast to the situation in "this nature" (ταύτῃ), which is unifying and regal.

103 "He who is his deputy" (ὁ δυναστεύων): as suggested by Andreeva, "Polemika," 10–11, this phrase probably refers to George Mouzalon in his capacity as chief minister or *mesazon*, a position known also ὁ παραδυναστεύων (Beck, "Der byzantinische 'Ministerpräsident,'" 310–20). Laskaris confesses above (§4, p. 140) his failure to introduce order among "the officials" (οἱ ἐν τέλει). Here, he presents his chief minister as being in charge of heavy-handed policies toward the officials.

arranging the battle order in the army, it is he who will put order into everything. Just as there is breath in any living body, he is in all of creation. Just as there is being in things existent, he is the Creator in being.

As regards perfection and constancy, I will say that he is the producer of everything, the distributor and the one who binds together, philanthropic and benevolent, all-powerful and almighty, perfective and generous, just and true, merciful and all-satisfying, powerful and full of pity, holy and heavenly, earthly and nonconfounded, situated in the middle and enclosing everything, revered and bestowing reverence, purifying and masterly, all things in all and container of things unsaid. What person who happens to encounter his illumination is truly not most blessed and, filling the cup of his soul with pleasure, will not live forever in happiness? To him belong jointly the power of wishing and the ability of acting. He sees that people living on earth do not think as he would wish, and yet he distributes his graces among them all: to some according to the measure of the virtue practiced by them, but to the rest he has mercy and forgives their mindlessness.

14. After having examined all these things with scientific knowledge and having gathered in myself the understanding of everything on its own, I came to recognize that understanding is twofold: the first is for pleasure and acquisition; the second is for pleasure alone. Hence there are many pleasures for me. As when someone enters the imperial treasury and gains a double fame with the things he takes, both through their splendor and acquisition, but in the case of the things that he does not take, he gains pleasure solely, as expected, because he is deprived of their possession—for he takes the former things to his own people, displays and enjoys them, while with regard to the latter [the thing seen in the treasury but not taken], he rejoices and delights in describing to his fellow men the pleasure alone derived from them—in like manner God has granted to the person who penetrates by divine will the affairs of life and investigates the world and things in the world.[104] Not all things are allotted to all, nor is an entire thing, whatever it is, allotted to every recipient of benefaction. But to one person one whole thing is allotted, to another person two whole things, and to another person ever more and more. For there is a great difference in the benefactions. God who has often bestowed on

Festa, p. 38

---

[104] The entry into the emperor's treasury for the purpose of deriving pleasure and obtaining gifts parallels a similar description of the riches made available by the emperor in the *Oration on Friendship and Politics*, §6, a work also dedicated to George Mouzalon.

us many benefactions added also knowledge that is raised high above all people, by which we have learned the things that are in the universe as they are by nature.

We dedicate to you this oration of ours that contains everything, because we know that you are honored with nobility of conduct, you are exalted in knowledge, you are adorned with excellent habits, and you shine with all the virtues all around. Wherever you cast well the net of your thoughts, you will draw out what I have taught you to draw. We consider the abiding and firm causes of your impulse in this direction to be your upbringing by us as well as our mutual loyalty and goodwill.

6

On What Is Unclear and a Testimony That the Author Is Ignorant of Philosophy

Explanation of the World, book 4

1. Since there are two leading terms, "the existent" and "the nonexistent"[1]—and as a consequence of them, "understanding" and "misunderstanding"—it is utterly necessary that, as a further consequence of them, there follows "knowledge"[2] and "ignorance," the former as a consequence following on the existent, the latter obeying an accidental thing, which is both nonexistent and unknown. Corresponding, then, to these aforementioned terms, namely knowledge and ignorance, there follows the profit of virtue. Knowledge follows on understanding, whereas the darkness of ignorance follows on misunderstanding. The end of knowledge is to know everything that is or exists, whereas ignorance dominates over misunderstanding, so that one can see neither existent things nor the properties of virtue.

Therefore, someone who pursues knowledge and truly perceives the reality of the existent things, as far as is possible, this person cuts by knowledge through ignorance and truly rises up toward being. But someone who is carelessly and crudely disposed to the understanding and truth of the existent things, and who will flood his mind with the darkness of ignorance in an ocean of misunderstanding, this

Festa, p. 39

---

1 On notions of "the existent" (τὸ ὄν) and "the inexistent" (τὸ μὴ ὄν), see above, p. 53.
2 "Knowledge" (ἐπιστήμη) corresponds to "understanding" (γνῶσις). The opposite of ἐπιστήμη is said to be ἀμαθία (ignorance), while the opposite of γνῶσις is ἀγνωσία (misunderstanding). Depending on the context, I have sometimes translated ἐπιστήμη as "scientific knowledge" and "science" in the Aristotelian sense: a superior knowledge based on demonstration from first principles (*Nicomachean Ethics* 1139b15–30; *Posterior Analytics* 71b10–15).

person, blinded by ignorance, is being carried along in a wretched way. Thus, those without affinity with virtue live in the worst way on the earth, whereas those, on the contrary, who cultivate virtue throughout their lives and who live by practicing it, they are truly acclaimed by everyone.

Festa, p. 40

2. What, then, shall I do? What on earth can I contrive, so that I can have my good share of fame without having any bit of knowledge in my mind? For those who look out for a recompense for their good deeds and who are engaged in a good manner with what is profitable come to enjoy the benefits at the right time, and they will take delight in the advancement of their virtue. But someone who is bereft of any advancement in virtue and who has not fully absorbed beforehand the fullness of knowledge, how would he have his share of fame? Or how would he deposit the fruits of virtue into his soul? For the knowledgeable person truly has knowledge and its possessor will truly possess abundantly, but someone who is deprived would not have a true understanding of all the things that have a real being.

For all these reasons I am well aware of the weakness coming from my ignorance and lack of knowledge, and I will use confession as a test.[3] Since I am devoid, so to speak, of everything and since I deliberately remove the veil over my deficiencies, I will be manifestly displaying to everyone my inner feebleness stemming from ignorance. In this way, in addition to my ignorance and lack of understanding, I will not be overwhelmed by lapsing into pride and pay double penalty as a truly unintelligent and unwise man.

3. For anyone who philosophizes has acquired a clear understanding of scientific knowledge; and having thus grasped it, he can indeed philosophize about the properties of existent things as they are by nature. He has recognized the divisions. He has recognized how he should express in a distinct manner the loud sound of his voice,[4] but also the genera and the specics, the proper and the accidental

---

3 The word ἔλεγχος, translated here as "test," means also "refutation." The author seems to exploit an ironic ambiguity. The learned descriptions of his supposed ignorance serve to test as well as to refute his claims of ignorance.

4 The wordplay here is notable. The word "voice" (φωνή) anticipates the five "voices" (φωναί), or predicables, listed later in the same sentence: species, genus, property, accident, and difference. These five predicables are a subject discussed in Porphyry's *Introduction*, known as the *Five Voices* (πέντε φωναί), to Aristotle's *Categories*. See also Th. L., *Ep.* 115.30–32 (p. 160).

On What Is Unclear

characteristics; and by mixing their differences in accordance with <the categories> that are ten in number,[5] he climbs on a ladder of greater perfection. He moves on from the possible propositions to those that are generally accepted, from the generally accepted to those that are truly necessary and unchanging,[6] both drawing up rules and syllogistically deriving in the three figures[7] through premises and conclusions what he deliberates about. In some places, by changing the matter in the premises and drawing out <a conclusion> from an impossible matter with an affirmative premise, he concludes about the nonexistent things as they are by nature.[8] For the *conclusion* always *follows from the weaker of the premises*.[9] In a similar fashion, he syllogistically derives generally accepted propositions from two matters, I mean from the possible and the necessary, as though setting up a mixture. Thus, by artfully implanting the uniqueness of the necessary matter, he concludes the most truthful proposition through the major and the minor premise.

Festa, p. 41

Such a person knows the forms of the arguments in order to make syllogisms artfully through induction. For by artfully shaping the inductive argument, he demonstrates that this is a sophistic syllogism regarding the issue at hand.[10] He knows the divisions, the corresponding demonstrations, and the artful conclusions resulting from them; the consequences and the concomitant circumstances; and how one should furnish premises. To put it simply, having grasped in knowledgeable fashion the rules, modes, definitions, matters, and figures of all these things, and having formed in his mind the precise knowledge of them, he discusses philosophically in the best way all the proper characteristics of nature.

---

5 Discussed in Aristotle, *Categories* (and listed in *Categories* 1b25–2a4).

6 The possible or the contingent (τὸ ἐνδεχόμενον), the accepted (τὸ ἔνδοξον), and the necessary (τὸ ἀναγκαῖον) are terms discussed in Aristotelian logic.

7 Discussed in the first book of Aristotle's *Prior Analytics*.

8 The "nonexistent things" (τὰ μὴ ὄντα) are defined in §1 as leading to ignorance and misunderstanding.

9 Themistius, *Quae fertur in Aristotelis analyticorum priorum librum, I: Paraphrasis*, ed. Wallies, 54.30–31; John Philoponus, *In Aristotelis Analytica priora commentaria*, ed. Wallies, 71.13–14.

10 Sophistic, or untrue, syllogisms are discussed in *On Sophistical Refutations* (see especially 169b, 171b). The author links the skill of logician with that of the rhetorician. The concept of the artful or artificial (τὸ ἔντεχνον) goes back to the discussion of proofs in Aristotle, *Rhetoric* 1355b35–39.

4. If someone lacks, just as I do, complete formation in all this, how would he discuss philosophically in the best way the properties of scientific knowledge? Or how would he deposit in his soul the perfection of virtue? For as I walk on the path of ignorance, I fear every day lest I should come across a man having a fair share of scientific knowledge. By arguing syllogistically in various ways with me, the unskilled one, he would cheat me because I am completely bereft of knowledge; and thus having met and cheated and ridiculed me, he will demonstrate that I am foolish in my thinking. For how would someone completely deficient in mathematics[11] become conversant with the *Organon*[12] of Aristotelian philosophy? This is why once upon a time the Platonic School bore the following inscription at the gate: *Let no one enter who does not know geometry!*[13] So if the inscription at the school of Plato is *Let no one enter who does not know geometry*, how will I dare touch the learning of Aristotle? For the works of the former stand apart from those of the latter. Hence, as I am lacking in both, I will never touch either of them.

5. But what can I say and utter, being bereft of mathematics? As I have not touched the knowledge of the *Organon*, how on earth could I have virtue in my soul? For who will enrich his soul with knowledge except someone who builds a bridge to his intellect through mathematics,[14] and having thus purified his soul's eye, rises from things on earth to those in heaven, guided through the bridge of mathematics? This is why the person scientifically trained in the axioms of mathematics truly possesses a bridge of understanding. Starting off from plane surfaces and expanding in height and length according to their ratio, he touches the most exalted matters. On the one hand, he calculates their proportional relationship <of height and length> with each other, and, on the other, arranging harmoniously and proportionately what comes from each, he fittingly assigns to both of them their

---

11 The author uses the word μαθήματα several times from this point on. Initially, he is referring to mathematics, but the concept also has the general meaning of "studies" and "learning."

12 The *Organon* was the name given to the six logical treatises of Aristotle: *Categories, On Interpretation, Prior Analytics, Posterior Analytics, Topics,* and *On Sophistical Refutations.*

13 David, *Prolegomena*, ed. Busse, 5.10–13; trans. Gertz, 87. See also Th. L, *Ep.* 121.19–20 (p. 168).

14 Mathematics had been discussed as a "bridge" to the intelligible world and the divine by the Neopythagorean author Nikomachos of Gerasa (*Introductio arithmetica* 1.3.6, ed. Hoche, 7.21–8.6) as well as in late antique philosophical schools (see David, *Prolegomena*, ed. Busse, 59.19–23; trans. Gertz, 143).

kindred nature; and through their ordering and union, he arrives at closest proximity to the movements of the stars.

The axiomatic principles in geometry are these: namely, to measure, fix, and make stable all figures. The axiomatic principles in arithmetic, *which is older than geometry*,[15] are to calculate the angles and frames of the figures, to assign proportionally to the figure parts of specific size, and to find terms for them. For as *quantity is double, that is, continuous and discrete*,[16] specificity about each is assigned in mathematics. In geometry, the continuous stays on forever and remains steady, but in arithmetic, which is older than geometry,[17] one finds the discrete. This being their mutual relationship as regards quantity, the former [the continuous] refers to the continuous quantity of a line and the latter [the discrete] refers to discreteness and numbering, and it gives the names to angles.

6. Hence, the relaxing character and intensity of sweetest music, the rhythm of the accented syllables,[18] the sizes of the figures, and the harmony of the lines constitute all the harmoniously assembled figures in mathematics. Where there is a line nine cubits in length—which is drawn out[19] as though in a triple segment and put together with another line drawn out in the same manner—it produces an oblong figure quadrilateral in shape.[20] The continuous linear extension (for this is the continuity of a line) is proper to geometry; the cubit being of a particular length is an axiomatic principle in arithmetic; the ability to make adjustment so as to form an oblong rectangle is, in fact, an eminently musical talent.

Festa, p. 43

Thus, all the figures are formed in a related way: the continuation of the continuous linear quantity comes from geometry; the terms for quantity and the best

---

15 Cf. Simplicius, *In Aristotelis Categorias commentarium*, ed. Kalbfleisch, 126.21–22 (ἔτι δὲ καὶ ἐκ τῶν ἐπιστημῶν, διότι, φασί, πρεσβυτέρα ἐστὶν ἀριθμητικὴ γεωμετρίας); Nikomachos, *Introductio arithmetica* 1.4.2–3, ed. Hoche, 9–10

16 Cf. Aristotle, *Categories* 4b20.

17 See n. 15 above.

18 Literally, "with accents on the last and the penultimate syllable" (ὀξύτονόν τε καὶ παροξύτονον).

19 Laskaris uses the verb γραμματίζω, from which derives the participle γραμματισθεῖσα, translated as "drawn out," with a meaning related to the noun γραμμή (line) rather than γράμμα (letter) as in the lexica. See LSJ and Lampe, s.v.

20 The description seems to be of two identical triangles that produce a parallelogram once they are connected.

proportions come from arithmetic (for first comes the number "three" and later the triangle is given shape); and from here, when it [arithmetic] is combined in a very musical fashion, as is necessary, with the figures and is joined to them by divine dispensation, all the figures harmoniously acquire shapes among themselves.

All these mathematical disciplines are like a ladder and bridge, as if drawing the mind away from the earthly and the material, and bringing it by an excellent and carefully devised progression near heaven; they unite the mind to the movements of the stars, cause it to mingle with them intellectually, and convince it to proceed smoothly and intelligently in its thoughts. For this reason, if the mind is enlightened by these more lofty sciences with real illumination,[21] it approaches divine theology as much as is possible. Hence, the man capable of scientific knowledge builds through mathematics a bridge over the obscurity of the divine concepts and easily traverses the earthly regions toward the intellectual and lofty ones.[22] For the drawn lines resemble wooden implements that, once they are professionally cut in a way characteristic of architecture, perform the function of the base of a bridge. The numbers are like nails that skillfully bind together and fix the junctures. Musical proportionality holds together, so to speak, the lines in a kind of harmony, impresses unitary patterns, and fittingly affixes them like *limbs and parts*[23] in the right proportion into a single breathing organism of the artfully designed product. As for the movements of the stars, they are like a panel presiding from on high and measuring the arithmetical, geometrical, and musical harmonic proportions.[24]

Festa, p. 44   Thus, when lines are harmoniously joined to each other in a natural relationship, and when both numbers and musical harmonies are put together proportionately and are well directed vis-à-vis the ordering of the stars, this mathematical

---

21   On the Neoplatonic notion of "illumination" (ἔλλαμψις), which was adopted by the early Greek church fathers and was discussed in Byzantine philosophy, see Ierodiakonou, "Rationality and Revelation," 27–32. Neoplatonic ideas of ascent of the soul permeate this section of the work.

22   On the author's view of the role of mathematics in theological discussions, see Angelov, *Byzantine Hellene*, 193–98.

23   For the word pair μέλη καὶ μέρη, often used by Greek authors, see, e.g., Plato, *Timaeus* 77a; Aristotle, *History of Animals* 486a.

24   Arithmetical proportion is based on addition and subtraction; geometrical proportion, on multiplication and division. On these and on harmonic proportion, see Nikomachos, *Introductio arithmetica* 2.22–26, ed. Hoche, 122–36.

On What Is Unclear

harmony is established as a truly divine bridge for the intelligent. Consequently, whoever acquires through scientific knowledge the understanding of these things in his mind moves beyond earthly matters as if approaching divine theology. But someone like me, whose motion of the soul is out of balance and whose intellectual eyes are blinded due to ignorance, how could he soar up to intellectual and exalted wonders and thoughts? For one comes to know what one fully understands, but one would not assign scientific and truthful rules to what he was never deemed worthy even of coming into contact with.

7. Since I am completely uninitiated in the abovementioned scientific teaching of Aristotle[25] and in the later lectures,[26] I will not observe rules that are unknown to me. But being inferior and more ignorant than men entirely uninitiated into science, I will follow a more humble path, one that leads me to instruction in prudence. Certainly, someone who wishes to learn can be taught what he lacks and the teacher pours out riches from his *good treasure*.[27] So let everyone who is ignorant like me of the properties of knowledge and understanding go to a teacher and learn them. No teacher will preside over the school of mathematics unless he has fully absorbed earlier the full range of learning on the subject with his entire mind. For the same reason, one should not appoint as generals men uninitiated into military practice lest they harm the army through their inexperience.

8. Who will ever say that a yokel can practice oratory, and who would encourage him at all to compose speeches for delivery within a set time frame[28]—a yokel who does not know how to give advice, how to get his tongue around words and make it pour forth refutations against arguments, how to plead at the law court against his opponents who contradict him, how to deliver a panegyric at oratorical contests? Whoever appoints this person <as a rhetorician> will automatically

---

25 A reference to the "knowledge (ἐπιστήμη) of the *Organon*," mentioned above at §5.

26 "Later lectures" (μετέπειτα ἀκροαματικοὶ λόγοι): the phrase is reminiscent of Aristotle's spurious letter to Alexander known to Laskaris, where ἀκροαματικοὶ λόγοι (literally, "discourses designed for hearing only") refer to Aristotle's treatises. See Hercher, *Epistolographi Graeci*, Ep. 6 (p. 174); Th. L., *Ep*. 125.44–46 (p. 175). The qualification of ἀκροαματικοὶ λόγοι as "subsequent," however, suggests that Laskaris may be envisaging commentaries on Aristotle.

27 Matt. 12:35; Luke 6:45.

28 Literally, "in relation to the water clock" (πρὸς ὕδωρ). On this proverbial expression, see above, *Satire of His Tutor*, §24, p. 87, n. 124.

concede the superiority of rhetoric. For tripped from both sides, the appointee will become tongue-tied and will ruin his speech along with his thoughts. An encomium will turn at once into a lament, a panegyric into an uncultured platitude, a counseling speech into the darkness and blindness of ignorance. To sum up, such a man will not be able to achieve anything at all in any way.

Festa, p. 45

Let the experts in the features of rhetoric explain in a clearer way all the rest— all that happens to be inappropriate for speech composition, all that is inapplicable to the figure of dialectical rhetorical argument,[29] all that concerns how and from where one should begin and in what way and how one should close his speech, all that concerns the formulations, the vivid descriptions,[30] the employment of detached phrases,[31] the impersonations,[32] all the simple language that will occur in elevated style,[33] all the inelegant things that will occur in the delineation of the circumstances[34] if these things are not written and spoken in the right sequence, and whatever else the experts deem both well-arranged and skillful. Namely, <the man falsely appointed as rhetorician> does not allegorically introduce a fable[35] at

29 "Dialectical rhetorical argument" (ἐπιχείρημα) is a type of argumentation laid out by Hermogenes, *On Invention* 3.5–9 (in *Opera*, ed. Rabe, 140–54). It was defined by Aristotle, *Topics* 162a16, as a dialectical syllogism in contrast to demonstrative syllogisms. Hence, it was seen in later centuries as appropriate for rhetoric, following Aristotle's views that the art of dialectic based on accepted opinions and common beliefs was characteristic of rhetoric. See Aristotle, *Rhetoric* 1354a, 1356a.

30 "Vivid descriptions" (διατυπώσεις) are discussed with specific examples by Alexander, *On Figures* 1.24, in Walz, *Rhetores Graeci*, 8:456.

31 For specific examples of the use of "detached phrases" (ἀποστάσεις) in rhetoric, see Hermogenes, *On Types of Style* 1.9, 10, in *Opera*, ed. Rabe, 267.101–2, 270.14–18.

32 "Impersonation" (ἠθοποιΐα) is a preliminary rhetorical exercise commonly practiced in late antique and Byzantine schools of rhetoric. See Hermogenes, *Progymnasmata*, no. 9, in *Opera*, ed. Rabe, 20–22.

33 The concept of the "elevated style" (δίαρμα) is mentioned by Hermogenes, *On Types of Style* 1.9, 2.9, in *Opera*, ed. Rabe, 264.17, 376.25–377.3.

34 On the six circumstances discussed in Hermogenes, *On Invention*, see above, *Satire of His Tutor*, §9, p. 66, n. 39.

35 The word μῦθος has many meanings, ranging from "word" (especially in Homer) to "story," "tale," "fable," and "fiction." The first preliminary rhetorical exercise in Aphthonios's and Hermogenes' handbooks on rhetorical compositions is called μῦθος: a fictional and morally beneficial fable, such as the fables of Aesop. See Hermogenes, *Progymnasmata*, no. 1, in *Opera*, ed. Rabe, 1–4; Aphthonios, *Progymnasmata*, no. 1, ed. Rabe, 1–2. Allegory and μῦθος converged in Byzantine interpretations of Homer. In the eleventh century John

a particular time and place, so that by making the narrated fable into an allegory and an example he would gain power through his persuasive speech, and so that he can magnify insignificant matters and play down lofty ones. For the special power of rhetoric truly boils down to this, magnifying and over-exalting the most insignificant among the lofty matters, and also sometimes completely belittling the more important among the things of lesser importance. And also <the man falsely appointed as rhetorician> does not vary the vocabulary with expert skill, nor does he know where to construct and where to cut and remove. Simply put, he lacks understanding of what we have said and recalled to mind. How would he speak as a rhetorician, even if someone will appoint him, and how would he take on the privileges of the rhetorical art without knowing its rules? But I know that even if he is appointed <as a rhetorician>, he fools himself in observing rules of what he has not grasped, just as has happened to me today.

9. Since I have not grasped the lessons of preliminary rhetorical training, have not felt the warmth of its fire, and have not been initiated earlier in its management or any sort of method or skill or practice, I am laying down laws unskillfully and unfittingly about what I never learned. However, I will speak the truth openly: I did not learn rhetoric, I did not learn poetry, I did not learn grammar.[36] How would someone advance to poetry who has not learned heroic verse, allegorical fable, ancient stories, and choice vocabulary? Those who know thoroughly the meter of heroic literature are capable of bringing this into proper order.[37] Fable dances allegorically among them on their tongues and in their minds, and choice and distinctive vocabulary keeps them company, and ancient stories will not run away from them. Because I am completely uninitiated into heroic thoughts and

Festa, p. 46

---

of Sardis, *Commentarium in Aphthonii Progymnasmata*, ed. Rabe, 10.3–9, gave an example from *Iliad* 1.197 (Athena seizing the son of Peleus by his fair hair is an allegory for the goddess capturing his mind). In the twelfth century, John Tzetzes composed allegorical interpretations of both the *Iliad* and the *Odyssey*, which would have been known to thirteenth-century learned audiences.

36 The comment is especially ironic for an accomplished author.

37 The meaning here is ambiguous because the verb ῥυθμίζειν, translated as "bring into proper order," has the connotations of both "teach" and "compose." See LSJ, s.v. This ambiguity runs through §10, where, in the context of grammar (below, p. 168), Laskaris refers to both "prescribing" and "composing" (κανονίζων τε καὶ λογογραφῶν).

devices of this kind and such importance, I prefer to maintain silence about them out of respect and affection.

10. The allegorizer ought to consider in what way the reconfiguring of tales that are told[38] matches whatever is his intention. Therefore someone who allegorizes at a later time, whether by nature or by convention,[39] should skillfully and poetically change what has been told earlier. Let the person who knows how to put all this together with a sure touch advance harmoniously to poetry. He [the allegorizer] will likewise research the interpretation of older works, provided that in his education from childhood he has focused his thoughts on books, has excerpted notes[40] from them, has treasured all this in his memory like gold, has frequented the doors of wise men as a hearer of their learned words, and possesses knowledge in his mind regarding the chance combination of all sorts of stories. Let him [the allegorizer] who has implanted in a fitting fashion the memory of earlier storytelling[41] into allegorical fiction[42] proceed naturally and harmoniously to

---

38 The translation of the phrase τὴν τῶν ἀγορευομένων λόγων μετάθεσιν as "the reconfiguring of tales that are told" takes into account the description of allegory in this passage as relevant to Homeric poetry, which recalls the allegorical interpretations of Homer by John Tzetzes and Eustathios of Thessaloniki. "Tales" is one of the many meanings of λόγος. Aesop was known as the λογοποιός (writer of fables) in antiquity and Byzantium. See Herodotus, *Histories* 2.134; John Doxapatres, in Rabe, *Prolegomenon Sylloge*, 154.12–14. Laskaris speaks of the allegory of fables (μῦθοι) and "new λόγοι" (ἡ τῶν μύθων εἴτ' οὖν τῶν καινῶν λόγων ἀλληγορία) in a letter commenting on a hymn composed by Demetrios Iatropoulos, an imperial official in Philadelphia. See Th. L., *Ep.* 140.2–3 (p. 197). The word μετάθεσις can refer to grammar ("metathesis" of sounds or syllables), rhetoric ("transposition" of an utterance to another speaker, as described by Phoebammon, *Scholia on Rhetorical Figures* 2, in Spengel, *Rhetores Graeci*, 3:52–53: περὶ μεταθέσεων), and methods of literary composition laid out by Dionysios of Halicarnassus, *On Composition* (see De Jonge, *Between Grammar and Rhetoric*, 367–90). On theories of allegory in the Greek literary tradition from late antiquity until the twelfth century, see Roilos, *Amphoteroglossia*, 114–30.

39 On "nature" (φύσις) and "convention" (θέσις) as philosophical principles of association, see above, pp. 53–54.

40 "Notes" (ὑπομνήματα): the sense here is that of learned notes or scholia, a meaning amply attested in Eustathios of Thessaloniki's twelfth-century commentaries on Homer and Dionysios Periegetes.

41 The expression τὴν πρώην ἱστορικὴν μνήμην is particularly puzzling. I take ἱστορική in connection with ἱστορίαι (stories) mentioned in the preceding sentence.

42 "Fiction" (μῦθος): the word refers here to a new allegorical composition, so "fiction" is preferable to "fable."

poetry. In a similar way, one ought also to know the choice vocabulary in the books of poets and tragedians, books in which heroic meter dances and takes shape. Let anyone who likes move ahead with them [the books] and let him, being intelligent and shrewd, pick out through laborious effort what would be beneficial from this gain. Drawing in this way on the segments and parts of the poetic arrangement, let him naturally and with joy obey the authority of the father of the *Iliad*.

Likewise, let people wishing to follow and practice the rules of the grammatical art consider what is by nature and what is by convention.[43] For they should observe the rules that it [grammatical art] has established with precision, even if someone will find without any trouble that through it [grammatical art] some things are both naturally prescribed and argued etymologically. For *sitos* [grain] has been called *sitos* from *seiesthai* [to be shaken]. Hence *krithe* [barley] too is shaken, and because both are shaken, both should have been called *sitos*. But the etymologies of words can never be interchanged, for wise men have established them by convention. *Tria* [three] is called among the disciples[44] of the arithmeticians *ateires* [stubborn] and *akataponetos* [inexhaustible], insofar as it is incapable of being split in two.[45] So every other odd number ought to have been called *trias* [triad] and *ateires* [stubborn], because it cannot be split in two, and so arithmeticians also do not divide up the monad. But since the number three is the first of the odd numbers and has acquired its own designation from etymology, and because the things argued etymologically are not interchangeable (for they have been established by convention), the number three takes first place among all the other numbers as *ateires* [stubborn], *akataponetos* [inexhaustible], and indivisible; it has fully assimilated in itself the name of the triad and holds on to this name in a permanent fashion, even if by convention. In a similar way, *ogdoas* [the number eight] is called *agodyas*[46] [I carry double], for when this is divided, it forms two

Festa, p. 47

---

43 See above, pp. 53–54.

44 For the rare meaning of παῖς as "disciple," see Lampe, s.v. The same meaning is encountered below, §13, p. 172: "the disciples of doctors" (ἰατρῶν παῖδες).

45 For this interpretation of the triad, see the Neoplatonic philosopher Iamblichus, *Theologoumena arithmeticae*, ed. de Falco, 18.9–11: ὅτι ὠνομάσθαι καὶ ταύτην τριάδα φασὶ παρὰ τὸ ἀτειρής τις εἶναι καὶ ἀκαταπόνητος· οὕτω δὲ λέγεται διὰ τὸ μὴ δύνασθαι αὐτὴν εἰς δύο ἴσα διαιρεῖσθαι.

46 On the designation of the number eight as ἀγοδυάς, see David, *Prolegomena*, ed. Busse, 54.5–19; trans. Gertz, 138.

in its parts, and therefore is called *agodyas*. Hence, any other number that forms two by division ought to have been called *agodyas*, such as the "six," the "four," the "twice eight," and similar numbers. But designations that have been and still are assigned by convention through etymology cannot at all be interchanged.

Therefore, let anyone wishing to dwell on the law of grammar first consider what comes by nature and what by convention in order to assign and arrange in the best way, both when prescribing and when composing, the rules and the terms, the declensions and the cases, the verbs and the adverbs, the pronouns, prepositions, and conjunctions, the steadfast observance in antistoichic matters[47]—and all the other things that have escaped my mind, whether by forgetfulness[48] or by ignorance. Having thus mastered the conventional power of all these, he will lay down the terms and rules of the grammatical art.

11. At present, I do not have precise knowledge of poetry, nor the established properties of grammar, nor the sense of the sonorous beauty and rhythm of rhetoric, nor the harmonic knowledge of mathematics, nor do I have a vague idea of the lofty Aristotelian knowledge. So how will I be able to rise to the level of being? I am truly bereft of all this and, being like a body lacking the corporal organs the five senses, I am mentally blinded, so to speak, in understanding discursive and intellectual sciences. I have thus been truly alienated from all knowledge and likewise from all understanding. For those with accurate understanding of things come to know them, but people whose uncertain understanding completely holds them in its grip, as is with me, will encounter what happens to me daily owing to my ignorance.

12. Indeed, as I said, I am truly bereft of everything, not only of philosophical arguments as well as arguments deriving from and resembling them, and those beyond them, but also of matters in which I received an active role by fortune. For God has entrusted me, even if unworthily, with governing in a top position of rule,

---

47 Namely, in matters of spelling involving homophone vowels and diphthongs. Riddles and humorous compositions with antistoichic words were the basis of schedography, as it emerged in the eleventh century and evolved in the twelfth. For a diachronic introduction to schedography and its contexts, see Nousia, *Byzantine Textbooks*, 49–92. On the twelfth century, see Efthymiadis, "L'enseignement secondaire à Constantinople"; Agapitos, "Grammar, Genre and Patronage in the Twelfth Century."

48 Forgetfulness (λήθη) implies knowledge, not ignorance, and underscores the author's irony.

as it best pleased him. Yet I did not learn how to put into practice the characteristics of the best virtue of government but am completely ignorant of its understanding and practice. These are the characteristics of the ruler:[49] (1) truth, (2) zeal, (3) mildness, (4) patience, (5) peaceable speech, (6) serenity, (7) absence of anger in the expression of his face, (8) forbearance, (9) generosity (which is more important than everything else), (10) steadiness, (11) a probing mind, (12) philanthropy, (13) goodness, (14) magnificence, (15) vehemence, (16) practical wisdom, (17) bravery, (18) justice, (19) moderation.

(1) Truth, so that he can separate appearance from reality;[50] (2) zeal, so that he can consume without partiality the growth of wickedness by the fire of most powerful authority; (3) mildness, so that he can pass judgment mildly on the wrongdoer; (4) patience, so that he will not pass sentence on the examined defendant before the trial; (5) peaceable speech, so that the subjects will consider and praise his voice as the voice of God; (6) serenity[51] in the expression on his face, because the loftiness and dignity of rulership naturally inspire fear (for should the eye[52] of the ruler take on a sterner appearance, the flock will truly tremble by the cliff edge and he would seem like a wild beast rather than a shepherd and teacher); (7) absence of anger,[53] so that even the wrongdoer can easily reform, the sinner can be called back, and the person drawn to vice would not be tormented by despair; (8) forbearance, so that even when chastising he will not give up on the chastised man as a hopeless case (for if forbearance is innate in the ruler and if he is generous while chastising, the chastised person—at once chastised and

---

49 These characteristics, or virtues, represent Laskaris's own views about the good and efficient ruler. Only some of the nineteen virtues also appear in the admonitory text on kingship, *Imperial Statue*, written by his teacher Blemmydes; parallels are indicated in the notes. The three royal virtues placed at the beginning—truth, zeal, and mildness—are those whose importance the author had already stressed in the imperial encomium on his father John III Vatatzes. See Th. L., *Op. rhet.*, 26.72–73, 50.615–18. Significantly, it is only at the end of the list of nineteen virtues that the four cardinal virtues appear: practical wisdom, bravery, justice, and moderation.

50 On the author's understanding of "truth," see Angelov, *Imperial Ideology*, 243–45.

51 Blem., *Imperial Statue* 35, 59–60 (pp. 54, 60–61).

52 Literally, the "lamp" or "light" (λύχνος). The "lamp of the body" (λύχνος τοῦ σώματος) is the eye in Matt. 6:22. On a similar reference to a stern (βλοσυρός) expression of the eyes, see *Oration on Friendship and Politics*, §6, p. 123.

53 Blem., *Imperial Statue* 34–48 (pp. 54–58).

Festa, p. 49 generously treated—will ungrudgingly put his own mind in a state of forbearance for the ruler); (9) generosity,[54] so that everyone who is strengthened and overjoyed by the cheerful effects of his charity[55] will deify the ruler as second in rank <after God> by God's grace—for to be charitable and generous to the subjects is an act of imitation and a characteristic feature of God; (10) steadiness, so that he cannot be dragged into injustice through deceiving words, nor will he lose his courage in wartime, being as if blown away by the wind, but, with unwavering steadiness of mind, he will turn to flight his seditious enemies;[56] (11) a probing mind, so that mixing it with his zeal, he will not favorably receive a party in a trial; (12) philanthropy, so that recognizing the failings of <human> nature and its afflictions, he can in fact expand his love of humanity to cover a wider scope; (13) goodness, so that the designs of the general public that do not gape at materiality can be proclaimed to be good;[57] (14) magnificence, which is especially appropriate for the ruler, so that he will not debase the entire body politic through trivialities with well-spoken words; (15) vehemence, so that in every way and every place he is committed to his own allotted duty, being utterly unbreakable like a diamond; (16) practical wisdom, because the ruler is entrusted with acting for the benefit of the people; (17) bravery, so that he can crush most bravely the force of pleasures, and also so that he can overcome with his bravery and steadfastness the attacks of the enemies; (18) justice, so that he can place in the judgment of his intellect the matters of government and the polity as well as the powers and qualities of all public affairs without exception, and can measure them as if with a balance and ruler, and can discern their essential characteristics and properties for *the preservation of the whole*;[58] (19) moderation, so that he can disregard as a spider's

54 Blem., *Imperial Statue* 69, 88 (pp. 64, 69).

55 The virtue of charity (ἔλεος) is particularly relevant to Nicaea, for Theodore II's father, the emperor John III Vatatzes, was remembered for his almsgiving and, by 1264, he was venerated as St. John the Almsgiver (ὁ ἐλεήμων). See Macrides, *George Akropolites*, 57–58, 277, n. 27.

56 A wordplay on two meanings of the word στάσις, "steadiness" and "sedition."

57 The manuscript reading μὴ πρὸς ὕλην βλέποντα τοῦ κοινοῦ is preferable to μὴ πρὸς ὕλην ῥέποντα τοῦ κοινοῦ suggested by Festa. For comparanda, see *Th. L.*, Ep. 1.3–4 (p. 1): ἐπειδὴ πρὸς τὴν ὕλην οἱ πλείους βλέπουσι, καὶ διὰ τοῦτο αὐτοὶ ὁρῶσι τὰ ὑλικά; Ep. 193.1–2 (p. 239).

58 Exactly the same expression, συντήρησις τῆς ὁλότητος, is found in Blem., *Imperial Statue* 4 (p. 44).

web the earthly and unstable aspects of material pleasure, because they will dissolve and change in a short time. All these [characteristics] are there in order that he be in the image of his most exalted Lord.

13. Even though I am designated with the name of all these [virtues] and say that I rejoice in their actions, I am carried along in ignorance by my lack of clarity. For whoever knows the rules and laws of those principles that we mentioned above, he is the person fit to govern. Someone like me, who is capable neither of observing the rules, nor putting them into practice, nor teaching them, such a man is indeed unfit to govern. *Festa, p. 50*

What an amazing thing! Along with my position as ruler, I am deprived of the position of general, for I completely lack knowledge of how to arrange the army in formation, or how to accomplish brave exploits in battle. Having mixed the distinctive characteristics of the general with those of rulership, I have nonetheless alienated both far from my soul. For the general, virtue consists of arranging the army in good battle order, skillfully adjusting the infantry formation, marching in security, instilling brave spirit into the troops, filling their souls with courage, foreseeing what may occur, taking a risk when called for, occasionally taking precautions, threatening from far afield, not pulling back when approaching the enemy, persevering when engaged in fighting, avoiding by all means conceit when winning, emboldening the zealous comrades when defeated. The general should surpass the rest in his hard work and should have courage in his soul, versatility in his tongue, and a hand ready, so to speak, to act with greatest generosity.

The person who mixes and combines all that benefits the ruler as well as the general, and who adorns, so to speak, his soul, he is truly a ruler and a general. But I am sad and downcast, as I am lacking in all these. In addition, I am bereft of simple military abilities, for I am incapable of mounting a horse easily, galloping speedily, and riding well. I do not know how to manage a lance and shield skillfully, nor do I know how to fit a quiver full of arrows into a bow and shoot. I cannot turn when riding, nor bend when jumping, nor whirl around as one should, nor mount without a saddle, nor set my ankles in motion, even if this happens to be the most enjoyable of all;[59] nor can I move, spin, throw, turn, lift, pass, suspend, return, shoot, and hold the little ball, and the other things that men eminently fit

---

59 "Setting the ankles in motion" (κινῆσαι σφυρά) appears to be a proverbial expression for a running exercise. See above, *Oration on Friendship and Politics*, §6, p. 123.

for military life practice with diligence in this beloved gymnasium;[60] nor can I lie persistently in ambush in the woods, nor do I know how to fire missiles, shooting them up from the flank around the army formation, nor how to move stealthily, nor am I able to march a full day and a full night with diligence.

Festa, p. 51

As I simply do not have any faint idea of these things and of things I have hesitantly left out <of my account>, I am harmed in my soul; and what is extraordinary, I do not know at all how to be useful in ruling, nor do I possess the characteristics of a subject. Anyone wishing to rule has knowledge of letters and devotes himself to laws and practices virtue—first, in order to reject with demonstrative arguments the sophistic and false bits <of reasoning>, and to wisely shepherd the flock with similarly intelligent counterarguments, and second, in order to rule lawfully and philosophically through virtue by forming a mixture of law and wisdom in his soul. Hence, as I am incompatible with the law and with letters, I do not have an understanding of government. Since I carry in my soul so much resentment, I am neither a ruler nor a subject. Due to inexperience on the one hand and due to my cantankerous mind on the other, I am consequently bereft of everything. I am bereft of the virtue of a general and a ruler, and of that of a soldier, and of the simplest and easily obtainable virtue, of letters and legal knowledge, of grammar and poetry, of rhetorical versatility and of the four higher disciplines,[61] of the argumentation and instruction of Aristotle, and his natural philosophy and doctrine, and of all the virtues—all the universal and all the particular ones—and, simply put, of all matters and methods altogether.

In this way, deceitful pleasure drags me down every day and I dance in the land of delusion as an ignorant man. As I am not conversant with the science of medicine, I thus dwell in ignorance like an incurably sick man. The disciples of doctors destroy with protective remedies illnesses caused by poison, give nourishment at the right time, feed with what is most beneficial, turn away what tends to destroy and corrupt the patient; they apply revulsions <of the humors>, drawings

---

60 The action related to the ball is a description of the game of polo. "This beloved gymnasium" seems to refer to a specific polo ground where the author practiced. The use of the vernacular verb γυρίζω is worth noting. Interestingly, Blem., *Imperial Statue* 128 (p. 84), criticizes polo as a useless distraction that does not lead to the development of military skills. George Pachymeres confirms that polo and jousting were favorite pastime for the Nicaean elite: see *History* 1.21, 2.9, ed. Failler, 1:95.8–12 (in Magnesia), 147.20–21 (in Nicaea).

61 That is, the so-called quadrivium: arithmetic, music, geometry, and astronomy.

On What Is Unclear

out,[62] amputations, salves and unguents, potions and plasters, and they urge exercise but also skillfully prescribe rest (for it is clear that inactivity is something helpful at the right time). When they explain and carry out all this in this way, they indeed make the ill body recover. But as I am incurable in my soul and have not touched this medical knowledge, I am sick like a truly unintelligent and ignorant man. And I would never elevate myself, given the uncertainty in my mind about life's affairs, about studies, arguments, and actions.

Festa, p. 52

14. What an amazing thing! Although I am crowned by the hand of God with independence and although I am good by my specific nature and am honored by the Word with the faculty of reason, I am bereft of reason through my ignorance and do not know the truth. Lack of understanding and clarity regarding studies and knowledge are the offspring of inexistence, but understanding and knowledge along with virtue are the offspring of the existent and good. But I will say something else. Reason is the *talent*[63] <of the scriptural parable>. Someone who buries and hides it in the comfort of his ignorance will undergo punishment in the fire <of hell>, but the person who invests it excellently in studies and knowledge will gain the kingdom above. As a matter of fact, every truly divine soul that has been permeated earlier in its parts with knowledge will take delight in a regal manner in the divine doctrines, for the glory of Christ, the first Word, Creator and God, for the divine praise of the Father, and for the worship and veneration of the all-holy Spirit.

---

62 The plural noun καθελκύσεις has a medical meaning that is hard to identify. The word is encountered in the singular in the *Moral Pieces*, §9, p. 109, and n. 24: ὡς ἐν καθελκύσει (as on a scale).

63 Matt. 25:14–30.

7

Oration on Hellenism

Book 7 of *Christian Theology, Second Oration against the Latins, or On the Procession of the Holy Spirit,* by the wisest emperor, lord Theodore Doukas Laskaris, composed after the full completeness[1] of his imperial rule.

1. The force that comes forth out of the Father and God, which has given completion to the edifice created by the Son of God, introduced order in the best way. Having first instituted full completeness[2] in the inanimate world, this [the Spirit] then also established the order of animate beings; and having by division settled the form of each one, it separated the reasoning from the unreasoning beings and ordered them in the best possible way; then, having set apart in rich variety the many-waved sea, it shaped it in infinite ways, giving a section to the land with its narrow strips, from there forming gulfs and bays. And once the different climate zones[3] were separated one by one, it spread out among them the

---

1 On "full completeness" (ἐντελέχεια) being a reference to the accession of Laskaris as the sole emperor in November 1254, see above, p. 130, n. 1.

2 The word, again, is ἐντελέχεια, as in the heading of the oration.

3 The phrase "climate zones" (κλίματα), literally "climes," is a key concept in Laskaris's Hellenocentric theory (on this theory, see below, §§3–7; on its ancient sources, see below, p. 177, n. 8). In the Ptolemaic scientific tradition, the seven climes (κλίματα) refer to circles of constant geographical latitude in the Northern Hemisphere defined by the longest day of the year. For a Byzantine summary, see Symeon Seth, *Conspectus rerum naturalium*, ed. Delatte, 24–26. Fascinated by the beneficial and adverse effects of climate on human nature, Laskaris was instead influenced by the ancient concept of the five climate zones (ζῶναι): two temperate climate zones (one in the Northern and one in the Southern Hemisphere), two frigid climate zones (again, one in the Northern and one in the Southern Hemisphere), and a torrid zone around the equator. The theory is developed in Aristotle's *Meteorology*

wise animal, the human kind, and filled with it [the human kind] the whole of the life-bearing earth (that distinct from the uninhabitable), in all its length and breadth, along the perimeter of the boundary and within the intervening land, as was appropriate.

2. With the earth containing the human kind in its regions, atmospheric changes—arranged throughout it according to the positions of the climate zones <and> the degree of proximity of the heavenly lights—brought about temperate climates and the opposite climates, as well as qualities of their mean. On this basis, the Intellect, the first cause of all,[4] caused the minds of human beings to be altered through the generation of quality and set into motion the qualities of peoples in accordance with their distance from the heavenly lights and the closeness to opposite regions—namely, those belonging to the temperate zone and its opposites. For those living in the North were fitted in one way by temperament, those in the South in another way, those in the areas around the North and South, and those in the East and in the West, in yet another; also different were those living along the coast and different again were those inhabiting islands. Then, according to the configuration vis-à-vis the extremes and the mean, he established the extent and adoption of skills,[5] wisely managing these matters, and through the setting of the quality of the regions of habitation, he introduced naturally clever and rougher dispositions. The capacity for knowledge and craftsmanship <comes into being> by the power of the configuration, and from these a best kind of understanding accumulates among people who wish to labor.

---

and elaborated by later authors. For a summary from Laskaris's circle based on ancient sources, see Nikephoros Blemmydes, *Epitome physica* 28.14–20, in PG 142:1273–77; George Pachymeres, *Quadrivium*, ed. Tannery, 376.20–34.

4 "The Intellect, the first cause of all" (πρωταίτιος νοῦς) is an epithet of God in Laskaris's *On the Divine Names*. See Th. L., *Chr. theol.* 4, 101.77–78. The idea is derived from Neoplatonic cosmology. See O'Meara, *Platonopolis*, 37–38, 42, 45, 51–52. On a similar expression of Neoplatonic origin, the "first intellects" (οἱ πρῶτοι νόες), meaning the angels in a Christian context, see above, *Moral Pieces*, §1, p. 101 and n. 2.

5 The theme of the invention and adoption of "skills" (τέχναι), that is, craft knowledge, is continued in §5, below.

3. Indeed, among the people of all languages,[6] the Greek stock is superior in its position and temperate climate,[7] and therefore in its natural intelligence and scientific knowledge.[8] This is so because the endless currents of the Sea of Marmara, the Black Sea, the Adriatic Sea, and the Gulf of Sicily[9] encircle and flood everything in the middle. Facing the North, the Adriatic Gulf, which is cut off to the South by Naupaktos and Epidamnos,[10] and which flows alongside Dalmatia, raises its neck above all of Mysia and Scythia. The Sea of Crete[11] mixes its waves via the Hellespont with the Sea of Marmara and extends the currents of its waters into the Black Sea. On one side, it surrounds the entire Peloponnese, Thrace, Byzantium, and Scythia Minor as far as the Don River, being overhung by the enclosed arm[12] of the Adriatic Sea. It [the Sea of Crete] flows thither as if in a straight line along the entire Doric and Ionic shore, the Hellespont, and Bithynia, but also along the whole of the Pontic shore as far as Sebastoupolis,[13] having as the beginning of its

---

6 "Among the people of all languages" is a periphrastic translation of ἁπασῶν γλωσσῶν (lit., "among all tongues"). Laskaris notably uses the word "tongues" (γλῶσσαι) in an ethnic sense, a rare usage attested in the Old Testament. See Isa. 66:18; Dan. 3:4; Jth. 3:8. In a linguistic tradition neighboring the Greek, the same semantics is commonly found in Old Church Slavonic, where the noun ꙗзꙑкъ was a translation for both γλῶσσα and ἔθνος. See Miklosich, *Lexicon*, s.v.

7 The Greek word for "temperate climate" (εὐκρασία) can also mean "good temperament," as it does below in §4.

8 Laskaris revives the Hellenocentric theory based on climatic determinism of Aristotle's *Politics* 1327b20–36. On ancient climatic determinism, see also Herodotus, *Histories* 3.106; Plato, *Timaeus* 24c; Hippocrates, *Airs, Waters and Places* 12.

9 Synonymous with the Sea of Sicily. See Eustathios, *Commentary on Dionysios Periegetes*, in Müller, *Geographi Graeci Minores*, 2:236.22–24.

10 Epidamnos is the ancient name of Dyrrachion (Durazzo, Durrës).

11 "The Sea of Crete" (τὸ Κρητικὸν πέλαγος) is roughly the Aegean Sea, although Laskaris gives a notably more expansive definition of this body of sea water. The geographical term is found in ancient authors (e.g. Thucydides, *Histories*, 4.53.3; 5.100.1) and is discussed by Eustathios, *Commentary on Dionysios Periegetes*, in Müller, *Geographi Graeci Minores*, 2:233.40–234.12, 237.3–12.

12 The word τράχηλος (neck) used several times in this paragraph has the rare meaning of "arm of the sea" or "gulf." See George Pachymeres, *History* 6.25, ed. Failler, 2:623.2 (Gulf of Nicomedia).

13 Sebastoupolis is present-day Sukhumi.

currents the entirety of Rhodes, the island of the Colossus.[14] From there, gushing mightily toward a bulging bay, it washes past the Syrian land, forming a sort of arm of the sea, which does not connect Cilicia and Iberia.[15] For a distance of about ten or more days remains from Trebizond to Tarsus.[16] Next, the rush of waters, lakes, and rivers flows into the two arms of the sea, which are hardly anything substantial in comparison with the entirety <of the sea>. The massive quantity <of water> of the Don, of the Sava and the Danube Rivers, and of countless streams flows into one arm of the sea. The currents of the Tigris and the Euphrates Rivers rushing toward the Syrian Gulf from the East flood owing to their proximity the other arm.[17] And also the currents from the Halys River[18] and others rivers pour into the Black Sea, completely watering and flooding it.[19]

---

14 The edition prints the text ἐκ Ῥόδου καὶ Κολοσαῖας ὅλης. Note, however, the manuscript reading Κολασσαῖας in Vat. gr. 1113, fol. 92r (Κολασαῖας in Barocci 97, fol. 78r). Κολασσαῖας derives from Κολασσαί, an alternative form of Κολοσσαί—namely, the ancient town Colossae in Asia Minor. The location poses a problem of interpretation. The Colossae known from Paul's epistle lay near Chonai along the Lycus River (a major tributary of the Maeander) and was in ruins in the Middle Ages. Laskaris was certainly thinking here of the island of Rhodes. Indeed, Colossae (Κολοσσαί) was sometimes used as another name for Rhodes, for the Colossus of Rhodes, one of the seven wonders of the world, was remembered in the Middle Ages as a famous historical feature of the island. See the eighth-century commentary on the poems of Gregory of Nazianzus by Kosmas of Jerusalem, *Commentary*, ed. Lozza, 226: Ἄγαλμα δέ ἐστιν ὁ ἐν Κολοσσαῖς τῇ λεγομένῃ Ῥόδῳ χαλκὸς ἀνδριάς. *Souda*, rho 205 (ed. Alder, 4:297), states that the inhabitants of Rhodes are known as Κολοσσαεῖς. The English pilgrim Saewulf, who traveled to the Holy Land in 1102–1103, fell for this misidentification when, after mentioning the ancient Colossus on Rhodes, he wrote that "it was to these Colossians that the blessed Apostle Paul wrote an epistle." The same error crops up in the fourteenth-century imaginary travels of John Mandeville. See *Saewulf*, trans. Brownlow, ed. Rogers, 4, 33; Mandeville, *Travels*, trans. Moseley, 54.

15 "Iberia" here refers to Georgia. On "Greater Iberia" (the Iberian Peninsula), see below, §5 and n. 25.

16 This specific piece of information suggests that on this occasion the author relied on oral information provided by contemporary travelers or their lost itineraries.

17 The two "arms" (τράχηλοι) of the sea refer, respectively, to the Black Sea and the Persian Gulf. The geographical term "Syria" as used in Byzantine texts can mean both Greater Syria and the core Abbasid areas in Iraq. See Durak, "The Location of Syria."

18 The Kızılırmak River in Asia Minor.

19 Reading περικλύουσαι (flooding) as in Vat. gr. 1113, fol. 92v, rather than περικλείουσαι as in Barocci 97, fol. 74v, and the edition.

4. It follows from this that the whole of Greece abounds in <fresh> water and in sea water.[20] Hence something wondrous happens. All the shores are covered with countless fields in their thousands of thousands and the leaves of the olive trees are more than the sands. This is another proof of the mildness of the atmosphere. For even if other lands possess flowing waters, yet they do not have such a great quantity of them, nor are they situated in the middle of the climate zones. That is why they benefit insufficiently from the cause of temperate climate and are insufficiently temperate. Only the land of the Greeks, by having the most central position in the climate zones and the fine air of sea waters, enjoys the mildest atmosphere. Thanks mostly to these, they [the Greeks] enjoy health in their bodies. Thanks to this well-being, they have natural intelligence[21] that eliminates any general tendency to wateriness, yet it introduces moisture by removing dryness. For the dampness of the sea waters gently dries and gently moistens, producing a good temperament. In this manner, the golden mean[22] of good temperament belongs to the Greeks. In this manner, the golden mean of good bodily condition is theirs. In this manner, the treasure of natural intelligence is theirs. By possessing the finest quantity of natural intelligence as an ornament from nature and by coming into contact later with the rather circular features of their location,[23] they are crowned with the garland of knowledge and understanding.

5. For the Greek people lie in the middle of all the limits of the inhabited world. It is well known that a skill originally conceived in a random place has been gathered—and is always gathered—among them by means of their central location. From the minor practical skills, greatest scientific knowledge has arisen. They [the Greek people] have like all others the capacity to invent on their own, but they possess an inalienable private treasure coming from their central location. Something like this happens because the impulses from the extremities meet in the middle if

---

20 The proximity of the Greeks to the sea was already noted by Aristotle, *Politics* 1271b34–35.

21 The εὐφυΐα of the Greeks is henceforth mentioned on several occasions. The abstract concept can mean "natural goodness," "good disposition," and "cleverness." I have consistently translated it as "natural intelligence," which corresponds to Laskaris's argument about the development of philosophy among the Greeks.

22 A translation of τὸ μέσον, following the Aristotelian concept.

23 The puzzling expression is soon explained through the circular diagram (fig. 2) in the following section (§5).

there is an outgoing movement. What do I mean? Let the letters on the diagram serve us: nu = Britain; omicron = Aornis;[24] lambda = Greater Iberia;[25] kappa = Egypt (Fig. 2). If some skill transfers, the gamma has been moved from nu to omicron (= Aornis) via alpha (= Greece[26]) or vice versa, from omicron through alpha to nu (= Britain); again, from lambda (= Iberia) it would go through alpha (= Greece) as far as kappa, or from kappa (= Egypt) through alpha (= Greece) as far as lambda. This is the complete move. But a partial move is like this: gamma has moved from nu as far as alpha, or from omicron as far as alpha, or from lambda as far as alpha, or from kappa as far as alpha. This is a partial move. Since the complete moves of skills pass through alpha to the limits, but the partial moves come from the limits to alpha, the accumulation of a skill in alpha is high in terms of its constancy and rapidity. Thus, the fullness of all knowledge lies in alpha, first because the gamma that comes from nu going to omicron does so via alpha, and second because what comes from nu goes as far as alpha: the former as a complete move and the latter as a partial move. Therefore, alpha is receiving in perpetuity what goes to the limits, and all the more rapidly, since the movements first pass via it and then are carried on to the other points. When the gamma has moved from nu and has passed through alpha and has settled in omicron, then the gamma is common to both the alpha and the omicron; nevertheless, because of its passage across the intervening space, it is more powerfully present in alpha. When the gamma moves from nu to alpha, then it belongs not to omicron but only to the alpha. In many ways Greece abounds in knowledge because of its middle position <in the inhabited world>.

6. Therefore, as it [Greece] is superior thanks to being surrounded by sea waters and to gathering the golden mean, it develops reason to the highest degree—first, because of its natural intelligence, for thanks to the temperate climate it enjoys abundant natural intelligence, and second, because of its position, for it possesses an assemblage of skills, the fruit of scientific knowledge. So natural intelligence and scientific knowledge are the finest among the Greeks, and it is

---

24 A mythical tall mountain in India near the shore of the Indian Ocean. See Dionysios Periegetes, *Description of the Known World*, l. 1151, ed. Lightfoot, 256 (text), 500 (commentary).

25 "Greater Iberia" (Ἰβηρία μεγάλη): "greater" is in contrast to the other Iberia, namely, Georgia (see §3 above).

26 The designation of Greece in §5 and §6 is ἡ Ἑλληνίς, whereas in the beginning of §4 Laskaris uses the concept of τὸ Ἑλληνικόν.

Oration on Hellenism

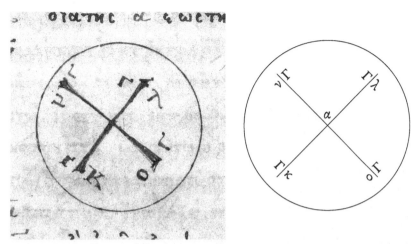

Figure 2. Theodore II Laskaris's diagram explaining the accumulation of knowledge in Greece. (a) As drawn in Barocci 97, fol. 80r (fifteenth century). Photo courtesy of the Bodleian Libraries, Oxford University. (b) Modern reconstruction. Drawing by the author.

from them that intellectual bliss has come to blossom. A long time ago among the Greeks the intellectual rivers were flowing in abundance upon the mortals, who were amply irrigated by the water of reason and poured out gold-flowing streams in all sorts of ways. And the more Greece flourished with all that was most divine and intellectual and the more it adopted from others[27] things of greater substance, the more it advanced to what was purer and clearer.

7. Here, Socrates produces philosophy, and Plato produces theology in a rhetorical fashion, enunciating in myths the former's philosophical thoughts. The Stagirite [Aristotle] discusses nature, learnedly putting logic into order, and transfers numbers out of chaos into quality, clarifying their unseen power in an immensely powerful way.[28] Pythagoras, who rises above matter, inclines toward learning and has been judged supreme over all for having discovered the principles in his intellect. Thales is the inventor of geometry, Euclid is the author of the

---

27 That is, from non-Greeks.

28 The reference is probably to the discussion of the Pythagoreans in the first book of Aristotle's *Metaphysics* (985b23–986b2).

Elements, with his connections with the great Theon,[29] and Ptolemy's astrological expositions[30] describe circular motion; the nobility of harmony is tuned thanks to the subtlety of the latter's mind. The beauty of letters is rhetoric, and to whom do Demosthenes, Hermogenes, and their followers belong? Poetry is a wonderful thing, and who is equal in rhythm with Homer? Medicine is a humane thing, and whence come Hippocrates and Galen? Which among the nations has studied grammar?[31] For a language by its vocabulary drives away arrogance, bearing witness to its own proof. I wish to say that theology, too, is Greek and that the Stagirite establishes the principles.[32] Proclus is a teacher of the elements[33] and together with him the godlike Plotinus. Prognostication, augury, and palmistry come from Calchas, and likewise from Adamantios[34] and Apollonios.[35] Divine signs are from Laurentios.[36] As for the astrological art of the observers <of heaven>, as for the *Data*,[37] the *Conica*,[38] the *Pneumatica*,[39] and the *Cylindrica*,[40] to whom do they belong other than Theon, Euclid, Apollonios, and Heron? Along with these, the art of magic and the practical skill of the secret philosophy[41] derive from Pythagoras. Indeed, all philosophy and knowledge, not to mention by name the sciences, are either the discovery of the Greeks or their improvement from something else; and

29 Theon of Smyrna (fl. 100 CE; see above, p. 72, n. 67) lived four centuries after Euclid.

30 The word διαθεματισμός is a hapax derived from διάθεμα (dispositions of the stars at the time of one's birth). The author has in mind Ptolemy's *Almagest*.

31 I have preferred to read the sentence as a question.

32 Aristotle, *Metaphysics* 1064b.

33 Proclus (fifth century CE), the author of *Elements of Theology*.

34 Adamantios (fifth century CE), the author of a treatise on physiognomy.

35 Apollonios of Tyana (second century CE), a Neopythagorean philosopher who had the reputation of a magician, astrologer, and prophet.

36 John Laurentios Lydos (sixth century CE), the author of *On Portents*, a high official and contemporary of Justinian I.

37 *Data* (Δεδομένα) is a work by Euclid.

38 *Conica* is a work by Apollonios of Perga.

39 *Pneumatica* is a work by Heron of Alexandria.

40 The author of the *Cylindrica*, Serenos of Antinoopolis, is omitted.

41 The "secret philosophy" refers to the occult sciences. See Magdalino and Mavroudi, introduction, 15–25; Angelov, *Byzantine Hellene*, 192, 309, n. 75.

the person seeking the full philosophical experience would learn[42] it by going through it in detail.

8. For mine is that most beloved and desired offspring gloriously adorned with the names of the scientists and sciences! But I stand up and ask, O Italian, after having established the foundation of my argument in the fullness of philosophy: Why do you boast arguing about these matters?

9. If reason did not display for a while its proper activity among the Greeks, you should know that it was not the absence of reason but the lack of the foundations that brought this about. Now the sword of the Greeks has taken a double revenge for the massacre of the Greeks in Constantinople by shedding the blood of the perpetrators. It laid low the arrogance in that place [Constantinople], but here it has liberated all the Greek people[43] and has directed their nature to return rapidly toward its habitual state. Therefore, it [the nature of the Greeks], which has been as if in a sleeping state, recovers through the awakening of reason its ability as never before and pursues philosophy. For heat is capable of doing the same when it is concentrated and shot forth. Now the city of the Nicaeans outrivals the city of Athens.[44] For we are Nicaeans not by ancestral stock but rather by our endeavor for the ancestral stock.[45]

10. And what is the reason? The communion of nature shows it.[46] A Greek can be stronger than another Greek, but an Italian cannot, regarding the highest things, the things in the middle, and the ends. Do compare highest things with the highest and so on, <O Italian>. You are great because you are incomparable. But I do not invent any novelties. You plunder in theology what is mine by historical right. I come from Athens, because I am an Athenian, and you forcibly take hold of an invention and pay attention to a newfangled philosophy; because the Lord's

---

42 I take the form of the verb to be μάθοι ἄν, an emendation from μάθοι ὄν in Vat. gr. 1113, fol. 98v. Barocci 97, fol. 83r, has μάθειεν, whereas the modern editor prefers μάθοιεν.

43 The word used here is τὸ πανελλήνιον.

44 The comparison of Nicaea to Athens also appears in an earlier work, Laskaris's encomium on the city of Nicaea. See Th. L., *Op. rhet.*, 71.90–72.110.

45 Νικαεῖς γὰρ ἡμεῖς οὐ τὸ γένος, ἀλλ' οὖν τῷ γένει ἐκ τῆς προθέσεως. The metaphor of this sentence rests on wordplay. "Nicaea" (Νίκαια) is derived from the word for victory (νίκη). Laskaris's compatriots are "Nicaean" (that is, victorious) by virtue of their military successes against the Latins on behalf of their "ancestral stock" (γένος)—namely, the Greeks.

46 See above, pp. 53–54.

statements are newfangled, you make them newfangled and invent what is newfangled among the newfangled. But you are no Athenian, for you have no regard for the Peripatetic school of Aristotle. For he toppled his master [Plato] with the argument of his doctrine, and although the former [Plato] was filling up the precinct of the school building, he [Aristotle] forced him to begin again from scratch. But you are a Stoic and always on the move. Why? I am at a loss in this regard. You say that you are watered <with knowledge>, and how come, O dry and wise soul? This is a current of dark water[47] and therefore you have a great difficulty with it. If you want, run to the lecture room and learn that studying philosophy comes from the Greeks, that in the ancient arrangement of the climate zones the middle portion <is allotted to the Greeks>, that the scientists come from us and that their sciences are ours, that the air they once breathed is now ours, that we are the ones who speak the Greek tongue, that we are those who descend from their blood, and that your arrogance stirs our indignation. Therefore our experience is great, and because our power stands far above all dominions, it gives us ease to relax. Relaxation <leads to> studying and studying <leads> to clarity through investigation. Therefore, we have all wisdom. Search for <our> wise men and you will not easily finish the count!

11. What wisdom is coming to us from you? It now belongs to you alone, you say. Why? For the sake of peace? And whose is all the turmoil? One *nation* among you *has risen up against a nation* of the same race[48] and your empire has been in turmoil.[49] Why is your peaceful Christ among us?[50] Is it to keep the schism in check, or to raise up a battalion of his good men among us?[51] For all battalions and every phraseology are found among you. You examine the divine essence and

---

47 Cf. Ps. 17:12. For the same scriptural metaphor, see above, *Satire of His Tutor*, §8, p. 65 and n. 35.

48 Cf. Matt. 24:7.

49 "Your empire" (ἡ βασιλεία ὑμῶν) seems to refer to the Roman imperial polity in the West rather than the Latin empire in Constantinople. After the death of the emperor Frederick II in 1250, it was engulfed in internal strife during the reigns of his sons Conrad IV (d. 1254) and Manfred (d. 1266).

50 A puzzling rhetorical question. Laskaris may be alluding to a specific Latin churchman in the delegation visiting Thessaloniki in 1256.

51 The notable military imagery is characteristic of Nicaean diplomatic correspondence with the papacy, which points to the latter's double role in initiating both crusades and a negotiated resolution of the schism.

Oration on Hellenism 185

you make syllogisms with a "from" or a "through."[52] You are in error, yes, in error, and do not hide the truth, doing this out of arrogance and pride. It is like an old man glorying in his old age without being a representative of weak people in his weakness. We, however, are weak in Christ.[53]

12. For that person [the arrogant old man] flexes his muscles with intense efforts, while his hair is growing white, in order to show that he is not at death's door. He remains active, being engaged in an untimely fashion in what is outside his season. And should somebody else do it, he performs that to show himself full of knowledge. Where is beauty? Rhetoric has breathed its last. Is there a proposition? There is no counterproposition. Reason has been restored among the Greeks. Who can resist? Nature and skill can, for each is truly royal with respect to the other. Without them nothing can be in accordance with truth. An assembly is taking place among the Greeks, and you <are there>, concerning the churches. This is for no other reason but because whenever you lay down doctrines you break the rules of philosophy and do not draw conclusions truthfully—at least not insofar as you appropriate philosophy for yourselves and practice theology.

13. Do not run to Gaius [Caligula],[54] for Philo had a very mocking attitude toward him. You bring up the name of Peter "the rock"[55] and do not contemplate grace. It was grace that dissolved the hardness of the Law. Have also in mind that John the Theologian, the mystical initiate of grace,[56] is superior to everyone.[57] I refer you especially to the definitions of faith and see that you make the framing

---

52 The Procession of the Spirit "from" the Father "through" the Son was discussed in theological disputes between Greeks and Latins during the 1250s, when Blemmydes wrote two works on the subject. For the first work, addressed to Theodore II Laskaris, see Nikephoros Blemmydes, *Oeuvres théologiques*, ed. Stavrou, 1:285 (date), 304–53 (text). For the second work, addressed to Jacob of Bulgaria, see *Oeuvres théologiques*, ed. Stavrou, 2:61 (date), 74–153 (text).

53 The scriptural allusion is to 2 Cor. 12:9 ("my power is made perfect in weakness").

54 The reference is to Philo of Alexandria's *Embassy to Gaius*, which portrays the emperor Gaius Caligula as a tyrant. The specific context suggests a veiled insult directed at the current Roman pontiff, Alexander IV (1254–1261).

55 Etymological wordplay found already in the gospel: Peter as the "rock" (πέτρα) of Christ (Matt. 16:18).

56 The name "John" of Christ's apostle and evangelist derives from *Yehôhanan*, which means in Hebrew "Yahweh is gracious."

57 Presumably as the "beloved disciple" (John 20:2).

of the definitions common [to both Peter and John].[58] How is this possible? Is the teaching not proper to the teacher and the mystery to the mystic?

14. You and I are not the latter [mystics], nor, if we had the former [the gift of teaching], would we speculate theologically about both [the apostles Peter and John] like fledgling theologians and experts who base their knowledge on shaky foundations. A ruler and a carpenter's square make out what is unequal, but you and I are additions to things equal.[59] This [statement] derives from our scientific knowledge. Do abandon, good sir, your faulty inquiring, from which comes harm rather than good. And as you have considered the matter, come to that wonderful saying: Do not close *the door of salvation*[60] on your soul, for perdition is very certain. If you do not agree, close your eyes willingly. For *you will hear me speaking*.[61]

15. Be a Philip, learner of the truth,[62] rather than a Peter, stone-like in matters of God.[63] Be an earth that bears the fruit of goodness rather than a rock lacking moisture.[64] Take strength for yourself upon the rock that is Christ lest the earthen mound of exaltation drag you into humiliation and you traverse in darkness the life-giving strait of life. If you hasten to take part in controversies, then eat and drink and excrete from your belly, and add your noises to the roar of the fathers. Is there a beast that will not crouch when the eagle takes flight? Similarly, no creature remains on the ground when the lion roars. But I have been distracted from making a speech about the subject with which I began the treatise[65] and have been diverted to correcting others—and this has been done in a Greek fashion. For the Christ-named glory of the Greeks is never dimmed.

---

58 The Greek is particularly elusive here. "Common to both Peter and John" seems to better fit the sense than "common to us both."

59 The implication is that the current theological discussions can harm the coequality of the three persons of the Trinity.

60 See, for example, John Chrysostom, *In Ep. ad Romanos*, Homily 5, in PG 60:446.

61 Cf. Exod. 19:9.

62 Based on John 14:8–11.

63 Another pun on Peter "the rock."

64 Cf. Matt. 13:5.

65 It is indicative of Laskaris's concept of the philosophical content of this work that he calls it "treatise" (πραγματεία) rather than "oration" (λόγος).

16. The doctrinal firmness of the great Greek spirit has compelled us to say that most divine thing[66] rather than appropriate philosophy for that [firmness of doctrine]. What else could be the reason? But the Italian is ignorant. He knows from where he received philosophy, yet he ignores that there is more water in the source. And this is the effect of his excessive knowledge! For my part, I do not step outside theology, nor do I hand over philosophy to the Italian, but through the alternating voices of both, or through propositions taken from each, I can show him to be the transgressor. If he abolishes the setting of principles, is he not a transgressor? Which of the two does he prefer: to accept the sayings of the Gospels as true and indemonstrable, or to revere their interpreters? The former, if it is the case, does not remove the latter, but the latter chases away the former. You act well, my brother, when you explain the words of the Lord with your carnal tongue wetted by the Spirit![67] Do you not notice Cornelius, are you not a Peter, and are you not learning from the *sheet*?[68] There [in the Acts of the Apostles], the most earthly explanation through the vision of comestibles brought true faith; but now, according to you, the sending to the gentiles of the Spirit out of the Son teaches that the Spirit is proceeding from the Son.

17. *Hear, O heaven! Give ear, O earth!*[69] Does anyone not know the mind of the Lord, or did anyone not know it? These people investigate the word of God and alter the Holy Spirit according to negations or propositions. This is an ironic mockery of the honor of Peter. You truly venerate the Holy Spirit! Peter in the up-above has spoken with the Holy Spirit and you tempt the Holy Spirit because of Peter.

18. I cannot bear you, tempters! Are you not aware that just as power abides in humility, so its opposite abides in conceit? Where are scientific knowledge, the experts in skillful argumentation, the theologians? Whenever you construct with sophisms your theology—for this is your theology—and whenever you unskillfully produce theology through philosophy, who on earth will debate[70] with you? Philosophy resides in matters of scientific knowledge, but theology lies in

---

66 Namely, that the Spirit proceeds from the Father alone.

67 An ironic statement.

68 A reference to the conversion of the centurion Cornelius and Peter's vision of a sheet with animals upon it, described in Acts 10:1–33.

69 Isa. 1:2.

70 Reading διαλέξεται (will debate) as in Barocci 97, fol. 88v, rather than διαδέξεται as in Vat. gr. 1113, fol. 105v, and the edition.

doctrines: you make common things that are separate. You say that the Spirit is sent by the Son: I agree. But please agree that the Spirit proceeds only from the Father and you will reconcile the members of the church with Christ, its only head. You remain stiff-necked. What do you want? Do you insist on philosophizing about imaginary topics? Come on then, invent, innovate, do not be afraid![71] You investigate the divine. And do fear judgment! Do not be tempted! However, if this is your custom, then branch out into novelties. For my part, I will remain in Christ. Which of two things do you want, the spiritual or the material? If it is the former, may you acquire a foundation in theology; but if the latter, then we will be like the pagan and the tax collector.[72]

19. As I rise higher than the bonds of Peter[73] and the chains of human thoughts and concepts, I gaze in a different direction, seeing that the former [the bonds of Peter] constitute—in the manner of likenesses of human comprehension—fetters and constraints lest somehow human comprehension advance to the most shameful matters, and that the latter [the chains of human thoughts and concepts] are like a most divine bond holding together the movement of reasoning thoughts. I honor that person [Peter], but I also embrace these [fetters and constraints]. I wholeheartedly confess the theology of John. I venerate the teaching of Paul, even if I do not perfect it, and the wounds of all the apostles.[74] You teach by abolishing <the teaching> and I hold back. Paul said that *every person must submit to the governing authorities.*[75] But you deliberately disregard that precept and intemperately send off your words to make a "sending" a "proceeding from,"[76] without

---

71 This sentence is treated as a question in the edition.

72 According to Christ's words in Matt. 18:17, his disciples were to shun both the pagan and the tax collector. Laskaris may be thinking here of the parable of the Pharisee and the tax collector (Luke 18:9–14), which presents the tax collector in a better light. See Laskaris's humorous interpretation of the latter parable: Agapitos and Angelov, "Six Essays," 44–45, 71–72 (essay 5).

73 An allusion to the imprisonment of Peter in Acts 12:6–11.

74 I have introduced a punctuation break here. The mention of the wounds of all the apostles, a likely echo from their whipping in Acts 5:40–41, seems to be a riposte to the Latin emphasis on the suffering of Peter.

75 Rom. 13:1.

76 The difference between "sending" (πέμψις) and "procession" (ἐκπόρευσις) was a key point made by Byzantine theologians in doctrinal disputes with the Roman Church on the *filioque*.

Oration on Hellenism

obeying the definitions of the fathers. I will change the sound of your flute and draw you toward salvation. For after I earlier aimed my blows at your intellect, which is the lord and teacher, I will now give you advice about what needs to be done. If you are not convinced just now, if you are not convinced in the things said, let me remain quiet in my judgment and let others pronounce what you deserve.

20. Listen to me! Each science and skill in this life has its own principles, from whose perfections this science is composed. The demonstration through a middle term in syllogism[77] is useful in the other sciences. In theology, which surpasses all [sciences], a middle term does not constitute a demonstration, but the proof of the things said is prophetic revelation. Therefore, an investigation into it [theology] is perilous. If the fathers and the apostles have already explained what you are saying, and if one has to abide by these [explanations], it does not follow that abidance is the same as making explanations. The latter is one thing and the former another. If Paul explained the Gospel, but you explain Paul, then another person explains you and yet another explains him, and the one after him explains that one, how uncertain and empty becomes the message <of the faith>. For Paul did not grant the honor of teaching even to angels.[78] If you indeed follow the Gospel and belong to Christ's doctrine, do not pervert his utterings, but taking your sincere inspiration from them, believe and you will discover eternal life. In this way, therefore, I address the Italian, or rather those Italians who come from Rome:[79] "You have mixed up theology and science. Enjoy their fruit, you joy lovers of our Church! For today the Greeks are flourishing through the word and wisdom of theology."

21. What goal does that man [the Italian] have but to claim that the Italian position is philosophical and derives from the Greeks? And what is his biggest goal but to demonstrate by induction that because something is wise it is also theological? Every Italian boasts about this thing, but does not perceive that other

---

[77] The middle term in a syllogism (τὸ μέσον) is the term present in the two premises but absent from the conclusion. Laskaris criticizes the nonscriptural middle term of theological syllogisms in his *First Oration against the Latins* as well and thus attacks the overuse of demonstrative logic in Latin scholastic theology. See Th. L., *Chr. theol.*, 127.111–128.124.

[78] Cf. Col. 2:18.

[79] In 1256 Pope Alexander IV dispatched the Dominican friar Constantine, bishop of Orvieto, to the empire of Nicaea as leader of a Latin ecclesiastical embassy. It is with Constantine of Orvieto and his entourage that Theodore held the disputations in Thessaloniki in the autumn of that year. See Gill, *Byzantium and the Papacy*, 97–100.

thing <the faulty mixing of theology and philosophy>, nor does he perceive his fatness and flabbiness, nor that his nourishment is inane and his self-will is strong. His arrogance and drunkenness are as unbreakable as a diamond. A worm comes from a pile of manure, yet boasts of the food without realizing that it consists of excretion made from food.

22. Whose is philosophy or whose is theology? *God always was and is and will be*, a wise and divine man from among ours [Gregory of Nazianzus] has said, broaching the subject through outer learning.[80] The quoted author was a theologian and philosopher all in one. But can it be that while we say what is ours, and they say what is ours, it is not we but they [the Italians] who are theologians to the greatest degree? What am I to do with this mother of arrogance? I want humility and she investigates the essence of God. The table of Jezebel every day mixes pride in human glory with blood and raises holy hands, both philosophical and theological.[81] I bow down and she [the mother of arrogance] is elevated. I guided her earlier to the areas of the climate zones,[82] supplied good temperament, rallied natural intelligence, gathered skill, and provided a home for scientific knowledge derived from skill. If she [the mother of arrogance] wishes to do so, let her believe. But if not, let her be sent back like a shot from a catapult, whirl around on herself, and learn her lesson from her ribaldry.

23. We take pride in divine love and the confession of the divine faith. But you, reverend men, priests and levites,[83] bishops and archpriests[84]—all of you along with the man superior to you all[85]—do not consent in any way at all to have futile or untimely disputations with the Italians. Do not have any respect for their objections or their towering arrogance. These things are their custom and ours is to reject them. What is right <should be treated> rightly, and the thing different from

---

80 Gregory of Nazianzus, *Oration 38* (*In Theophania*) 7.1, ed. Moreschini, 114; *Oration 45* (*In Sanctum Pascha*), PG 36:625.

81 The table of the false prophets gathered by Queen Jezebel is mentioned in 3 Kings (1 Kings) 18:19. Laskaris's description seems to be a jibe at the Roman eucharistic service.

82 A reference to the earlier discussion of climate, §§3–6.

83 That is, deacons.

84 "Bishops and archpriests" (ἀρχιθῦται καὶ πρωτοθῦται): the wordplay in the invocation, which is lost in the translation, is worth noting.

85 That is, Patriarch Arsenios Autoreianos (1254–1259, 1261–1264), who is known to have been present at the reception of the papal delegation in Thessaloniki in the autumn of 1256.

Oration on Hellenism

that should be destroyed. For if theology is being reinvented by them, how can we not strike with our argument those who speak like that? If honor is being debased, how can we not condemn the thieves? If God is being treated badly, how can we not mock those who treat him so? Fear not!

24. Stand fast in your faith, crush their weapons, deprive them of strength with arguments that come from analytic science,[86] and drive away their poison with defensive and holy remedies if there is soundness in the remedies. Do everything with vigor and courage, so that you may break their heads on account of philosophy, science, theology, and piety, and raise up a trophy of piety. By the natural order of things, you have been shown to be naturally superior to them in accordance with the principles of reason, and may you also appear utterly unrivaled with regard to them from a theological point of view.

25. However, you, O Word, and O divine and timeless Spirit proceeding from the Father and consubstantial with the Word, although <the Father is> the cause of the procession and generation of both of you, O Triad that is primal and equal in honor, do keep us among those who are yours. As for those who in their weakness are fond of controversy because of an unprecedented doctrine, bring them to goodness, so that by binding together your church, as is necessary, in the place of instruction here, you will display to all opponents that she is immovable. May you feed her with the heavenly bread in the future dreadful confession of deeds and may you in your kindness have mercy on us, who subscribe to every word and knowledge and custom among those who are yours, thanks to the intercession of the guardianship of the Mother of God.

---

[86] "Analytic science" (ἀναλυτικὴ ἐπιστήμη) refers here to the mystical teaching of pseudo-Dionysios, as it does in Th. L., *Ep.* 105.50–51 (p. 145). Interestingly, "syllogistic and analytical science" (συλλογιστικὴ καὶ ἀναλυτικὴ ἐπιστήμη) also signifies logic in a much-cited passage on the inappropriate application of logic to theology in Gregory of Nyssa, *On the Soul and the Resurrection*, in PG 46:52. See, for example, Nikephoros Gregoras, *History* 10.8, ed. Schopen, 1:509.

8

Letter on Royal Duty, Taxation, and the Army
Ep. 44 to Nikephoros Blemmydes

1. The inheritance of the emperor is to guard the empire from the harm of neighboring enemies from all directions, and this is a most excellent thing. The inheritance and glory of the wise man is the complete understanding and construction of arguments as well as the decision on and initiation of action through teamwork, and this is a matter of supreme importance.[1] The inheritance of a wise man who is above all an emperor is virtue, praise, laudation, honor, and glory—this is well known to wise men.

2. What am I saying? That you surely are a most wise man and you recognize from his actions the person who has an inheritance and what he has inherited. For what special and most honorable lot is there for wise emperors other than truth, discernment, and justice? If the power of judgment somehow takes no notice,[2] the judge hardly judges with a power of judgment. But if he examines what is just down to the finest details with righteousness, he will never be condemned unjustly.[3] If truth seeks by means of the light what belongs to truth, not what belongs to darkness and secrecy, how would truth ever be darkened? How would it be concealed? This is known by knowledgeable people, but is wholly unknown to those outside this circle.

Festa, p. 56

---

1 A translation of τοῦτο τῶν μάλιστα.
2 In keeping with the manuscript reading λανθάνει. The editor Festa emended it to μανθάνει, but the former is preferable, as noted by Papadopoulos-Kerameus in his 1899 review of Festa's edition (551).
3 For the idea of the judge being judged by God, see above, *Representation of the World, or Life*, §3.

3. You certainly are a very close friend to us, and because you are a friend to us, you are also a friend to the authorities. There was indeed a time when there was no friendship on your part toward the authorities.[4] But now your friendship to us has brought you very well in line with the authorities too. Is there something you are telling us, or rather something you are telling the authorities? Are we to wholly abandon the rights of the authorities or to follow the truth? Are we to search for justice according to reason or to cancel the judgment[5] out of philanthropy? For if we remove judgment from human nature, humankind will live chaotically. Where and how will the ruling power govern? There also is judgment lacking in discernment when the stumbler stumbles without discernment or without examination, going against conscience.

Festa, p. 57

4. What are you saying? Would you force us with your wise words to forgo the right of the imperial office concerning the people who inappropriately hold what was given them for a reason?[6] For my father did these things, and we seek to do what he did with reason. It is quite true that his work was also that of reason. For his works show his sense of purpose, his true knowledge, his patriotic rationale, his judgment concerning the subjects, and all the best things about him. Consider carefully the Triballians,[7] the land near Dyrrachion,[8] and think about Tripolis,[9]

---

4 On the relations between Blemmydes and Laskaris during the latter's reign, see above, pp. 49–51.

5 The specific decision against which Blemmydes had objected cannot be identified. Andreeva, "Polemika," 9, n. 28, linked it with his successful intervention on behalf of an accused official described by Nikephoros Blemmydes, *Autobiography* 1.87–88, ed. Munitiz, 43–44.

6 The cryptic reference appears to be to officials from aristocratic families.

7 A classicizing name for the Serbs.

8 The geographical places listed here, along with the mention of the neighboring Serbs, convey the territorial limits of the expanding empire of Nicaea. Dyrrachion was ceded to Nicaea as part of the arrangement made with Michael II Komnenos Doukas in the autumn of 1256. See above, p. 43.

9 Tripolis was a heavily fortified town lying on the Maeander River at the border between the empire of Nicaea and the sultanate of Rum. See George Akropolites, *History* 41, ed. Heisenberg and Wirth, 67–70 (trans. Macrides, *George Akropolites*, 221–22); Angelov, *Byzantine Hellene*, 49, 95, 170, 172.

Rhodes,[10] and Karambis,[11] and measure the extent of the territory by perimeter and diameter, and investigate the neighboring lands and peoples with their manifold shapes. Look at the battles, examine the plots, the intrigues, the schemes, the conjunctions of rogueries, the contrivances, the designs wickedly set in place in one world[12] with a united mind. And please pass judgment, most wise one, on all these.

5. I ask again: What are you saying? Are these troops needed or not? If that is the case, pay most wisely the levy[13] and the expenditure. If you want battles but say that the wages should not be paid by those for whom the battles are fought, explain how you came to this opinion. There is indeed gold, as well as precious material and silver bullion collected for the entirety <of the polity>, and if you identify therein the assets[14] for necessary army expenditure, you will find no gold in a little while. After establishing the bad habit for the subjects, you will ask for a loan for use and you will draw no money <through taxation>, and the harm from the said thing will be great.

6. What shall we do, we who are being criticized? Are we practicing virtue, or are we doing evil? For as we hold on to virtue, we are criticized for what is being done. As we proceed toward the praises, which I would never designate as virtue, we keep as our judge that wretched power of ours. What shall we do? Shall we keep

---

10 Rhodes was the location of a Nicaean victory against the Genoese, an event dated to 1248–50. See George Akropolites, *History* 48, ed. Heisenberg and Wirth, 86–88; trans. Macrides, *George Akropolites*, 246–49, with further discussion.

11 Cape Karambis (Kerembe Burnu) marked the easternmost boundary of the empire of Nicaea along the Anatolian Black Sea coast.

12 The expression "in one world" (ἑνὶ κόσμῳ) encapsulates Stoic views of a single universe. See Marcus Aurelius, *Meditations* 7.9. The same idea underpins Laskaris's reflections in *Representation of the World, or Life*.

13 "Levy" (ναῦλος): the precise meaning of the term is difficult to determine. In the eleventh and twelfth centuries, *naulon* was a commercial tax collected from ships crossing the Hellespont and carrying goods to Constantinople. See Rouillard, "Taxes maritimes," 282; Smyrlis, "Trade Regulation and Taxation," 72–75 (detailed discussion); Leveniotis, *Η Ἄβυδος*, 407, 410, 428–29, 560. The word also means "a passage fare," "a freight charge." See Constantine Harmenopoulos, *Hexabiblos* 2.11.21, ed. Heimbach, 332. Laskaris probably has in mind specific fiscal obligations of Blemmydes' monastery of Christ-Who-Is. In his autobiography Blemmydes mentions his opposition to soldiers who acted unjustly in collecting taxes (εἰσφοραί) from his monastery. See Nikephoros Blemmydes, *Autobiography* 2.79, ed. Munitiz, 81.

14 The Greek word is ἀφορμή.

silence for a while and see the sinews of imperial power cut? Shall we speak out as is our custom and incur the blame—I will say this again—of wise people? What is this then? Do we lavish gold for extravagant purposes? Do we abuse what is finest for many follies, for abuses without benefit? What unreasonable thing are we doing? Do we spend the gold in the pursuit of hunting? Do we spend it for a great feast with sumptuous dining tables? For immoderate drinks, inane luxuries, hated innovations? For what toy or latest pastime are we spending the gold—we who are in the prime of our life, but have grown old in soul and pay special honor to matters of philosophy?

When the sun rises, care for the infantry soldiers is awakened from bed with us at the same time. As the sun mounts higher and is carried around loftier heights, there is our preoccupation for ambassadors, for their reception and dismissal. While the sun is still rising, we arrange the order of the troops. When the sun is in the middle at noon, the task of receiving petitioners is undertaken and performed, and we proceed on horseback in order to hear people who are unable to join those at the gates of the palace. When the sun is bowing low, we pass judgments for those who bow before us. When the sun sets, we taste food as is normal, forced by the bond of soul and matter, and even then we do not cease to speak about our allotted duty. And when the sun turns and hides at the shores of the ocean, we make plans concerning campaigning and equipment. What are we doing idly? For what are we being criticized? We keep vigil as we give thanks to God, and especially when we fret powerlessly. And this is in accordance with righteousness, because he appointed us, the unworthy ones, to be carers of many people.

After we do this, God raises other concerns on the following day. Hostility against the common people is stirred up and the foreigners are fighting against us. Who will be our helper? How will the Persian[15] help the Greek? The Italian rages especially, the Bulgarian most manifestly.[16] The Serb is pressured by force and restrained. The person who perhaps is ours is perhaps not truly one of ours. Only the Greeks give aid to themselves, deriving their inclination from within themselves.[17] Do we order the army to be cut or the money, thanks to which the

---

15 That is, the Seljuk Turks.

16 In the years 1255–1256, Laskaris fought a war against the Bulgarians. See Angelov, *Byzantine Hellene*, 151–66.

17 "Deriving their inclination from within themselves" (οἴκοθεν λαμβάνον τὰς ἀφορμάς) poses a translation difficulty owing to the allusive meanings of the words ἀφορμή and

army has been formed? If we do the former, we help our enemies. But if we do the latter, we are abandoning the army, because we are abandoning the money that supports the army, and I say again that we are helping our enemies. This is no sophistry, but clearer than any other truth.

7. For there is one truth for me, one purpose, and one pursuit: always to hold together God's flock and preserve it from enemy wolves. For what reason are we being criticized? Why are we considered miserly? And why are we especially uncharitable? Spare me the lie, my <heavenly> Lord! Why do we struggle as emperor to hold on to the allotted power of governing and why do we deliberately choose to be dishonored when we truly dedicate for the sake of God's flock our soul and body, our material and our immaterial essence, our intellect, senses, mind, reasoning capacity, intellectual and divine nature, mathematical knowledge, learning disposition, schooling, teaching, philosophy, sophistry, likeness to the divine, and divinity? Is this a reason of shame for me? With Paul I will cry out, *I will become a spectacle for angels and people*.[18] I will give my body, for I will have an honor superior to the body. I will give my spirit and will take my recompense from God, namely *the fragrance of God*[19] and life, in order to obtain that blessed, divine, and ineffable state of well-being. I have learned to act not in appearances but in truth. If in fact I am put to the test, those who see me fight on behalf of what exists in truth and who blame me will themselves rather be blamed by the One Who Is.[20] What shall I do? With whom shall I fight? Whom shall I refute? By whom shall I be refuted? I want everyone to criticize me, but not for petty sophistries. I have learned them thoroughly and nobody will outwit me. But whoever will train a wise man, may he receive his proper reward from the Absolute Wisdom above.

Festa, p. 59

οἴκοθεν. If ἀφορμή is taken to mean "assets," the sentence would run: "Only the Greeks give aid to themselves, drawing assets from within their own financial resources." The ambiguity may well have been intended.

18 Laskaris has slightly adapted the phrase in 1 Cor. 4:9 (θέατρον ἐγενήθημεν τῷ κόσμῳ καὶ ἀγγέλοις καὶ ἀνθρώποις), putting it into the future tense.

19 In keeping with the manuscript reading εὐωδίαν and the quote from Romanos Melodos, *Cantica*, 5, no. 53, §27.4, ed. Grosdidier de Matons, 5:448. The editor Festa emended the word to ἐξουσίαν.

20 The One Who Is (ὁ ὤν) alludes to the epithet of Christ in the name of the monastery of Christ-Who-Is at Emathia near Ephesos. Blemmydes was both its founder and its abbot at the time of the letter's composition. See above, pp. 48–49.

The subject of all that has been said is life, virtue, evil, and intention. The first [life] is the predicate as a middle term in syllogism,[21] but the latter [virtue and evil] become apparent when placed alongside the predicate [life].[22] It is intention that demonstrates virtue and evil. If virtue on behalf of the flock of God appears to be evil, we accept the dishonors, we tolerate the painful affronts, and we submit to receiving all sorts of slanderous accusations![23] But if, thanks to virtue and God's flock, we receive the judgments unjustly, we do fear God's judgment lest he judge according to the customary judgment. I do say these things to your Holiness, but the assessment of the arguments will be made among the later generations. May the prayer of your Holiness be forever granted to me.

---

21 On τὸ μέσον as the middle term in syllogism, see also *Oration on Hellenism*, §20, p. 189, n. 77, above.

22 Lived experience as the basis for philosophical thought is one of themes of *Representation of the World, or Life*.

23 "Accusations" (ἀφορμαί): on this rare meaning, see Kriaras, s.v.

BIBLIOGRAPHY

Abbreviations

Blem., *Imperial Statue*	H. Hunger and I. Ševčenko, *Des Nikephoros Blemmydes* Βασιλικὸς Ἀνδριάς *und dessen Metaphrase von Georgios Galesiotes und Georgios Oinaiotes* (Vienna, 1986).
BZ	*Byzantinische Zeitschrift*
CAG	*Commentaria in Aristotelem Graeca*, 23 vols. (Berlin, 1882–1909).
CCSG	Corpus christianorum, series graeca
CFHB	Corpus fontium historiae byzantinae
CPG	E. V. Leutsch and F. W. Schnedewin, *Corpus paroemiographorum Graecorum*, 2 vols. (Hildesheim, 1958).
CSHB	Corpus scriptorum historiae byzantinae
DOP	*Dumbarton Oaks Papers*
DOS	Dumbarton Oaks Studies
ΕΕΒΣ	Ἐπετηρὶς ἑταιρείας βυζαντινῶν σπουδῶν
GdSAI	*Giornale della Società Asiatica Italiana*
JÖB	*Jahrbuch der Österreichischen Byzantinistik*
JÖBG	*Jahrbuch der Österreichischen Byzantinischen Gesellschaft* (after 1968, *JÖB*)
Kriaras	E. Kriaras, *Λεξικό της Μεσαιωνικής Ελληνικής Δημώδους Γραμματείας, 1100–1669*, 22 vols. to date (Thessaloniki, 1968–).
Lampe	G. W. H. Lampe, *A Patristic Greek Lexicon* (Oxford, 1961).
LBG	*Lexikon zur byzantinischen Gräzität*, 8 fasc. (Vienna, 1994–2007).

LSJ	H. G. Liddell, R. Scott, and H. S. Jones, *A Greek–English Lexicon*, 9th ed. (Oxford, 1940).
PG	J. P. Migne, *Patrologiae cursus completus, series graeca*, 161 vols. (Paris, 1857–66).
REB	*Revue des études byzantines*
SC	Sources chrétiennes
Th. L., *Chr. theol.*	Ch. Krikonis, Θεοδώρου Β΄ Λασκάρεως περὶ χριστιανικῆς θεολογίας λόγοι (Thessaloniki, 1988).
Th. L., *Ep.*	N. Festa, *Theodori Ducae Lascaris epistulae CCXVII* (Florence, 1898).
Th. L., *Op. rhet.*	L. (Aloysius) Tartaglia, *Theodorus II Ducas Lascaris: Opuscula rhetorica* (Munich, 2000).
TLG	Thesaurus Linguae Graecae Digital Library. Ed. Maria C. Pantelia. University of California, Irvine.

Works by Theodore Laskaris

Agapitos, P., and D. Angelov. "Six Essays by Theodore II Laskaris in Vind. Phil. Gr. 321: Edition, Translation, Analysis." *JÖB* 68 (2018): 39–75.
Angelov, D. "The *Moral Pieces* by Theodore II Laskaris." *DOP* 65–66 (2011–12): 237–69.
Festa, N. "Κοσμικὴ Δήλωσις." *GdSAI* 11 (1897–98): 97–114.
Festa, N. "Κοσμικὴ Δήλωσις." *GdSAI* 12 (1899): 1–52.
Georgiopoulou, S. "Theodore II Dukas Laskaris (1222–1258) as an Author and an Intellectual of the XIIIth Century." PhD diss., Harvard University, 1990.
Tartaglia, L. *Satira del pedagogo*. Naples, 1992.

Primary Sources

Alexander, *On Figures*. Edited by C. Walz in *Rhetores Graeci*, 8:414–86. Stuttgart, 1835.
Alexander Romance, ε recension. See *Anonymi Byzantini vita Alexandri regis Macedonum*, under Primary Sources.
Anna Komnene. *Annae Comnenae Alexias*. Ed. D. Reinsch and A. Kambylis. 2 vols. CFHB 40/1–2. Berlin, 2001.
Anonymi Byzantini vita Alexandri regis Macedonum. Ed. J. Trumpf. Stuttgart, 1974.
Aphthonius. *Aphthonii progymnasmata*. Ed. H. Rabe. Leipzig, 1926.

Arsenios Autoreianos, *Letter*. Edited by L. Pieralli, "Una lettera del Patriarca Arsenios Autorianos a Papa Alessandro IV sull'unione delle Chiese." *JÖB* 48 (1998): 171–88.
Byzantine Monastic Foundation Documents: A Complete Translation of the Surviving Founders' Typika and Testaments. Ed. J. Thomas and A. Hero. 5 vols. DOS 35. Washington, DC, 2000.
Constantine Harmenopoulos. *Constantini Harmenopuli Manuale legume sive Hexabiblos*. Ed. G. Heimbach. Leipzig, 1851.
Constantine Manasses. *Breviarium chronicum*. Ed. O. Lampsidis. 2 vols. CHFB 36. Athens, 1996.
David. *Prolegomena et in Porphyrii Isagogen commentarium*. Ed. A. Busse. CAG 17.2. Berlin, 1900. Translated by Sebastian Gertz in *Elias and David: Introductions to Philosophy, with Olympiodorus: Introduction to Logic*, 83–176. London, 2018.
Demetrios Chomatenos. *Demetrii Chomateni Ponemata diaphora*. Ed. G. Prinzing. CFHB 38. Berlin, 2002.
Dio Chrysostom. *Dionis Prusaensis quem vocant Chrysostomum quae exstant omnia*. Ed. J. von Arnim. 2 vols. Berlin, 1893–96.
Diodorus Siculus, *Bibliotheca* 1. Edited by P. Bertrac, trans. by Y. Vernière, *Bibliothèque historique: Livre I*. Paris, 1993.
Dionysios Periegetes. *Description of the Known World: With Introduction, Translation, and Commentary*. Ed. and trans. J. L. Lightfoot. Oxford, 2014.
Ecloga: Das Gesetzbuch Leons III. und Konstantinos' V. Ed. L. Burgmann. Frankurt, 1983.
Eustathios, *Commentary on the Iliad*. Edited by M. van der Valk, *Eustathii archiepiscopi Thessalonicensis commentarii ad Homeri Iliadem pertinentes*. 4 vols. Leiden, 1971–87.
Eustathios, *Commentary on Dionysios Periegetes*. In G. Müller, *Geographi Graeci Minores*, 2:201–407. Paris, 1861.
Evagrios Pontikos, *Praktikos*. Edited and translated by C. Guillaumont and A. Guillaumont, *Traité pratique, ou, Le moine*. 2 vols. SC 170–71. Paris, 1971.
Florilegium Baroccianum (Florilegium Patmiacum). Edited by E. Sargologos, *Un traité de vie spirituelle et morale du XIe siècle: Le florilège sacro-profane du manuscrit 6 de Patmos*. Thessaloniki, 1990.
Foss, C. *Nicaea: A Byzantine Capital and Its Praises: With the Speeches of Theodore Laskaris, "In Praise of the Great City of Nicaea," and Theodore Metochites, "Nicene Oration."* Trans. J. Tulchin. Brookline, MA, 1996.
Frederick II Hohenstafen, *Greek Letters*. Edited by E. Merendino, "Quattro lettere greche di Federico II." *Atti della Accademia di Scienze, Lettere e Arti di Palermo*, 4th ser., 34.2 (1974–75): 293–343.
Galen, *On the Different Kinds of Pulse*. In *Claudii Galeni opera omnia*, ed. C. G. Kühn, 8:493–765. Leipzig, 1824.
Galen, *Synopsis on the Pulse*. In *Claudii Galeni opera omnia*, ed. C. G. Kühn, 9:431–533. Leipzig, 1825.

George Akropolites, *History*. In *Georgii Acropolitae opera*, ed. A. Heisenberg and
P. Wirth, 1:1–189. 2 vols. Stuttgart, 1978. Translated by R. Macrides as *George
Akropolites: The History*. Oxford, 2007.
George Pachymeres, *History: Relations historiques*. Vols. 1–2, ed. A. Failler, trans.
V. Laurent. CFHB 24/1–2. Paris, 1984. Vols. 3–4, ed. and trans. A. Failler. CFHB
24/3–4. Paris, 1999.
George Pachymeres, *Quadrivium*. Edited by F. Tannery, *Quadrivium de Georges
Pachymère*. Vatican City, 1940.
Gregory of Nazianzus, *Oration 31*. Edited and translated by P. Gallay, in *Discours 27–31*,
276–343. SC 250. Paris, 1978.
Gregory of Nazianzus, *Oration 38 (In Theophania)*. Edited by C. Moreschini, translated
by P. Gallay, in *Discours 38–41*, 105–49. SC 358. Paris, 1990.
Gregory of Nazianzus, *Oration 43 (Funeral Oration for Basil of Caesarea)*. Edited and
translated by J. Bernardi, in *Discours 42–43*, 117–306. SC 384. Paris, 1992.
Heisenberg, A. *Aus der Geschichte und Literatur der Palaiologenzeit*. Munich, 1920.
Hercher, R. *Epistolographi Graeci*. Paris, 1873.
Hermogenes. *Hermogenis opera*. Ed. H. Rabe. Leipzig, 1913.
"Heron of Byzantium." *Siegecraft: Two Tenth-Century Instructional Manuals by "Heron of
Byzantium."* Ed. and trans. D. F. Sullivan. Washington, DC, 2000.
Iamblichus. *Iamblichi theologoumena arithmeticae*. Ed. V. de Falco. Leipzig, 1922.
John Argyropoulos, *Katablattas*. Edited by P. Canivet and N. Oikonomides, "La Comédie
de Katablattas: Invective byzantine du XVᵉ siècle." *Diptycha* 3 (1982–83): 5–97.
John Chrysostom. "A Comparison between a King and a Monk." In PG 47:387–92.
Translated by D. Hunter in *A Comparison between a King and a Monk; Against the
Opponents of the Monastic Life: Two Treatises*, 69–76. Lewiston, NY, 1988.
John Italos. *Quaestiones quodlibetales*. Ed. P. Joannou. Ettal, 1956.
John Philoponus. *In Aristotelis Analytica priora commentaria*. Ed. M. Wallies. CAG 13.2.
Berlin, 1905.
John of Sardis. *Ioannis Sardiani commentarium in Aphthonii Progymnasmata*. Ed. H.
Rabe. Leipzig, 1928.
John Sikeliotes, *Commentary on Hermogenes, On Ideas*. Edited by C. Walz in *Rhetores
Graeci*, 6:56–504. Stuttgart, 1834.
John Tzetzes. *Allegories from the Verse Chronicle*. Edited by H. Hunger, "Johannes Tzetzes,
Allegorien aus der Verschronik," *JÖBG* 4 (1955): 18–33.
Kosmas Indikopleustes. *Christian Topography*. Edited by W. Wolska-Conus, *Topographie
chrétienne*. 3 vols. SC 141, 159, 197. Paris, 1968–73.
Kosmas of Jerusalem, *Commentary*. Edited by G. Lozza, *Commentario ai Carmi di
Gregorio Nazianzeno*. Naples, 2000.
Leo VI, *Novels*. Edited and translated by P. Noailles and A. Dain, *Les Novelles de Léon VI
le Sage*. Paris, 1944.

Libanius, *Progymnasmata*. Edited and translated by C. Gibson, *Libanius's Progymnasmata: Model Exercises in Greek Prose Composition and Rhetoric*. Atlanta, 2008.
Livistros and Rodamne. Edited by P. Agapitos, Ἀφήγησις Λιβίστρου καὶ Ροδάμνης: Κριτικὴ ἔκδοση τῆς διασκευῆς α. Athens, 2006. Translated by P. Agapitos as *The Tale of Livistros and Rodamne: A Byzantine Love Romance of the 13th Century*. Liverpool, 2021.
Mandeville, John. *The Travels of Sir John Mandeville*. Trans. C. Moseley. Harmondsworth, 1983.
Menander. *Menandri sententiae: Comparatio Menandri et Philistionis*. Ed. S. Jäkel. Leipzig, 1964.
Menander Rhetor. Edited and translated by D. A. Russell and N. G. Wilson, *Menander Rhetor*. Oxford, 1981.
Michael Psellos, *Historia syntomos*. Edited and translated by W. J. Aerts, *Michaelis Pselli Historia syntomos*. CFHB 30. Berlin, 1990.
Michael Psellos. *De omnifaria doctrina*. Ed. L. Westerink. Nijmegen, 1948.
Miklosich, F., and J. Müller. *Acta et diplomata graeca medii aevi sacra et profana*. 6 vols. Vienna, 1860–90.
Nemesius, *De natura hominis*. Edited by M. Morani, *Nemesii Emeseni De natura hominis*. Leipzig, 1987. Translated by R. W. Sharples and P. J. Van der Eijk as *On the Nature of Man*. Liverpool, 2008.
Nikephoros Basilakes, *Progymnasmata*. Edited and translated by A. Pignani, *Progimnasmi e monodie*. Naples, 1983.
Nikephoros Blemmydes, *Autobiography*. Edited by J. Munitiz, *Nicephori Blemmydae autobiographia sive curriculum vitae necnon epistula universalior*. CCSG 13. Turnhout, 1984. Translated by J. Munitiz as *A Partial Account*. Leuven, 1988.
Nikephoros Blemmydes, *Monastic Rule*. Edited by A. Heisenberg in *Nicephori Blemmydae curriculum vitae et carmina*, 93–99. Leipzig, 1896.
Nikephoros Blemmydes. *Oeuvres théologiques*. Ed. and trans. M. Stavrou. 2 vols. SC 517, 558. Paris, 2007–13.
Nikephoros Gregoras, *History*. Edited by L. Schopen, *Nicephori Gregorae Byzantina historia*. 3 vols. CSHB 19. Bonn, 1829–55.
Niketas Choniates. *Nicetae Choniatae Historia*. Ed. J.-L. van Dieten. CFHB 11. Berlin, 1975.
Nikomachos, *Introductio arithmetica*. Edited by R. Hoche, *Nicomachi Geraseni Pythagorei introductionis arithmeticae libri ii*. Leipzig, 1866.
Philo of Alexandria. *Opera quae supersunt*. Ed. L. Cohn and P. Wendland. 6 vols. Berlin, 1896–1915.
Phoebammon, *Scholia on Rhetorical Figures*. Edited by L. Spengel in *Rhetores Graeci*, 3:43–56. Leipzig, 1856.

Phyllada of Alexander the Great. Edited by G. Veloudis, Ἡ φυλλάδα τοῦ Μεγαλέξαντρου: Διήγησις Ἀλεξάνδρου τοῦ Μακεδόνος. Athens, 1977. Translated by R. Stoneman as *The Book of Alexander the Great: A Life of the Conqueror.* London, 2012.

Physiologus. Ed. F. Sbordone. Rome, 1936.

Proclus, *Commentary on Plato's Timaeus.* Edited by E. Diehl, *Procli Diadochi in Platonis Timaeum commentaria.* 3 vols. Leipzig, 1903–06.

Proclus, *Theologia platonica.* Edited and translated by H. D. Saffrey and L. G. Westerink, *Théologie platonicienne.* 6 vols. Paris, 1968–97.

Pseudo-Dionysios, *Celestial Hierarchy.* Edited by G. Heil in *Corpus Dionysiacum,* ed. G. Heil and A. M. Ritter, 2:5–59. Berlin, 1991.

Pseudo-Galen, *On the Humors.* Edited by C. G. Kühn in *Claudii Galeni opera omnia,* 19:485–96. Leipzig, 1830.

Pseudo-Gregory of Corinth, *On the Four Parts of the Perfect Speech.* Edited by W. Hörandner, "Pseudo-Gregorios Korinthios, Über die vier Teile der perfekten Rede," *Medioevo greco* 12 (2012): 87–131.

Pseudo-Kodinos. Edited and translated by R. Macrides, J. Munitiz, and D. Angelov, *Pseudo-Kodinos and the Constantinopolitan Court: Offices and Ceremonies.* Farnham, 2013.

Pseudo-Maximos the Confessor. Edited by S. Ihm, *Ps.-Maximus Confessor: Erste kritische Edition einer Redaktion des sacro-profanen Florilegiums Loci communes, nebst einer vollständigen Kollation einer zweiten Redaktion und weiterem Material.* Stuttgart, 2001.

Rabe, H. *Prolegomenon Sylloge.* Leipzig, 1931

Rhalles, G., and N. Potles. Σύνταγμα τῶν θείων καὶ ἱερῶν κανόνων. 6 vols. Athens, 1852–59; repr., Athens, 1992.

Romanos Melodos, *Cantica.* Edited and translated by J. Grosdidier de Matons, *Hymnes,* 5 vols. SC 99, 110, 114, 128, 283. Paris, 1964–81.

Saewulf. Translated by W. R. Brownlow, *Saewulf (1102, 1103 A.D.),* 1–30 [Latin ed. by A. Rogers, 31–52]. Palestine Pilgrims' Text Society 4.2. London, 1892.

Sargologos, E. *Un traité de vie spirituelle et morale du XIe siècle: Le florilège sacro-profane du manuscrit 6 de Patmos.* Thessaloniki, 1990.

Simplicius. *In Aristotelis Categorias commentarium.* Ed. K. Kalbfleisch. CAG 8. Berlin, 1907.

Souda. Edited by A. Adler, *Suidae lexicon.* 5 vols. Leipzig, 1928–38.

Spingou, Foteini, ed. *The Visual Culture of Later Byzantium (c. 1081–c. 1350).* Sources for Byzantine Art History 3. Cambridge, 2022.

Strömberg, Reinhold. *Greek Proverbs: A Collection of Proverbs and Proverbial Phrases Which Are Not Listed by the Ancient and Byzantine Paroemiographers.* Göteborg, 1954.

Symeon Seth, *Conspectus rerum naturalium (Σύνοψις τῶν φυσικῶν).* Edited by A. Delatte in *Anecdota Atheniensia et alia,* vol. 2, *Textes grecs relatifs à l'histoire des sciences,* 17–89. Liège, 1939.

Synesios of Cyrene. *On Kingship.* Edited by J. Lamoureux, translated by N. Aujoulat, in *Synésios de Cyrène,* vol. 5, *Opuscules II,* 84–141. Paris, 2008.

Syrianus. *Syriani in Hermogenem commentaria.* Ed. H. Rabe. 2 vols. Leipzig, 1892–93.

Themistius. *Quae fertur in Aristotelis Analyticorum priorum librum, I: Paraphrasis.* Ed. M. Wallies. CAG 23.3. Berlin, 1884.

Theodore Skoutariotes (?), *Synopsis chronike.* Edited by K. Sathas in *Μεσαιωνικὴ Βιβλιοθήκη,* 7:1–556. Venice, 1894.

Theognostos, *Treasury.* Edited by J. Munitiz, *Theognosti Thesaurus.* CCSG 5. Turnhout, 1979. Translated by J. Munitiz as *Treasury.* Turnhout, 2014.

Theon. *Progymnasmata.* Edited by C. Walz in *Rhetores Graeci,* 1:145–257. Stuttgart, 1832.

Theon of Smyrna, *On Mathematics Useful for Reading Plato.* Edited by E. Hiller, *Theonis Smyrnaei philosophi Platonici expositio rerum mathematicarum ad legendum Platonem utilium.* Leipzig, 1878.

Theophanes. *Chronographia.* Ed. C. de Boor. 2 vols. Leipzig, 1883–85.

Theophilos Protospatharios, *On the Pulse.* Edited by F. Z. Ermerins in *Anecdota medica graeca,* 3–77. Leiden, 1840.

Theophylaktos Simokattes. *Historiae.* Ed. C. de Boor and P. Wirth. Stuttgart, 1972.

Thomas Magistros, *On Kingship.* Edited by P. Volpe Cacciatore, *La regalità.* Naples, 1997.

Secondary Sources

Agapitos, P. "Blemmydes, Laskaris and Philes." In *Byzantinische Sprachkunst: Studien zur byzantinischen Literatur gewidmet Wolfram Hörandner zum 65. Geburtstag,* ed. M. Hinterberger and E. Schiffer, 1–19. Berlin, 2007.

Agapitos, P. "Grammar, Genre and Patronage in the Twelfth Century: A Scientific Paradigm and Its Implications." *JÖB* 64 (2014): 1–22.

Agapitos, P. "The Insignificance of 1204 and 1453 for the History of Byzantine Literature." *Medieovo Greco* 20 (2020): 1–58.

Agapitos, P. "Literature and Education in Nicaea and Their Legacy: An Interpretive Synthesis." *Medieovo Greco* 21 (2021): 1–37.

Agapitos, P., and D. Angelov. "Six Essays." See under Works by Theodore Laskaris.

Andreeva, M. "Polemika Theodora II. Laskaria s Nikiforom Vlemmidom." In *Mémoires de la Société royale des sciences de Bohême, classe des lettres, année 1929,* 1–36. Prague, 1930.

Andreou, A., and P. Agapitos. "Of Masters and Servants: Hybrid Power in Theodore Laskaris' *Response to Mouzalon* and in the *Tale of Livistros and Rodamne*." *Interfaces: Journal of Medieval European Literatures* 6 (2019): 96–129.

Angelov, D. *The Byzantine Hellene: The Life of Emperor Theodore Laskaris and Byzantium in the Thirteenth Century*. Cambridge, 2019.

Angelov, D. "Classifications of Political Philosophy and the Concept of Royal Science in Byzantium." In *The Many Faces of Byzantine Philosophy*, ed. B. Bydén and K. Ierodiakonou, 22–49. Athens, 2012.

Angelov, D. *Imperial Ideology and Political Thought in Byzantium, 1204–1330*. Cambridge, 2007.

Angelov, D. "The *Moral Pieces*." See under Works by Theodore Laskaris.

Angelov, D. "Theodore II Laskaris on the Sultanate of Rum and the Flight of 'Izz al-Dīn Kay Kāwūs II." In *In Memoriam Angeliki Laiou*, ed. C. Kafadar and N. Necipoğlu, special issue, *Journal of Turkish Studies* 36 (2011): 26–43.

Angold, M. *A Byzantine Government in Exile: Government and Society under the Laskarids of Nicaea, 1204–1261*. Oxford, 1975.

Astruc, C. "La tradition manuscrite des oeuvres oratoires profanes de Théodore II Lascaris." *Travaux et Mémoires* 1 (1965): 393–404.

Beck, H.-G. "Der byzantinische 'Ministerpräsident.'" *BZ* 48 (1955): 309–38.

Berg, B. "Manfred of Sicily and the Greek East." *Byzantina* 14 (1988): 263–89.

Chitwood, Z. *Byzantine Legal Culture and the Roman Legal Tradition, 867–1056*. Cambridge, 2017.

Constantinides, C. N. *Higher Education in Byzantium in the Thirteenth and Early Fourteenth Centuries, 1204–ca. 1310*. Nicosia, 1982.

De Jonge, C. *Between Grammar and Rhetoric: Dionysius of Halicarnassus on Language, Linguistics and Literature*. Boston, 2008.

Döberl, M. "Berthold von Vohburg-Hohenburg, der letzte Vorkämpfer der deutschen Herrschaft im Königreiche Sicilien: Ein Beitrag zur Geschichte der letzten Staufer." *Deutsche Zeitschrift für Geschichtswissenschaft* 12 (1894–95): 201–78.

Dölger, F. "Zur Bedeutung von φιλόσοφος und φιλοσοφία in byzantinischer Zeit." In his *Byzanz und die europäische Staatenwelt*, 197–208. Ettal, 1953.

Dölger, F., and I. Karagiannopoulos. *Byzantinische Urkundenlehre*. Munich, 1968.

Duffy, J. "Hellenic Philosophy in Byzantium and the Lonely Mission of Michael Psellos." In *Byzantine Philosophy and Its Ancient Sources*, ed. K. Ierodiakonou, 139–56. Oxford, 2002.

Durak, K. "The Location of Syria in Byzantine Writing: One Question, Many Answers." In *In Memoriam Angeliki Laiou*, ed. C. Kafadar and N. Necipoğlu, special issue, *Journal of Turkish Studies* 36 (2011): 45–55.

Efthymiadis, S. "L'enseignement secondaire à Constantinople pendant les XIe–XIIe siècles: Modèle éducatif pour la Terre d'Otrante au XIIIe siècle." *Nea Rhome* 2 (2005): 259–75.

Festa, N. "Κοσμικὴ Δήλωσις." See under Works by Theodore Laskaris.
Franchi, A. *La svolta politico-ecclesiastica tra Roma e Bisanzio (1249–1254): La legazione di Giovanni da Parma: Il ruolo di Federico II*. Rome 1981.
Gardner, A. *The Lascarids of Nicaea: The Story of an Empire in Exile*. London, 1912.
Georgiopoulou, S. "Theodore II Dukas Laskaris." See under Works by Theodore Laskaris.
Gill, J. *Byzantium and the Papacy, 1198–1400*. New Brunswick, NJ, 1979.
Heisenberg, A. *Aus der Geschichte und Literatur*. See under Primary Sources.
Hinterberger, M. "From Highly Classicizing to Common Prose (XIII–XIV CE): The *Metaphrasis* of Niketas Choniates' *History*." In *Varieties of Post-Classical and Byzantine Greek*, ed. K. Bentein and M. Janse, 179–200. Berlin, 2020.
Hinterberger, M. "The Language of Byzantine Poetry: New Words, Alternative Forms, and 'Mixed Language.'" In *A Companion to Byzantine Poetry*, ed. W. Horändner, A. Rhoby, and N. Zagklas, 38–65. Leiden, 2019.
Hinterberger, M. "The Rose and the Dung Beetle: Theodore Laskaris on 'Friendship' and 'Envy.'" In *After the Text: Byzantine Enquiries in Honour of Margaret Mullett*, ed. L. James, O. Nicholson, and R. Scott, 191–204. Abingdon, Oxon., 2022.
Horrocks, G. "Georgios Akropolitis: Theory and Practice in the Language of Later Byzantine Historiography." In *Toward a Historical Sociolinguistic Poetics of Medieval Greek*, ed. A. Cuomo and E. Trapp, 109–18. Turnhout, 2017.
Horrocks, G. *Greek: A History of the Language and Its Speakers*. 2nd ed. Chichester, 2010.
Hunger, H. "Philanthropia: Eine griechische Wortprägung auf ihrem Wege von Aischylos bis Theodoros Metochites." *Anzeiger phil.-hist. Klasse. Österreichische Akademie der Wissenschaften* 100 (1963): 1–20. Reprinted in Hunger, *Byzantinische Grundlagenforschung* (London, 1973), Study XIII.
Ierodiakonou, K. "A Logical Joust in Nikephoros Blemmydes' *Autobiography*." In *Logic and Language in the Middle Ages: A Volume in Honour of Sten Ebbesen*, ed. J. L. Fink, H. Hansen, and A. M. Mora-Márquez, 125–37. Leiden, 2013.
Ierodiakonou, K. "Rationality and Revelation in Eleventh and Twelfth Century Byzantium." In *De usu rationis: Vernunft und Offenbarung im Mittelalter*, ed. G. Mensching, 19–31. Würzburg, 2007.
Jeffreys, E., ed. *Rhetoric in Byzantium: Papers from the Thirty-fifth Spring Symposium of Byzantine Studies*. Aldershot, 2003.
Jouanno, C. "Alexander's Friends in the *Alexander Romance*." *Scripta Classica Israelica* 32 (2013): 67–77.
Kaplan, M. *Les hommes et la terre à Byzance du VIe au XIe siècle: Propriété et exploitation du sol*. Paris, 1992.
Kiesewetter, A. "Die Heirat zwischen Konstanze-Anna von Hohenstaufen und Kaiser Johannes III. Batatzes von Nikaia (Ende 1240 oder Anfang 1241) und der Angriff des Johannes Batatzes auf Konstantinopel im Mai oder Juni 1241." *Römische historische Mitteilungen* 41 (1999): 239–50.

Laiou, A. "'Consensus Facit Nuptias—Et Non': Pope Nicolas I's *Responsa* to the Bulgarians as a Source for Byzantine Marriage Customs." *Rechtshistorisches Journal* 4 (1985): 189–201.

Laiou, A. "Economic Thought and Ideology." In *The Economic History of Byzantium: From the Seventh through the Fifteenth Century*, ed. Laiou, 3:1123–44. 3 vols. Washington, DC, 2002.

Laurent, V. " Ὁ μέγας βαΐουλος, à l'occasion du parakimomène Basile Lécapène." *ΕΕΒΣ* 23 (1953): 193–205.

Leveniotis, G. *Η Άβυδος του Ελλησπόντου και η περιοχή της*. Thessaloniki, 2017.

MacDonald, P. S. *History of the Concept of Mind: Speculations about Soul, Mind and Spirit from Homer to Hume*. Aldershot, 2003.

Macrides, R. *George Akropolites: The History*. Oxford, 2007.

Macrides, R. "Trial by Ordeal in Byzantium: On Whose Authority?" In *Authority in Byzantium*, ed. P. Armstrong, 31–46. Farnham, 2013.

Macrides, R., J. Munitiz, and D. Angelov, *Pseudo-Kodinos*. See pseudo-Kodinos, under Primary Sources.

Magdalino, P., and M. Mavroudi. Introduction to *The Occult Sciences in Byzantium*, ed. Magdalino and Mavroudi, 11–37. Geneva, 2006.

Marciniak, P. "The Art of Abuse: Satire and Invective in Byzantine Literature: A Preliminary Survey." *Eos* 103 (2016): 349–62.

Marinis, V. *Death and the Afterlife in Byzantium: The Fate of the Soul in Theology, Liturgy, and Art*. Cambridge, 2016.

Miklosich, F. *Lexicon palaeoslovenico-graeco-latinum emendatum auctum*. Vienna, 1862–65.

Mullett, M. "Byzantium: A Friendly Society?" *Past and Present* 118 (1988): 3–24.

Nicholas, N. "The Passive Future Subjunctive in Byzantine Texts." *BZ* 101 (2008): 89–131.

Nilsson, I. *Writer and Occasion in Twelfth-Century Byzantium: The Authorial Voice of Constantine Manasses*. Cambridge, 2020.

Nousia, F. *Byzantine Textbooks of the Palaeologan Period*. Vatican City, 2016.

O'Meara, D. *Platonopolis: Platonic Political Philosophy in Late Antiquity*. Oxford, 2003.

Papadopoulos, J. "La Satire du Précepteur, oeuvre inédite de Théodore II Lascaris, empereur de Nicée." In *Compte-rendu du deuxième Congrès international des études byzantines*, ed. D. Anastasijević and P. Granić, 27. Belgrade, 1929.

Papadopoulos-Kerameus, A. Review of *Theodori Ducae Lascaris epistulae CCXVII*, ed. N. Festa (Florence, 1898). *Vizantiiskii vremennik* 6 (1899): 548–54.

Politis, N. "Γοργόνα." *Parnassos* 2 (1878): 259–75.

Prato, G. "Un autografo di Teodoro II Lascaris imperatore di Nicea?" *JÖB* 30 (1981): 249–58.

Richter, G. *Theodoros Dukas Laskaris: Der Natürliche Zusammenhang: Ein Zeugnis vom Stand der byzantinischen Philosophie in der Mitte des 13. Jahrhunderts*. Amsterdam, 1989.

Roilos, P. *Amphoteroglossia: A Poetics of the Twelfth-Century Medieval Greek Novel.* Washington, DC, 2005.
Rouillard, G. "Les taxes maritimes et commerciales d'après les actes de Patmos et de Lavra." In *Mélanges Charles Diehl: Études sur l'histoire et sur l'art de Byzance*, 1:277-89. 2 vols. Paris, 1930.
Ševčenko, I. "A New Manuscript of Nicephorus Blemmydes' 'Imperial Statue,' and of Some Patriarchal Letters." *Byzantine Studies/Études Byzantines* 5 (1978): 222-32.
Siegel, R. *Galen's System of Physiology and Medicine.* Basel, 1968.
Simpson, A. *Niketas Choniates: A Historiographical Study.* Oxford, 2013.
Smyrlis, K. *La fortune des grands monastères byzantins (fin du Xe-milieu du XIVe siècle).* Paris, 2006.
Smyrlis, K. "Trade Regulation and Taxation in Byzantium, Eleventh-Twelfth Centuries." In *Trade in Byzantium: Papers from the Third International Sevgi Gönül Byzantine Studies Symposium*, ed. P. Magdalino, N. Necipoğlu, with the assistance of I. Jevtić, 65-87. Istanbul, 2016.
Svoronos, N. "Le serment de fidélité à l'empereur byzantin et sa signification constitutionnelle." *REB* 9 (1951): 106-42.
Tartaglia, L. *Satira del pedagogo.* See under Works by Theodore Laskaris.
Trapp, E. "Learned and Vernacular Literature in Byzantium: Dichotomy or Symbiosis?" *DOP* 47 (1993): 115-29.
Verpeaux, J. "Les οἰκεῖοι: Notes d'histoire institutionnelle et sociale." *REB* 23 (1965): 89-99.

INDEX OF SCRIPTURAL PASSAGES

Old Testament

Genesis
- 3:19   101n1

Exodus
- 15:1   88n130
- 19:9   186n61
- 20:5   140n44
- 29:20   121n19

Leviticus
- 1:10   112n29
- 8:24   121n19

Deuteronomy
- 6:5   127n36
- 6:15   140n44
- 11:14   117n9
- 28:35   62n17
- 32:10   121n18
- 32:24   152n95

Joshua
- 10:7   140n45

Judge
- 11:1   140n45

3 Kings (1 Kings)
- 18:19   190n81

Psalms
- 2:2   81n96
- 9:21   122n24
- 16:8   121n18
- 17:12   65n35, 184n47
- 17:33   61n10
- 23:4   140n40
- 29:2   76n80
- 31:9   80n91, 105n14
- 49:1   149n84
- 56:5   65n34
- 64:7   61n10
- 67:19   99n24
- 88:23   84n110
- 90:13   112n32
- 101:16   81n96
- 102:14   101n1
- 103:21   86n118
- 103:24   70n57
- 108:19   61n10
- 109:5   81n96
- 118:45   104n11
- 123:5   147n72
- 123:8   83n107
- 128:7   137n28, 137n31
- 132:3   89n137
- 133:3   83n107
- 136:8–9   128n39
- 137:14   81n96
- 148:11   81n96

Proverbs
- 2:18   110n26
- 10:24   112n31
- 13:1   112n31
- 13:15   112n31
- 22:8a   121n21
- 26:11   149n85

Ecclesiastes
1:9	70n57
6:14	28n42
49:1	107n21

Isaiah
1:2	66n38, 187n69
1:8	140n46
5:8	142n55
9:14	147n74
11:6	65n33
40:4	88n132
44:20	136n21
59:5	112n32
61:2	97n16
63:4	97n16
65:25	65n33
66:18	177n6

Jeremiah
5:8	86n117
5:24	117n9
11:19	112n29
16:17	140n43

Daniel
2:47	149n84
3	82n102
3:4	177n6
3:5	123n25
3:7	123n25
3:10	123n25
3:19	82n101
5	83n102
14:1–22	83n102

Hosea
6:3	117n9

Joel
1:6	97n19
2:23	117n9

Micah
4:2	127n37

Habakkuk
3:6	88n131

Zechariah
10:1	117n9

New Testament

Matthew
3:2	122n22
5:15	70n56
6:22	169n52
6:27	82n99
7:10	69n51
12:35	163n27
13:5	186n64
15:19	106n15
16:18	185n55
17:14–18	69n52
18:17	188n72
22:14	96n14
22:37	127n36
23:12	72n65
24:7	184n48
25:14–30	37, 173n63
25:21	120n16
25:23	120n16

Mark
1:25–26	69n54, 70n55
1:43	69n53
4:21	70n56
7:21	106n15
12:30	127n36

Luke 2:108 9n134
2:35	106n15
4:35	69n54, 70n55
6:45	163n27
9:47	106n15
10:19	76n81
10:27	127n36
11:11–12	69n51, 131n7
11:33	70n56
12:25	82n99
14:11	72n65
15:8–10	127n35
15:22	121n20
16:19–31	151n91
18:9–14	188n72
18:14	72n65
24:38	106n15

INDEX OF SCRIPTURAL PASSAGES

John
    10:11   128n38
    11:35   106n17
    13:37–38   128n38
    14:8–11   186n62
    15:13   128n38
    20:2   185n57

Acts
    5:40–41   188n74
    10:1–33   187n69
    10:42   83n108
    12:6–11   188n73

Romans
    8:33   96n14
    9:21   105n13
    11:29   99n25
    13:1   188n75
    14:9   83n108

1 Corinthians
    4:9   197n18

2 Corinthians
    1:3   91n143
    12:9   185n53

Ephesians
    1:3   91n143
    4:8   99n24

Colossians
    2:18   189n78
    3:12   96n14

1 Thessalonians
    2:9   120n17

2 Timothy
    1:12   133n12

Titus
    1:1   96n14

1 Peter
    2:9   91n144

Apocryphal/Deuterocanonical Books

Judith
    3:8   177n6

Wisdom of Solomon
    4:12   98n21
    7:15   128n41
    8:3   70n58, 76n83

Psalms of Solomon
    9:5   112n31
    17:22   112n31

GENERAL INDEX

Theodore II Laskaris is referred to as Laskaris in this index's subheadings.
Scriptural references precede this index.

Adam and Eve's fall, 127n34, 150n86
Adamantios, 182, 182n34
adoption, metaphorical use of term, 131n6, 134
Akropolites, George, 3, 8, 17–18, 17n23, 43
Alcibiades, 31, 141, 141n53
Alexander III (Alexander the Great), 26–29, 115–16, 125–26
   spurious letter from Aristotle to, 163n26
   statues in Alexandria of, 126n32
Alexander IV (pope), 41, 185n54, 189n79
Alexander romance, 29, 126n32
Alexios V Mourtzouphlos, 67n43
Anatolia, 3
Angeloi dynasty (1185–1204), 18, 63, 63n20
Aphthonios, 20
Apollonios of Perga, 182n38
Apollonios of Tyana, 182, 182n35
Argyropoulos, John: satire of Katablattas, 20
Aristotle, 36, 97, 130n1, 132, 146n71, 163, 181, 182, 184
   author's feigned ignorance of, 36, 163
   Blemmydes' mastery of Aristotelian logic, 50, 72
   Categories, 30, 108n23, 136n23, 158n4, 159n5, 160n12
   History of Animals, 162n23
   Metaphysics, 75n78, 181n28
   Meteorology, 175n3
   natural philosophy of, 29n50, 45, 48, 53, 54, 154n101, 172
   Nicomachean Ethics, 29, 117n11, 157n2
   On Colors, 71
   On Generation and Corruption, 108n22, 110n27, 154n101
   On Interpretation, 160n12
   On Sophistical Refutations, 159n10, 160n12
   Organon, 160, 160n12, 163, 163n25. *See also* logic, Aristotelian syllogistic
   Physics, 111n28
   Politics, 177n8, 178n20
   positive vs. privative, 30–31, 136–37, 136n22
   Prior Analytics, 159n7, 160n12
   Rhetoric, 159n10
   spurious letter to Alexander, 163n26
   Topics, 160n12
arithmetic. *See* mathematics and mathematical disciplines
army
   army reform and finance, 5, 42–43, 50, 195, 197
   military abilities of the author, 36, 73, 171–72
   taxation required to maintain army, 42, 50, 195
Arsenios Autoreianos (patriarch of Constantinople), 41, 41–42n62, 190n85
Atlas (Greek Titan), 144, 144n65

Bacchus (Greek god), 44
Balkans
    Blemmydes in, 3
    John III's campaign in, 3, 4, 16, 17, 87, 194
    Laskaris on campaign in, 5, 16, 17, 87
    Manfred of Sicily's anti-Nicaean alliance in, 43
    map of, 6
    Nicaean expansion into, 2, 4–5, 42, 43, 194, 194n8, 195n10
Basilakes, Nikephoros, 96n13
Basil of Caesarea, 117n6
Bel (pagan god), 82, 82–83n102
Béla IV (Hungarian king), 2
Berthold of Hohenburg, 4, 101
Blemmydes, Nikephoros
    as abbot of Christ-Who-Is monastery, 4, 49, 195n13, 197n20
    as abbot of St. Gregory the Miracle Worker monastery, 3
    Aristotelian logic used by, 50, 72
    Autobiography, 18, 50, 60n8, 194n5, 195n13
    changing relationship with Laskaris, 8, 34, 37, 42–43, 47–51, 143n59, 194
    critical of empire's tax policies, 50, 195, 195n13
    Epitome physica, 48n77, 108n22, 110n27, 111n28, 176n3
    The Imperial Statue, 4, 22–23, 27, 27n39, 28, 48, 49, 79n89, 96n12, 97n18, 98n20, 103n8, 138nn32–33, 141n53, 147n75, 169n49
    as influence on Laskaris, 3–4, 8, 48, 49, 51
    invited to become patriarch of Constantinople in exile, 50
    Laskaris asking for prayers and medical advice of, 51
    Laskaris's earliest letters to, 18
    as Laskaris's teacher of philosophy in *Satire of His Tutor*, 17–18, 17n23, 72–73, 72n66, 82
    resisting purported unjust decisions of Laskaris as emperor, 50
    theological views on the Trinity, 49–50, 154n101, 185n52

Brutus, 31, 141, 141n53
Bulgaria. *See also* Elena (wife of Laskaris); Ivan Asen II
    alliance with (1235), 2
    Bulgarians 196
    Bulgarian territories, 71
    war against (1255–56), 5, 143n59, 196n16
Byzantine proverbs and expressions, 63n21, 65n32, 83n106, 85n116, 87n124
    from Cyrus the Elder, 28n42
    "divine fire," 134n14

Calchas, 182
Caligula (Roman emperor, Gaius), 141n51, 149nn81–82, 185, 185n54
Carinus (Roman emperor), 104, 104n9
Cerberus (dog guarding gates to Hades), 73, 151
Chimera (monster), 83, 83n103
Chomatenos, Demetrios, 134n14
Choniates, Niketas, 47
Christ
    epithet of The One Who Is, 197n20
    lamentation of, 106
    references to miracles of, 69
Christian Theology (Laskaris)
    chronological placement among Laskaris's works, 7, 13
    First Oration against the Latins, or, On the Procession of the Holy Spirit (book 6), 41, 42, 189n77
    On the Divine Names, 9, 47, 49n78, 128n40, 176n4
    Second Oration against the Latins, or, On the Procession of the Holy Spirit (book 7), 41
Claudius. *See* Ptolemy, Claudius
climate theory, 38–39, 176
Colossae and Colossus of Rhodes, 178, 178n14
Conrad IV (Hohenstaufen king of Germany and Sicily), 4
Constantine (Dominican bishop of Orvieto), 41, 189n79

GENERAL INDEX

Constantinople
  Byzantine exodus from and government in exile, 2, 64n28
  fall of (1204, Fourth Crusade), 14, 39, 64, 64n27, 67n44, 141n47
  Laskaris's lament over, 31, 141n47
  as megalopolis, 141n47
  Nicaeans fighting to reclaim, 2, 183, 183n45
  reconquest (1261), 2, 7
Constanza-Anna of Hohenstaufen (Nicaean empress, stepmother of Laskaris), 4, 16, 17n22, 22, 87n126
convention vs. nature, 53–54, 105, 105n12, 134n13, 166, 166n39, 167–68
corruption, 24, 30, 31, 52, 102–3, 105, 107, 136, 136n24, 140, 140n39
Croesus, 104, 148, 148n77
Cronus (Greek Titan), 62, 62n14
Cynosarges (Athenian temple of Heracles), 95n6
Cyrus the Elder (king of Persia), 28n42, 28n44, 138, 138n33, 148

Demosthenes, 66n37, 87, 182
devil. *See* Satan
Diophantos. *See* Idiophantes
divine fire, associated with Plato, 134, 134n14
doctrinal disputes between the papacy and the Byzantine church, 187, 188–89, 188n76. *See also* Procession of the Holy Spirit
Dyrrhachion (Adriatic city), 5, 43, 177n10, 194

Echetos (Epirote king), 85, 85n113, 151, 151n89
Eirene Laskarina (mother of Laskaris), 2, 65, 65n30
Eirenikos family, 19–20
Eirenikos, Nicholas (*chartophylax* at patriarchate), 16–17, 19

Eirenikos, Niketas, as possible tutor of Laskaris, 19, 20
Eirenikos, Theodore II (patriarch of Constantinople resident in Nicaea), 19
Elena (wife of Laskaris), 2, 4, 25, 52, 101, 112, 112n30
Epiros, 2, 4, 5, 43, 50, 194n8
epistolography, 7, 8
etymology. *See* vocabulary and new words
Euclid, 72, 181–82, 182n37
Eustathios of Thessaloniki, 77n85, 177n11
existence vs. nonexistence, 24, 35, 51, 52–53, 106–10, 157, 159n8
Explanation of the World (Laskaris). *See also* On What Is Unclear and a Testimony That the Author Is Ignorant of Philosophy; Revelation of the World, or Life
  chronological issues of, 34–35
  Dedicatory Preface to, 5, 10, 33, 37, 38, 130–34
  four treatises of, 7, 33
  in miscellany collection of late works (1258), 13
  On the Elements (book 1), 8, 33, 131n8, 132
  On Heaven (book 2), 8, 33, 132, 132n9
  title, meaning of, 132
eye of the soul, 102, 102n4

First Council of Lyons (1245), 23
Florilegium Baroccianum (*Florilegium Patmiacum*), 28n43
Fourth Crusade, 1, 2, 52, 64n27
Frederick II Hohenstaufen (medieval Western emperor), 16, 22–23, 184n49
friendship. *See* Oration on Friendship and Politics

Galen, 90n139, 145n70, 182
geometry. *See* mathematics and mathematical disciplines

God
    names of, 47, 49n78, 128n40. *See also Christian Theology* for *On the Divine Names*
    nature alongside, 54
    as omnipresent, 33, 154
    protection of Laskaris against tutor, 70
    writing in praise of, 131
golden mean, 179, 180
Gorgon, 145, 145n67
grammar, 47
Greek identity. *See* Hellenic identity
Greeks
    access to water and agriculture, 39, 179
    accumulation of knowledge and natural intelligence, 39, 40, 179n21, 180–81
    adoption of skills invented elsewhere, 39, 179–81
    "Greek people," use of term, 119n14, 179, 183
    notable writers, philosophers, and scientists, 39, 181–83
    residing in ideal location and superior to rest of inhabited world, 39, 177–78
Greek proverbs, 64n23, 87n124
Gregory of Nazianzus, 40, 65n32, 117nn6–7, 178n14, 190
Gregory of Nyssa, 191n86

Hades, 15, 25, 32, 80, 113, 146. *See also* Cerberus
Hannibal, 31, 141
Hellenic identity, 1, 4, 8, 38–42, 43, 50, 54, 115, 179–89, 196
Heraclitus, 103, 103n7
Hermes (Greek god), 44, 68, 68n50, 73, 73n71, 116, 116n5
Hermogenes, 87, 182
    On Invention, 66n39
    On Types of Style, 68n48, 135n18
    Progymnasmata, 93n1
Herodotus, 86n119, 148n77, 177n8

Heron of Alexandria: *Pneumatica*, 66, 67n41, 182, 182n39
"Heron of Byzantium," 106n18
Hesiod, 137n27
Hippocrates, 177n8, 182
Homer, 60, 72, 102, 182
    Iliad, 62n16, 63n18, 83n103, 97n18
    Odyssey, 77n85, 85n113, 139n36, 145n68, 151n89
humor, 14, 44, 46, 54, 68
hymnography, 7

Idiophantes (Diophantos), 60, 60n8, 72, 72n68
Isaac II Angelos (r. 1185–1195, 1203–1204), 63n20, 67n43
Isaiah (biblical), 30, 140–41, 147
Italians
    display of arrogance, 40, 184–85
    erroneous philosophy and theology, 40, 42, 183–91, 186n59
    erroneous syllogisms on Procession of the Holy Spirit, 39, 49–50, 154n101, 185, 185n52, 188–89, 189n77, 191
    inferior to Greeks, 39, 54, 183–84
    as interlocutors in *Oration on Hellenism*, 39–40, 189–90
    military and political turmoil, 39, 184
Ivan Asen II (Bulgarian king), 2

Jeremiah (biblical), 106, 106n16
Jerusalem, 31, 140–41, 141n47
Jesus. *See* Christ
Jezebel (biblical), 190, 190n81
John (apostle), 40, 185–86, 185nn56–57, 188
John III Vatatzes (father of Laskaris), 2
    Balkan campaign of, 3, 4, 16, 17, 87, 194
    celebration of marriage to Constanza-Anna, 16–17, 17n22, 87, 87n126
    engaging tutor for son Laskaris, 65, 65n30
    Frederick II's letters to, 23
    Laskaris following in legacy of, 4, 42, 194

GENERAL INDEX

Laskaris's speech in praise of, 4, 8, 49
Michael VIII Palaiologos and, 143n59
referring to Tornikes as his "brother," 130n2
John IV Laskaris (son of Laskaris), 2, 7
John Chrysostom, 127n33, 140n38, 186n60
Joshua (biblical), 147
Judas (biblical), 16
judicial ordeals by red-hot iron, 134n14

Klaudioupolites, Constantine (bishop of Ephesos and patriarch-elect of Antioch), 18

Lancia family, 4
Laskaris. *See* Theodore II Laskaris; Theodore II Laskaris, works by
Laurentios (John Laurentios Lydos), 182, 182n36
law
  pessimistic view of, 31, 139, 139n35
Letter on Royal Duty, Taxation, and the Army (Laskaris), 42–43, 193–98
Libanius, 28
Licinius (tetrarchic emperor), 32, 149, 149n80, 149n83
literary style, 43–44. *See also* wordplay and puns
Livistros and Rodamne (Greek vernacular romance), 45, 45n69
logic, Aristotelian syllogistic, 36, 38, 40, 50, 71, 72, 159–62, 159n10, 160n11, 164n29, 198
Lucian, 102n4
Lykos River valley, 5

Macro (praetorian prefect of Caligula), 32, 149, 149n81
Manasses, Constantine, 44
Manfred of Sicily, 43
Maria (daughter of Laskaris), 41n62

mathematics and mathematical disciplines, 152–53, 153n97, 161–62
  arithmetic proportion and geometrical proportion, 162, 162n24
  as bridge to intelligible world and the divine, 160n14, 162–63
  music and, 36, 161–62
  in theological discussions, 162, 162n22
Maximian (tetrarchic emperor), 32, 149, 149n80, 149n83
Maximos the Confessor, 28
Memorial Discourse on Emperor Frederick II, 21–23, 93–99
Menander, 22, 28n42
Methodios II (patriarch of Constantinople resident in Nicaea), 18
Metochites, Theodore, 44
Michael II Komnenos Doukas (Epirote ruler), 41n62, 43, 194n8
Michael VIII Palaiologos (Byzantine emperor), 5, 7, 143n59, 149n83
Michael Asen (Bulgarian king), 5
Mongols, 5, 71n60
Moral Pieces Describing the Inconstancy of Life (Laskaris), 23–26, 101–13
Moses (biblical), 88, 147
Mouzalon, George
  assassination of, 7
  Dedicatory Letter to George Mouzalon, 10, 13, 33–34, 129, 135n16
  Explanation of the World addressed to, 130
  as guardian of Laskaris's writings, 30, 55, 134–35
  as Laskaris's close friend and chief minister, 5, 8, 30, 52, 125n28, 131n6
  Laskaris's reference to as his "brother," 130n2, 131n6
  Oration on Friendship and Politics addressed to, 5, 27, 35, 115, 128
  as regent for John IV Laskaris, 7
  Representation of the World, or Life addressed to, 5, 30, 33, 51, 129, 133–36, 154n103, 156
  titles granted to (1255), 34, 130nn3–5

natural good, 118–20, 118n12, 123–24
natural philosophy. *See* Aristotle
nature
  convention vs., 53–54, 105, 105n12, 134n13, 166, 166n39, 167–68
  God and, 54, 79, 124
  human nature, 23–24, 31, 102–7, 143
  seasonal changes linked to human conduct, 32, 35, 137, 146–51
Navatos. *See* Novatian
Nebuchadnezzar, 82–83, 82n102
negative (apophatic) theology, 38, 132n11
Neoplatonism, 38, 93n2, 134n14, 162n21, 167n45, 176n4
Nerva (Roman emperor), 22, 147n75
Nestor (king of Pylos), 71
Nicaean aristocracy
  Laskaris's relations with, 5, 27, 28, 52, 119, 127
  Michael VIII Palaiologos as champion of, 7
Nikomachos of Gerasa, 160n14
nobility
  as moral characteristic, 25, 32, 109, 140, 147–48
Novatian (Navatos), 16, 85, 85n116
numerology, 29, 152–53, 153n97

Odysseus, 77n85, 139n36. *See also* Homer
On the Divine Names. *See* Christian Theology
On What Is Unclear and a Testimony That the Author Is Ignorant of Philosophy (Laskaris), 8, 35–38, 95n8, 157–73
Oration on Friendship and Politics (Laskaris), 26–30, 115–28
Oration on Hellenism (Laskaris), 8, 38–42, 50, 175–91

Palaiologos. *See* Michael VIII Palaiologos
Paul (apostle), 40, 178n14, 188, 189, 197
Perseus (king of Macedonia), 16, 85, 85n115

Peter (apostle), 40, 185–86, 185–86nn55–58, 188, 188n73
Phalaris (tyrant of Agrigentum), 151, 151n89, 151n90
philanthropy (*philanthropia*), 95nn8–9, 170
Philip (apostle), 186
Philip (king of Macedonia), 138, 138n33
Philo of Alexandria, 141, 141nn50–51, 149n81, 185, 185n54
philosophers
  as exception to custom of exchanging flatteries, 51, 145
  Laskaris as literary figure and philosopher, 1, 7–9, 51–55, 52n91, 79
philosophy
  definitions of, 15, 17, 74–75, 74nn74–75, 75nn77–78, 76n79, 76n82, 107n20
  exceptional knowledge of Laskaris and direct access to Lady Philosophy, 32–33, 49, 52, 54, 151, 153
  feigned ignorance of, 36, 132–33, 158–60
  Italians' erroneous philosophy, 40, 42, 183–91
  as Laskaris's main pursuit and love, 14–15, 17, 30, 69, 70, 72, 77–79, 135, 151–54
  philosophical irony, 37
  relationship with theology, 38, 40, 42, 53, 181, 187, 191, 191n86
  role in rulership, 21
  as "royal science," 79, 79n88
Phyllada (post-Byzantine Alexander romance), 29n48
Plato, 72, 181
  Aristotle and, 184
  "circular motion of the soul" as concept from, 102n3
  "eye of the soul" as concept from, 102n4
  "healing the soul" as concept from, 126n30
  inscription at school of, 160
  Laches, 126n30
  mathematical disciplines attributed to, 153n97
  philosopher-king, idea of, 31, 139–40, 139n38

GENERAL INDEX 221

Phaedo, 75n77, 116n4
Republic, 102n4, 139n38
"royal science" as philosophical term derived from, 79n88
Sophist, 74n76
Theaetetus, 74n74
Timaeus, 102n3, 134n14, 162n23, 177n8
Platonic School's gate, 160
Plotinus, 182
Plutarch, 29n50
Poimanenon, Battle of (1224/25), 2
political thought, 8, 23. *See also Memorial Discourse on Emperor Frederick II*; *Oration on Friendship and Politics*
Polydeukes (Pollux, half-brother of Castor), 144n64
Polyphemus, 77n85
Porphyry, 158n4
Poseidon, 77, 77n85
Procession of the Holy Spirit, 39, 41, 49–50, 154n101, 185, 185n52, 188–89, 189n77, 191
Proclus, 134n14, 182, 182n33
Prodromos, Theodore, 44
Psellos, Michael, 104n9
pseudo-Aristotle, 152n93
pseudo-Dionysios, 101n2, 191n86
pseudo-Galen, 145–46n70
pseudo-Kodinos, 124n27, 130n3
pseudo-Maximos the Confessor: *Loci Communes*, 28, 29n45, 101n2
Ptolemy, Claudius, 72, 73, 175n3, 182, 182n30
puns. *See* wordplay and puns
Pythagoras, 72, 74n75, 76n79, 76n82, 151n90, 181, 182
Pythias of Massalia, 83n105

questions-and-answers literature, 27
Quinisext Council (691/92), 71n63

Representation of the World, or Life (Laskaris), 30–35, 134–56
rhetoric, 7, 14, 28, 30, 36, 66n39, 163–65, 168
Hermes as inventor of, 68n50, 116n5
Rhodes, 178, 178n14, 195, 195n10
royal justice, 21, 22, 23, 95–96, 99. *See also* virtues of the ruler
corruption of judges, 30, 52, 136, 136n24, 140, 140n39

Saewulf (English pilgrim to Holy Land), 178n14
Sardanapalus (Assyrian king), 63, 63n19, 138, 138n32
Satan, 16, 69, 73n73, 76, 86, 90n140
satire, 3, 7, 8
Satire of His Tutor (Laskaris), 13–20, 59–92
Seljuk Turks
  as Persians 196
Semiramis, 141
Serbs 196
  as Triballians, 194
Serenos of Antinoopolis, 182n40
Sesostris (mythical Egyptian king), 48, 103, 103n8
Sirens, 145nn67–68
Skoutariotes, Theodore, 41
Socrates, 37, 38, 72, 85n114, 96n13, 132, 181
Solomon (biblical), 70
Solon (Athenian sage), 148, 148n77
Souda, 20, 96n13
Souliardos, Michael, 89n135
Stagirite. *See* Aristotle
Stoic philosophy, 143n60, 184, 195n12
Strategopoulos, Alexios, 143n59
syllogisms. *See* logic, Aristotelian syllogistic; Italians
Synesios of Cyrene, 104n9
Synopsis chronike (anonymous, attrib. to Theodore Skoutariotes), 41

tax collection, 31, 32, 140n39, 140n41, 143n58, 147, 147n73, 148n79, 188n72. *See also* army
Thales, 181
Themis (goddess of justice), 87, 87n123
Theodore I Laskaris (maternal grandfather of Laskaris), 2
Theodore II Laskaris (Laskaris *in this index*), iv
  accession as sole emperor (November 1254), 130n1, 175n1
  autobiographical self-representation, 8, 20, 23, 25, 51–52
  Balkan campaign with his father, 16, 17, 87
  children of, 2, 41n62
  daily routine and duties as emperor, 21, 42–43, 52, 78, 97–98, 119–20, 193, 196–97
  education of, 3, 18n24, 52, 65. *See also Satire of His Tutor*
  illness of, 5, 51
  internal policies of, 5. *See also Letter on Royal Duty, Taxation, and the Army*
  legacy as concern of, 54–55
  legacy of his father and, 4, 42, 194
  as literary figure and philosopher, 1, 7–9, 51–55, 52n91
  Michael VIII Palaiologos and, 143n59
  military expeditions led by, 4–5
  relationship with Blemmydes. *See* Blemmydes, Nikephoros
  sorrow upon death of wife Elena, 4, 24, 25, 52, 101, 112, 112n30
Theodore II Laskaris, works by. *See also Christian Theology; Explanation of the World; Letter on Royal Duty, Taxation, and the Army; Memorial Discourse on Emperor Frederick II; Moral Pieces; On What Is Unclear and a Testimony That the Author Is Ignorant of Philosophy; Oration on Friendship and Politics; Oration on Hellenism; Representation of the World, or Life; Satire of His Tutor*
  Encomium on Nicaea, 1
  Encomium on the Spring and the Charming Man, 7
  grammar, 47
  literary style, 43–44
  mix of genres, 20, 22, 44
  Mouzalon as guardian of, 55
  Natural Communion, 9, 53, 53n94, 105n12, 134n13
  Sacred Orations, 4, 13
  speech in praise of his father John III Vatatzes, 4, 8, 49
theology
  disagreement between Laskaris and Blemmydes over, 49–50
  Italians' erroneous theology, 40, 42, 183–91, 186n59. *See also* Procession of the Holy Spirit
  mathematics in theological discussions, 162, 162n22
  negative (apophatic), 38, 132n11
  relationship with philosophy, 38, 40, 42, 53, 181, 187, 191, 191n86
Theon of Smyrna, 72, 72n67, 74n76, 153n97, 182, 182n29
Thersites, 16, 62n16, 82, 85
Thessaloniki, church council attended by papal and Nicaean representatives (1256), 41, 184nn50–51, 189n79, 190n85
Thucydides, 177n11
Tornikes, Constantine, 143n59
Tornikes, Demetrios Komnenos, 130n2
Trajan (Roman emperor), 147, 147n75
Treaty of Regina (1256), 5
Trinitarian treatises, 9
Tripolis on the Maeander, 194, 194n9
truth, 42, 49, 96, 96n11, 128, 169, 186, 193, 197
tutor, 3, 18
  birth, 14, 19, 61–62, 61n13, 66, 67n41
  character of, 14, 59–61, 63, 66–67, 81–86, 90n141, 91
  identity of, 18–20
  machinations against pupil and philosophy, 14–15, 48, 66, 70, 71, 73–77, 82–83,
  physical appearance and dress, 14, 15, 62–63, 66n40, 71, 81–82, 81n98, 85

Tzetzes, John, 83n105
virtues of the ruler, 36, 49, 96n11, 119–20, 169–71. *See also* philanthropy (*philanthropia*); royal justice
vocabulary and new words, 12, 36, 44–47, 54. *See also* Byzantine proverbs and expressions; wordplay

wordplay and puns, 12, 37, 43, 45–46, 97n18, 112n32, 158n4, 185n55, 190n84

Xerxes (king of Persia), 138, 138n32, 148

Zabareiotes, Niketas, as possible tutor of Laskaris, 19, 19n27, 20